The Lynching of Language

Edited by
SANDRA L. RAGAN
DIANNE G. BYSTROM
LYNDA LEE KAID
CHRISTINA S. BECK

Foreword by
JULIA T. WOOD

The Lynching of Language

Gender, Politics, and Power in the Hill-Thomas Hearings

UNIVERSITY OF ILLINOIS PRESS

URBANA AND CHICAGO

1   2   3   4   5   C   P   5   4   3   2   1

This book is printed on acid-free paper.

Library of Congress Cataloging-in-Publication Data
The lynching of language : gender, politics, and power in the Hill–
Thomas hearings / edited by Sandra L. Ragan . . . [et al.].
     p.   cm.
Includes bibliographical references and index.
ISBN 0-252-02126-6. — ISBN 0-252-06517-4 (pbk.)
   1. Thomas, Clarence—1948–   . 2. United States. Supreme Court—
Officials and employees—Selection and appointment. 3. Sexual
harassment of women—Law and legislation—United States. 4. Hill,
Anita. 5. Law and politics. 6. Truthfulness and falsehood.
I. Ragan, Sandra L.
KF8745.T48L96   1996
347.73´2634—dc20
[347.3073534]   95-32458
                                                            CIP

Contents

Acknowledgments

A project of this scope, with colleagues across the country, necessarily involves the support and assistance of a number of people. First, we are grateful to our contributors for making this volume possible. For their assistance in the study presented in the essay "Tracking Reactions: Audience Evaluations of the Hill-Thomas Hearings," thanks are also due to Professor Anne Johnston of the University of North Carolina at Chapel Hill, who helped gather data, and John Ballotti, a doctoral student in the University of Oklahoma Department of Communication, for videotaping the original hearings. We also wish to acknowledge the assistance of Carolyn Seratte of the University of Oklahoma, who helped prepare the manuscript for publication, and Marie Mathos of the Political Communication Center, who assisted in corresponding with our contributors and publisher, as well as our editors at the University of Illinois Press—Karen Hewitt, senior editor, and Jane Mohraz, manuscript editor—for their support, patience, and editorial contributions. Finally, we are grateful for the encouragement and understanding of our families—Mark Acker; Keith, Christopher, and Elizabeth Bystrom; Cliff Jones; and Wade, Brittany Nicole, and Chelsea Meagan Pangburn—in the development, preparation, and publication of this volume.

Foreword: Continuing the Conversation about Hill and Thomas

JULIA T. WOOD

Recently I witnessed an age-old scene between my five-year-old niece Michelle and her playmate Steven. The earthshaking issue over which they argued was whether he had eaten the last cookie in the cookie jar. "You did," Michelle accused. "I did not," Steven protested. "Did too," "did not," "did too," "did not," they continued in endless iterations of the classic dialogue.

As I listened, trying to disguise my amusement at what they clearly considered a momentous matter, I recalled the Hill-Thomas hearings of 1991. Though Anita Hill and Clarence Thomas did not have the excuse of being only five years old, their testimony resembled Michelle's and Steven's "did too—did not" dialogue. Just as I was unable to determine whether Steven did devour the last cookie, many people, scholars and laypersons alike, cannot decide with certainty whether Clarence Thomas sexually harassed Anita Hill. Even those of us who have firm opinions about who told the truth in the 1991 hearings are unable to marshal indisputable evidence to support our judgments and refute rival ones.

Interest in the Hill-Thomas hearings cuts across lines of class, race, and gender that often partition attention to topics of social life. White- and blue-collar workers were equally glued to the televised drama; women and men passionately debated what had "really" happened; blacks and whites were equally, though differently, invested in the charges and countercharges and in the conduct of the inquiry. The Hill-Thomas hearings in particular and sexual harassment in general have drawn all of us into a continuing conversation about what happened then and what it means now.

Widespread interest in the hearings and in the larger issue of sexual harassment gave birth to a torrent of publications of conspicuously unequal quality. As often happens when an issue captures the public limelight, myriad writers, both popular and scholarly, exploit the latest topic by jumping on the bandwagon of its appeal. The result, with several important exceptions, is a rash of trendy books, poorly researched and hastily composed. Other than producing royalties for the authors, most books on the Hill-Thomas hearings have little enduring merit. They provide fireworks more than illumination.

In contrast to the plethora of shallow books and articles that materialized almost instantly in the wake of the 1991 hearings, *The Lynching of Language* is a sustained, serious, and significant analysis of an event that continues to shape public life and personal identity in the United States. This volume stands out from most discussions of sexual harassment in several ways. Most important, the contributors to this book took the time required to conduct substantial research and to let their ideas and analyses benefit from seasoning. *The Lynching of Language* extends prior research and theorizing by posing questions and suggesting answers that are both astute and original.

This volume is noteworthy for its complexly layered analysis of events and issues that have too often been reduced to simplistic, one-dimensional accounts. The hearings, and the larger context of gendered interaction within which they were embedded, involve multiple and intimately intertwined issues. Among those issues are race and racism, sexuality and sexism, codes of professional conduct, and the nature of public inquiry in Western society. In concert, the essays in this book provide sophisticated and often subtle insights into the Hill-Thomas hearings on two levels, both of which enlarge understanding of the ways in which cultural consciousness is shaped.

On one level, *The Lynching of Language* focuses on the dispute between Anita Hill and Clarence Thomas about what happened between them in the 1980s. In pursuing this issue, the authors tackle questions that must be asked about the 1991 drama: "Did Thomas harass Hill?" "Who told the truth in the hearings?" "How can we tell when someone is lying?" Many people, including academics, attorneys, talk show hosts, serious journalists, tabloid writers, workers, and employers across the nation, have pondered these questions. *The Lynching of Language,* however, provides better informed and more convincing answers to these questions than most analyses.

Several of the essays in this volume present previously unpublished analyses of the testimony of the leading characters in this drama. Readers will gain new insights into clues of deception and candor as they read the essays in this collection. Although readers may not unshroud the absolute truth by reading these essays, they will discover more and less tenable ways of evaluating personal credibility and public claims. The analyses in this volume are distinguished from a host of others that have been published by the authors' attention to *communicative* dimensions of the hearings.

The close readings of testimony offered by contributors to this volume illuminate ways in which the language of Hill and Thomas and the language that other participants in the hearings used to describe them sculpted perceptions of sexual harassment and the disputants' honesty and integrity. In showing how communication during the trial influenced perceptions of Hill and Thomas, this volume highlights the power of language to shape thought and judgment.

On a second level, this volume extends what others have previously noticed about the hearings and their meaning. In addition to offering new, communication-based insights into the credibility of Hill and Thomas, the authors of the essays that follow wrestle with a much larger issue—one that both encompasses and transcends the specifics of the dramatic 1991 hearings that bound even the most inveterate nonwatchers to their television sets.

A distinctive and important contribution of *The Lynching of Language* is its attention to the role of discourse, or language, in reproducing or contesting prevailing ideologies. The authors make a convincing case that discourse shaped understandings of what the hearings were. Although the chair's opening remarks asserted that the hearings were not a trial, the communication throughout the three-day affray belied that claim. The senators conducted themselves in lawyerlike ways; Hill, Thomas, and others who testified were treated as witnesses in a court trial; and the senators acted as a jury, doing what a jury conventionally does—rendering a verdict. Thus, the communication during the hearings turned them into a trial, whether officially or not.

This volume's focus on communication sheds light on the radical transformation that occurred early in the hearings/trial. Originally the assembly was called to judge Anita Hill's accusation that Clarence Thomas had sexually harassed her. In this scenario Hill was the plaintiff and Thomas the defendant who must refute charges against him or justify his actions. The tables quickly turned, however, and Anita Hill became the defendant who was on trial to defend herself against not only Thomas's claims that she was lying in claiming he harassed her but also a deluge of other charges that impugned her professional competence, personal integrity, sanity, and sexual normalcy.

The authors of this volume contribute to understanding how this remarkable turnabout transpired. By highlighting the language senators used to refer to Hill and Thomas and to interrogate them, the authors show how Hill's identity was transformed from that of a plaintiff who had been victimized to that of a spiteful, untrustworthy defendant who was assumed to be in the wrong. One communicative act pivotal in this transformation was Thomas's comparison of the hearings to a "high-tech lynching." That linguistic strategy, as several authors in this volume demonstrate, evoked a racist legacy in which black men, like Thomas, were barbarously hung by white men, like the senators. The image was powerful in reversing perceptions of who was on trial and what the trial/hearings themselves were.

Another discursive dimension of the hearings was their force in defining sexual harassment as an important issue. The nationally televised three-day spectacle named sexual harassment dramatically and wrote it indelibly onto the American agenda. The hearings thus contributed to public awareness of sexual harassment and fortified institutional and judicial motivation to address the problem.

But the hearings were not just about Anita Hill and Clarence Thomas. They were about all of us—women and men of all races, ages, and ethnicities. The hearings reflected how we see each other and how we judge conduct between us, and they shaped how we do and will deal with each other, especially in professional settings. The events behind the prime-time drama of 1991 continue to surface in factories and schoolrooms throughout the nation. As Hill and Thomas debated one another and as viewers debated what they said, we began what is an extended struggle to define what is and is not acceptable, normal, and customary in interaction between women and men in professional contexts.

Focusing on the formative power of language allows the authors in this volume to situate the 1991 proceedings within the larger social issues that the hearings highlighted. Existing scholarship on the discursive construction of social life is rich and growing. By drawing from this line of inquiry, the authors of *The Lynching of Language* enhance our understanding of how discourse creates the meaning of issues and identities in both public and private settings.

The Anita Hill–Clarence Thomas hearings concluded in 1991, yet their impact continues. Then we asked what the hearings meant; now we still do. Then we asked who told the truth; now that question continues to haunt us. Then we wondered what it said about Western society's views of women and sexual harassment that following the hearings Clarence Thomas was appointed to the highest court in the land; now that question, as well as how we answer it, shapes our thinking and our political choices. Then the hearings were a dramatic spectacle; now they are an emblem that signifies the intersecting issues of sexual activities, personal rights, and professional relationships.

Then we launched a conversation that had been silenced for too long; now we continue to engage in the dialogue that Anita Hill brought to the public stage. Although much remains murky about the hearings and their aftermath, one certainty is that the public conversation begun in 1991 will continue for many years to come. *The Lynching of Language* is an important contribution to this ongoing conversation that affects us all.

Introduction to a Communication Event: The Hill-Thomas Hearings

SANDRA L. RAGAN, CHRISTINA S. BECK,
DIANNE G. BYSTROM, AND LYNDA LEE KAID

In 1991 President George Bush nominated Judge Clarence Thomas to replace retiring Justice Thurgood Marshall on the U.S. Supreme Court. In so doing, he unwittingly set the stage for a national drama that would be played out on Capitol Hill and transmitted across America on prime-time television. Thomas's quest to become the second African American to serve on the Supreme Court became more than the usual Washington clash between conservatives and liberals, Republicans and Democrats. Professor Anita Hill's allegations that Thomas had sexually harassed her when she worked for him at the U.S. Department of Education and the Equal Employment Opportunity Commission (EEOC) in the early 1980s surfaced publicly just days before the U.S.

Senate was scheduled to vote on Thomas's nomination in early October 1991 and stirred an immediate debate that transcended party lines and impacted much more than Thomas's bid for the court.

This book was born of a sincere conviction, shared by the four coeditors as well as by many in the communication discipline, that the Anita Hill–Clarence Thomas hearings of October 1991 marked an unusual and significant communication event—unusual in the sense that no sexual harassment complaint had ever received the intense national attention and scrutiny that Hill's elicited and significant because the event sparked immediate ramifications and long-range reverberations.

Although numerous public officials and political nominees have been confronted with allegations of past improprieties as they pursue election, reelection, or political appointment, the treatment of Hill's claim by members of the Senate Judiciary Committee and by Judge Thomas during the hearings attracted unprecedented attention from the mainstream media (including prime-time coverage on the three major networks and front-page reports of the proceedings in national newspapers). Of the many ironies of the hearings (including that a former head of the EEOC was now being charged with sexual harassment in the workplace), perhaps the most profound was that the hearings themselves so closely resembled prototypical sexual harassment cases. Hill was a classic sexual harassment victim, remaining silent about the harassment for many years and maintaining professional ties with her former (harasser) employer. Although they protested to the contrary, the senators on the Judiciary Committee participated in the hearings as if they understood neither sexual harassment in general nor Hill's situation in particular.

Unfortunately, in 1991, these senators were not alone. The issue of sexual harassment in the workplace had been addressed in laws passed by Congress and in a number of subsequent court rulings, yet it had not attracted widespread attention or been discussed by most employers and employees or the public. As with Hill, victims tended not to talk about their experiences because they feared that they would not be believed and that there could be adverse career consequences if they spoke out. Further, as in Hill's case, harassed individuals who did report their harassers faced the challenge of convincing others that they were telling the truth, frequently without the benefit of eyewitnesses or actual evidence to offer as "proof." Thus, until the Hill-Thomas hearings in 1991, sexual harassment remained a workplace offense that few discussed and even fewer pursued in the courts. The hearings gave the issue a public forum that, owing to the very nature of sexual harassment, it had lacked.

As the hearings ensued, the participants worked to define themselves and each other as well as what should be treated as paramount in understanding what was occurring during the hearings. Participants repeatedly attempted to put their own "spin" on what should and should not count as salient to the hearings by charging others with political intrigue, party politics, ethical and procedural errors by senators and their staffs, racial stereotypes and bias, gender stereotypes and bias, and, of course, sexual harassment by Thomas. From senators' open accusations that colleagues in the Senate unethically released confidential documents and used Hill as a political ploy to Thomas's insinuation that his foes employed racial stereotyping, each participant's verbal and nonverbal contributions to the hearings were deliberately rhetorical. Such contributions also were consequential to the hearings and to each participant's self-presentation and public persona during and following the hearings.

For example, all of the senators felt compelled to present themselves as unbiased "judges" of the "facts" while also maintaining their political allegiances to either Hill or Thomas. Thomas's advocates faced the challenge of appearing sensitive to the issue of sexual harassment while speaking in favor of Thomas or attacking specific portions of Hill's testimony. After Thomas introduced the race issue when he referred to the proceedings as a "high-tech lynching," the senators needed to position themselves on race and to distance themselves from the appearance of possible racial stereotypes or bias. Furthermore, Thomas (who was still very much seeking confirmation to the Supreme Court and who had been challenged by liberals earlier in the hearings on his stands on women's rights and abortion) and the senators had to deal with Hill and the issue of sexual harassment in a manner that would not indicate a disregard for women, women's rights, or fair treatment for women in the workplace. From the senators on the Judiciary Committee to Professor Hill to Judge Thomas (and, to some extent, to the experts and advocates on the issues who were paraded before the public on the nightly news), their respective abilities to engage the discourse of the hearings (i.e., to articulate their perspectives and to tell their stories) literally facilitated or precluded their effective presentation of themselves and their views of the many complex issues to each other and to the public.

Indeed, the authors in this volume take the position that discourse (verbal and nonverbal) constituted many of the complex issues of the hearings and that discourse made the issues relevant to the participants in the hearings and encouraged them to explore these issues. The nature of Thomas's indignant self-defense; Hill's calm and quiet description of Thomas's alleged harassment; and the senators' orations about justice, fairness, and truth contributed to the ongoing creation of the hearings and of each participant in the hearings. Through such verbal and nonverbal interaction the participants advanced preferred images of themselves and their views of what should be treated as fact or fiction, significant or insignificant, appropriate or inappropriate.

Furthermore, the manner in which the participants interacted became the catalyst for making the hearings assume an importance beyond determining whether Thomas should be confirmed to the Supreme Court. The nature of the discourse itself during the hearings sparked the outrage of citizens who felt that the entire tenor of the hearings was unprofessional and that the overall conduct of the senators on the Judiciary Committee displayed a lack of respect for the confirmation process, for Judge Thomas, for Professor Hill, and, perhaps most damning of all, for the American citizenry. Moreover, because the way in which the senators, Hill, and Thomas presented themselves and treated each other mirrored what experts on sexual harassment knew to be typical in such cases, the hearings stirred an unprecedented public debate on the issue of sexual harassment between those who viewed the hearings as offensive to the victim and those who perceived them to be unfair to the accused. In a sense, that debate came to epitomize, symbolize, and, in some instances, polarize an ongoing, larger struggle between harassed and harasser, employer and employee, and even between women and men. The frequent accusation that "they just don't get it" and the much-cited phrase "he said/she said" attest to the clash and polarization that characterized not only the Hill-Thomas hearings but much of the discourse over sexual harassment and sexual politics in general. Because the nature of the interaction between the participants was central to the hearings and remains key to the ongoing dialogue about sexual harassment, we believe that this volume—which seeks to illuminate the hearings from a number of communication perspectives, approaches, and methodologies—will enhance our understanding of how the Hill-Thomas hearings unfolded.

Since the hearings were both audio and videotaped, they became immediately accessible to communication researchers intent on mining the discourse of the judiciary interactions. Several researchers presented the results of their investigations at the May 1992 annual meeting of the International Communication Association. By the November 1992 annual meeting of the Speech Communication Association (SCA), entire panels were devoted to the Hill-Thomas hearings, including panels sponsored by such divisions as Language and Social Interaction, Rhetorical and Communication Theory, Political Communication, Mass Communication, and the Feminist and Women's Caucus. Four essays, first presented as papers on a panel titled "The Clarence Thomas–Anita Hill Controversy: The Co-Creation of Social Activities and Selves through Language and Social Interaction," became the core of this volume. Subsequently, other researchers who had presented their work on the Hill-Thomas hearings at the 1992 and 1993 SCA annual meetings were invited as contributors. Of the book's thirteen essays, we solicited only three from researchers who did not originally present their work at these two communication conferences. Communication researchers' immediate and overwhelming response to the hearings at the November 1992 SCA meeting was a communication phenomenon in itself. No one national event had ever evoked the intensity of scholarly reaction among communication researchers as did the Hill-Thomas hearings.

In this volume, we are concerned with three different aspects of the communicative significance of the Hill-Thomas hearings: how language use and strategy in conversational practice create social meaning, how speaker credibility is maintained and destroyed through the discourse of cross-examination, and how the hearings have impacted communication in politics and the workplace. The thirteen essays of the book are divided into three sections, representing these aspects of the controversy: Language and the Creation of Meaning in the Hearings, Communication and the Creation of Credibility, and Implications of the Hearings for Politics and the Workplace.

In the first section, Language and the Creation of Meaning in the Hearings, we address the question of how the discourse of the hearings aided in the construction of their social meaning. In answering this question, researchers utilize several approaches to examine the language and the conversational interaction of the exchanges between the Senate Judiciary Committee, Hill, and Thomas. In "Analyzing the Testimony from a Legal Evidentiary Perspective: Using Judicial Language Injudiciously," Shirley A. Weigand, a law professor and colleague of Anita Hill at the University of Oklahoma School of Law who accompanied Hill to the hearings, analyzes the legal language of the hearings to discover that politics, rather than proper legal procedure, governed their conduct. Whereas the actual text of the hearings is replete with legal references, lawyerly authority, and the pretense of impartiality, the subtexts Weigand uncovers are anything but impartial and serve to promote Thomas's nomination while discrediting Hill's allegations.

In "The Doing of Gender through Cross-Examination," Christina S. Beck, Sandra L. Ragan, and Lynda Lee Kaid employ a conversation analytic approach to analyze how the cross-examination in the hearings results in the politicalization of sexual harassment. Despite the fact that Hill did not fit the senators' gender, racial, or professional stereotypes, the authors' analysis reveals that the interaction of the hearings served as catalyst for the perpetuation of perceived gender differences, which had the effect of severely undermining Hill's credibility. In "Sex, Race, and Politics: An Intercultural Communication Approach to the Hill-Thomas Hearings," Cynthia S. Roper, Mike Chanslor, and Dianne G. Bystrom deal with the overlapping roles of race, gender, and politics in the hearings. Utilizing a model of intercultural communication that explains how communication transpires between strangers, these authors reveal that the Senate Judiciary Committee's biases against an African American woman helped to undercut her credibility.

"Who Is Anita Hill? A Discourse-Centered Inquiry into the Concept of Self in American Folk Psychology," concerns the psychological construct of "self" as created through the discourse of the hearings. Erica Verrillo concludes that persons in powerful positions (e.g., Thomas) can attain and maintain power by controlling "self" image whereas lower-status persons (e.g., Hill) are permitted less control over self-definition. Her analysis thus supports those of others in this section that demonstrate how the discourse of the hearings discredits Hill while elevating Thomas. In "Impression Management Mismatch on Capitol Hill: The Anita Hill–Clarence Thomas Confrontation," Dale G. Leathers analyzes the impression management strategies of Clarence Thomas and concludes that while the Republican impression managers skillfully achieved their short-term goals, they did so at the expense of both ethical considerations and long-range credibility for Thomas and for themselves.

In each of these five essays, a careful investigation of the use of language and conversational strategy in the hearings demonstrates how prejudice and politics shape the hearings' outcome. Although the authors make no claim about the senators' intention to treat Anita Hill unjustly, their analyses show how the discourse of the hearings works inevitably to discredit Hill. Skillful manipulation of the language subverts ostensibly appropriate legal procedure, such that Hill becomes the political victim of powerful white male senators rather than the victim of sexual harassment by an also powerful black male.

The second section, Communication and the Creation of Credibility, concerns the verbal and nonverbal detection of deception as manifested in the discourse of the hearings. Essentially, the focal point of essays in this section is the credibility of Hill and Thomas, as perceived by researchers who investigated the verbal and nonverbal content of the exchanges as well as by the public in its immediate and subsequent response to the hearings. Focusing on the verbal messages of the hearings, Curtis D. LeBaron in "Looking for Verbal Deception in Clarence Thomas's Testimony" utilizes deception detection techniques advanced by the FBI Academy. He discovers clusters of presuppositions, mannerisms, and omissions throughout Thomas's testimony that, according to the FBI, indicate deception; LeBaron, however, does not subject Hill's testimony to this scrutiny.

In "Detection of Deception in the Hill-Thomas Hearings: An Analysis of Nonverbal Behavior," Valerie Cryer McKay looks at nonverbal behaviors of both Hill and Thomas during the hearings for possible clues about who was telling the truth. Researchers coded three classes of nonverbal behavior (body, facial, and vocal) but found no significant differences between Hill and Thomas on the nonverbal behaviors indicating deception. McKay suggests that we must pose the question of verity in a communication gestalt broader than the coding of nonverbal behaviors allows.

In "Believability: Narratives and Relational Messages in the Strategies of Anita Hill and Clarence Thomas," Judith K. Bowker attempts to discover why the public overwhelmingly believed Thomas at the time of the hearings and then shifted its support to Hill five months after the event. Through a multifaceted research approach incorporating survey as well as interpretive methodology, Bowker contends, among other findings, that the public's education on sexual harassment issues in the intervening months might have prompted this attitude shift. Lynda Lee Kaid, John Tedesco, and Clifford A. Jones in "Tracking Reactions: Audience Evaluations of the Hill-Thomas Hearings" use an experimental research design to measure the effects of the hearings and to gauge changes in audience evaluations. They find that males and females differed substantially in their evaluation of Hill and Thomas at every stage in the hearing process and that audiences were more favorably impressed with Thomas's vehement denials than with Hill's qualified, equivocal statements and her failure to refute the charges leveled against her character.

Utilizing the method of rhetorical criticism, Thomas J. Darwin in "Telling the Truth: The Rhetoric of Consistency and Credibility in the Hill-Thomas Hearings" traces the rhetorical strategies Republican senators employed to discredit Hill. Because such strategies display Hill's behavior as inconsistent with culturally defined roles, they portray her as liar rather than as sympathetic victim. Relying on the public's expectation that one must adopt acceptable roles (or idealized versions of these roles) to be credible, Republican senators managed to erode Hill's credibility totally.

The third section of the book, Implications of the Hearings for Politics and the Workplace, focuses on the pragmatic and long-range importance of the hearings for sexual politics. Darrin Hicks and Phillip J. Glenn in "The Pragmatics of Sexual Harassment: Two Devices for Creating a 'Hostile Environment'" suggest that one must define sexual harassment in terms of its occurrence in interaction instead of attempting to define harassment and "hostile environment" as independent of their communication contexts. They examine the Hill-Thomas hearings in the light of how Thomas asymmetrically manipulated the conversational context of the former work relationship between the two. The authors thus suggest that workplace training should focus on the practical effects of communicative behaviors instead of listing isolated behaviors or topics to be precluded from workplace interaction.

A further examination of how the Hill-Thomas hearings may have affected the dialogue between women and men regarding sexual harassment appears in "'Giving' Voice to Sexual Harassment: Dialogues in the Aftermath of the Hill-Thomas Hearings" by Leda M. Cooks, Claudia L. Hale, and Sue De-Wine. These authors interviewed sixteen professional women and men concerning their definitions of and experiences with harassment. Centering their discussion on the themes of power, choice, responsibility, and surveillance, they contend that the complexity of power relations in the workplace makes it difficult to regulate private identities through corporate policies.

In the concluding essay, "Beyond the Hearings: The Continuing Effects of Hill vs. Thomas on Women and Men, the Workplace, and Politics," Dianne G. Bystrom summarizes how race and gender have shaped the public's evaluation of the hearings—and who was telling the truth—as well as the construction of the sexual harassment allegations. She argues that no matter whom one believed, the hearings raised the nation's consciousness on the issue of sexual harassment, affected how men and women communicate in the workplace, and prompted the election of a record number of women to political office in 1992. The "Anita Hill effect" continues to exert significant influence, both in the traditional contexts of American politics and in the more generic "political" arenas for women and men—the workplace and the home.

The reader may be slightly troubled by two aspects of this volume: first, excerpts from the hearings are frequently cited by authors in support of their claims, yet these excerpts come from several different "verbatim" transcripts of the hearings rather than from one standardized transcript. We trust that transcript differences will not prove disconcerting. On a second, perhaps more problematic note, we wish to respond in advance to a potential criticism that our authors tend to favor Anita Hill and that this volume does not present a balanced account of the Hill-Thomas hearings. In fact, most academics at the University of Oklahoma, in the communication discipline, and in academia in general, *were* disposed to believe Professor Hill's testimony. We make no apologies for this partiality. She is one of our own, and her story rang true to us at the time of the hearings, as it now rings true for the majority of the American public. We hope that the authors represented in this volume, regardless of explicit or implicit bias, are convincing in their arguments. In most instances, they have let the transcript data speak for itself. Through their thoughtful, reasoned analyses, interviews, and experiments, they should at least persuade you to consider the merits of their individual cases. That is what the communicative process is all about.

When combined, the essays in this volume make a compelling argument for the claims that Professor Hill was telling the truth and that her ability to make her case to the Senate Judiciary Committee and to the viewing public was hindered severely by the way in which the hearings were conducted and the manner in which she and Thomas were treated by the senators and by each other. Each of the studies in this volume, conducted independently and from a variety of theoretical and methodological perspectives, supports such claims. This volume is unique in its offering of such a combination of empirical studies that pursue the Hill-Thomas hearings. As such, we contend that it is an important contribution to our understanding of this pivotal event for the entire issue of sexual harassment as well as male-female politics.

Part I

Language and the Creation of
Meaning in the Hearings

This is not a trial, this is not a court room. . . . This is a fact-finding
hearing. . . . this is not a trial, we are just trying to find out the
truth. . . .
SENATOR JOSEPH BIDEN

I want to assure [Judge Thomas and Professor Hill] at the outset that
they will be dealt with fairly.
SENATOR STROM THURMOND

I don't think that this body can serve as a judicial system. . . . this is a
political body, I don't think it can serve as a judicial system.
CLARENCE THOMAS

Analyzing the Testimony from a Legal Evidentiary Perspective: Using Judicial Language Injudiciously

SHIRLEY A. WIEGAND

On October 11, 12, and 13, 1991, Anita Hill, Clarence Thomas, and numerous witnesses appeared before the Senate Judiciary Committee to give their
versions of what happened ten years earlier. When they entered the Russell
Senate Office Building, they were ushered to the large doors of Room SD-
325, where the Judiciary Committee hearings were taking place. When the
doors opened, they saw a large imposing room filled with spectators, video
equipment, dozens of television and newspaper reporters, and, at the front
of the room, a long table behind which sat fourteen white men with micro-
phones in front of them and a long line of young assistants standing or sit-

ting behind them.[1] Witnesses were led to a wooden table, were supplied with a microphone and a chair, and were seated with their backs to the spectators and media so that they could face the fourteen senators. Witnesses did not speak unless asked a specific question, and they were expected to answer directly the questions put to them. Spectators were reminded to remain quiet upon threat of expulsion from the room. No one was allowed to enter the room without permission from the federal officials guarding the doors. The spectacle looked and sounded remarkably like any well-publicized trial in any other courtroom in the United States.

As in any trial, participants relied on well-defined rules designed to maintain decorum, fairness, and order. Witnesses reasonably expected that *someone* was in charge of ensuring that proceedings would run smoothly. Certainly the distinguished senators on the Judiciary Committee could be relied on to exercise evenhanded control over the hearings. After all, most of them were lawyers,[2] trained to articulate and enforce courtroom rules. Indeed, the rules governing these hearings were clearly stated from the beginning. But, as became obvious early in the proceedings, these rules were often set aside for reasons that can only be termed political.

Many who watched the hearings were not surprised by the political direction they took. After all, the committee was made up not of neutral judges appointed for life (as all federal judges are) but of politicians who are answerable to the electorate every six years. Who would not expect occasional posturing for the public and moments of argumentative bickering?

But for some who watched the hearings, and certainly for many who participated in them, the rules originally set by the committee were perceived as safeguards, guaranteeing that the process would be fair for all involved. After all, the man who had been named a Supreme Court nominee had been accused of sexual harassment during his term as director of the Equal Employment Opportunity Commission and would face accusations of the most intimate nature. His accuser, a scholarly law professor, would be called on to share the sordid details of her story with millions of television viewers. Ordinary citizens would be asked to come forward and testify, often reluctantly and at great personal expense, all for the good of their country. Surely these persons deserved at least minimal safeguards. Was it too much to expect that they might be treated with the same respect accorded witnesses in any courtroom?

This essay examines the verbal communications of the Judiciary Committee members and analyzes the text and subtexts of the committee hearings on

October 11, 12, and 13, 1991. The text was imbued with legal/judicial refer-ences, lawyer authority, and a pretense of impartiality. The subtexts were often simple politics. In most instances, the underlying subtexts served to promote Clarence Thomas's nomination and to discredit Anita Hill's allegations.

Rules as Safeguards

Modern trials in this country are designed to determine the truth. They have replaced older methods that we now deem "uncivilized." For example, in early English history, trial by ordeal resolved legal disputes. People accused of theft, assault, or witchcraft would be thrown into the river. If they sank, the water had accepted them, and they were deemed innocent. If they floated, the wa-ter rejected them, and they were deemed guilty.[3] Or, the accused might be made to walk across hot coals and the extent of their guilt would be deter-mined by the quality and extent of their scars. In this country's history, prior to the nineteenth century, when two persons disagreed about the rightness of their positions, they might resolve their dispute by engaging in a duel. Such truth-seeking ordeals have now been replaced with a formalized, structured system designed to allow the presentation of all relevant evidence in a civi-lized, orderly fashion.

All trials in this country employ two bodies of rules, both of which serve as a framework for the presentation of evidence. The federal (in federal courts) or state (in state courts) rules of civil procedure determine how a case should be handled prior to trial.[4] Those rules dictate the form and substance of the original complaint, provide time restrictions for each stage of pretrial prepa-ration, and determine which documents and other relevant information must be divulged prior to the trial.

Such a formal framework serves the same purpose that rules of a game do. It is designed to ensure that the parties are all playing the same game by the same rules. The legal framework attempts to prevent overreaching by one party who might have greater expertise, more resources, or better political connections than the other. If the "stronger" party refuses to follow the game rules, the weaker party can ask for the court's assistance in enforcing the rules. The judge serves as the administrator of this framework: "We count . . . on the guiding presence of the judge, who can employ a number of measures to lessen the impact of distributional inequalities" (Fiss, 1984, 1077).

Once the trial begins, the federal (in federal courts) or state (in state courts) rules of evidence provide the same formal guidance. These rules dictate when evidence can be presented, the form it will take, and under what circumstances evidence will be excluded. The evidence rules rest on two important axioms: (1) only facts having rational probative value are admissible, and (2) all facts having rational probative value are admissible, unless some specific rule forbids it (Wigmore, 1983). The judge determines whether any proffered fact has a rational probative value (i.e., that it contributes in a meaningful way to the discovery of the truth).

The rules of evidence play another very important role: to maintain decorum, civility, and order in the courtroom. Without these rules, the presentation of evidence could quickly result in chaos, with parties and witnesses competing to win the jury's or judge's favor by blurting out statements that are both prejudicial and unreliable. Evidence rules define in advance of trial the kinds of statements that lack rational probative value and should be excluded from the courtroom. Both sets of rules thereby provide a road map to litigation, from the filing of the original complaint through trial.

During the trial, the judge serves as enforcer of the rules. By ensuring their enforcement, the judge is able to control (to some extent) the behavior of the attorneys, their clients, and the witnesses. The judge is able to prevent badgering or abuse of witnesses and to arbitrate disputes about the admission of evidence. By following the rules, both parties have access to the same kinds of information prior to trial and are allowed the same opportunities for presentation of evidence during trial. The judge employs the rules to balance the scales of justice.[5]

The Senate Judiciary Committee Hearings: Setting the Rules

Ten of the fourteen members of the Senate Judiciary Committee were lawyers. They surely were cognizant of these evidentiary and procedural rules and the purposes they serve. What the committee members lacked, however, was an understanding of the proper role the committee itself served. Were they to act as the judge, enforcing committee rules and arbitrating disputes among the participants, or were they to serve as jurors, deciding which witnesses were credible and which were not?[6] If they assumed the role of jurors, who was in charge of enforcing the rules and maintaining decorum? Were they acting as prosecutors representing the government's position against an accused? If so, who was the accused? Or were they simply advocates, pseudoattorneys, for one party or the other? An examination of their conduct at the hearings reveals a profoundly confused process that resulted in a hearing no one seems to have found fair, civil, or even truth-determinative.

At the beginning of the hearings and throughout the three-day ordeal, Senator Joseph Biden, chair of the Judiciary Committee, attempted to impose order and decorum on the august body. Early on, he made the following statements:[7]

> This is a hearing convened for a specific purpose, to air . . . allegations which may be true or may not be true.

> This is not a trial, this is not a court room. At the end of our proceedings, there will be no formal verdict of guilt or innocence, nor any finding of civil liability. Because this is not a trial, the proceedings will not be conducted the way in which a sexual harassment trial would be handled in a court of law. . . . the rules of evidence that apply in court rooms will not apply here today. Thus, evidence and questions that would not be permitted in the court of law must, under Senate rules, be allowed here. This is a fact-finding hearing, and our purpose is to help our colleagues . . . determine whether Judge Thomas should be confirmed to the Supreme Court. We are not here, or at least I am not here to be an advocate for one side or the other with respect to the specific allegations . . . and it is my hope and belief that my colleagues here today share that view.

> In this setting, it will be easy and perhaps understandable for the witnesses to fear unfair treatment, but it is my job, as Chairman, to insure as best as I possibly can fair treatment, and that is what I intend to do. . . .

> The Chair does have the power to rule out of order questions that are not relevant to our proceedings. Certain subjects are simply irrelevant to the issue of harassment, namely, the private conduct out of the workplace relationships, and intimate lives and practices of Judge Thomas, Professor Hill and any other witness that comes before us.

> The committee is not here to put Judge Thomas or Professor Hill on trial. . . . the best way to do our job is to ask questions that are non-judgmental and open-ended, in an attempt to avoid questions that badger and harass any witness.

> The primary responsibility of this committee is fairness. (Transcript, October 11, 1991, 3–6)

This said, Senator Biden provided all participants with his vision of his proper role, most analogous to that of judge. He articulated the framework for the proceedings and the foundation of fairness that was to undergird this framework. The foundation and framework were both designed to protect all witnesses from unfairness and overextension and to determine ultimately the truth. But this framework was quickly attacked and ultimately dismantled; its foundation—fairness—also disintegrated.

Despite the destruction every viewer observed, the committee continued to employ judicial language and process to disguise what in fact had become merely a textual artifice. By doing so, the committee members hoped to convince both the media and the public that the hearings were fair, evenhanded, and truth-determinative. In the process, they diminished both their own reputations and the reputation of the country's judicial system, demonstrating that the line between judicial power and legislative ambition can become blurred in the political arena. An examination of several key judicial principles demonstrates the problem.

Burden of Proof

Our judicial system has created several different burdens of proof that either the plaintiff or the defendant bears during a trial. In a civil case (i.e., a non-criminal case), plaintiffs are generally required to convince the jury of the truth of their allegations by a mere "preponderance" of the evidence, defined as a finding that "the existence of the fact . . . is more probable than not" (Gifis, 1975, 159). Or, in rarer cases, they might have to prove their case by "clear and convincing" evidence; this burden is heavier than the preponderance burden and is defined as "such that it will produce . . . a firm belief as to the facts" (Gifis, 1975, 33). Neither burden is as heavy as that imposed on the government in a criminal case: beyond a reasonable doubt. In the criminal case, defendants are presumed innocent unless the government proves its case so conclusively and completely "that all reasonable doubts of the fact are removed from the mind" (Gifis, 1975, 170).

Every senator on the Judiciary Committee knew that the hearings did not constitute a criminal trial. No one had been charged with a criminal offense, no one had filed a formal complaint, and no one faced penal sanctions in the form of a fine or a jail sentence. The reasonable doubt standard simply played no role in the hearings.

Furthermore, because no one had brought any formal charges against anyone else, the hearings may not even have raised the applicability of either of the lower standards used in a civil case. In any event, the senators did not refer to either of the lower burdens. They did from time to time question whether either Clarence Thomas or Anita Hill bore any burden of proof. In the end, it was obvious that the senators' communications about the applicable standard were designed to confuse and influence the public rather than to maintain decorum and fairness.

Senator Orrin Hatch was the first to raise the issue. On the first day of the hearings, he cast the hearings in a criminal context by asserting, "I think it is time to be fair to the nominee. . . . He is the one who is being accused. They have the burden of showing that he is not telling the truth here . . ." (Transcript, October 11, 1991, 29).

Later that day, he emphasized the point in pure judicial terms: "I hope that nobody here, either on this panel or in this room, is saying that, Judge, you have to prove your innocence, because I think we have to remember and we have to insist that Anita Hill has the burden of proof or any other challenger, and not you, Judge. The fact of the matter is, the accuser, under our system of jurisprudence and under any system of fairness, would have to prove their case" (Transcript, October 11, 1991, 301). Moments later, Senator Alan Simpson added that Clarence Thomas must "be given the benefit of the doubt. . . . and if there is any doubt, it goes to Clarence Thomas, it does not go to Professor Hill" (302).

The next day, October 12, Senator Hatch again reminded the public of this important point, this time inventing a novel legal principle: "The burden of proof is certainly not on Judge Thomas. This is America. This is America. The burden of proof is on those *who use statements that are stereotypical statements*" (Transcript, October 12, 1991, 48, emphasis added).

This same day, Senator Biden repeatedly emphasized that the presumption of innocence rested with Clarence Thomas, in language designed to cast the hearings in terms similar to a criminal trial, with Clarence Thomas as the accused and Anita Hill as his accuser. In one speech, Senator Biden stated to Thomas, "And lastly, Judge, with me, from the beginning and at this moment, until the end, the presumption [of innocence] is with you. . . . This is not a right and wrong, until it comes down to a decision about you, and the presumption is with you. With me, the presumption is with you, and in my opinion it should be with you until all the evidence is in and people make a judgment" (Transcript, October 12, 1991, 179–81).

These numerous references to the burden of proof served to recharacter-ize the committee and the hearings. Committee members who adopted such judicial language hoped thereby to strengthen their public image as authori-tative judges. Their frequent lectures about the burden of proof were designed to serve as "jury instructions"—in this case, for the public as jury. In addi-tion, committee members attempted to treat the "fact-finding" hearings as a criminal trial, with Clarence Thomas as the accused cloaked with a mantle of innocence and Anita Hill as his accuser. In the eyes of several senators and many in the public, she became just one more woman seeking to destroy a successful man with charges of sexual harassment. At one point, Senator Howell Heflin even equated the charges with date rape. His purpose was to note that in sexual harassment cases, as in date rape cases, "there are no wit-nesses" (Transcript, October 12, 1991, 113). The effect, however, was to lump Anita Hill with other such accusers who often face an uphill battle in prov-ing their cases.

The Committee as Judge, Jury, Witness, and Prosecutor

Although the committee's chair initially portrayed the committee as a body of fact finders, this role quickly developed into a variety of roles, depending on political points to be gained. Various committee members trotted out var-ious hats at various times, now serving as judge, now jury, now witness, now prosecutor. In each instance, they employed judicial text to bolster their own credibility. The confusion of roles contributed to the confusion of result.

Senator Hatch was most active in obfuscating his role.[8] The first morning of the hearings when the questioning of Clarence Thomas had just begun, Sena-tor Hatch interjected, "This is the nomination process of a man to become a Justice of the Supreme Court of the United States, and he has been badly ma-ligned. I might add that I have a lot of sympathy for Professor Hill, too, and I am not going to sit here and tolerate her attorneys telling you or me or anybody else that, now that she has made these statements in writing, with what is, if the Judge is telling the truth—and I believe he is—scurrilous allegations, that that statement cannot be used" (Transcript, October 11, 1991, 24). At that point, the hearings already had begun to disintegrate into chaotic bickering, and the committee recessed to resolve the problems that had developed. Senator Hatch made it clear from the beginning of the hearings that he refused to remain neu-tral and viewed his role as Clarence Thomas's advocate.

Senator Arlen Specter, too, assumed a role other than neutral judge, despite his initial disclaimers. He first told Anita Hill, "I do not regard this as an adversary proceeding. . . . And my purpose, as the purpose of the hearing, generally, is to find out what happened" (Transcript, October 11, 1991, 64). Shortly thereafter, though, Senator Specter questioned her credibility and then commented on it. She had just explained why she believed it important to maintain a cordial professional relationship with Clarence Thomas after she had left his employ. Senator Specter responded, "All right. I am prepared to leave it at that. There is some relevancy to that continuing association questioning your credibility, but you have an explanation. I will leave it at that" (124).

Moments later, he questioned her again: "How reliable is your testimony in October of 1991 on events that occurred eight, ten years ago, when you are adding new factors, explaining them by saying you have repressed a lot? And in the context of a sexual harassment charge where the Federal law is very firm on a six-month period of limitation, how sure can you expect this committee to be on the accuracy of your statements?" (Transcript, October 11, 1991, 125). Here, Senator Specter served as an advocate for Clarence Thomas, again relying on his legal expertise to bolster his argument. He noted several times that had Anita Hill been filing a formal sexual harassment complaint against Clarence Thomas, federal law required her to do so within six months. She was not filing such a claim, yet his reliance on this law served to denigrate her testimony.

Later that afternoon, Senator Simpson joined Senator Specter in advocating Clarence Thomas's nomination, using the language of an attorney cross-examining Anita Hill. Although he had yet to hear from any witnesses other than Hill and Thomas, he noted that "Senator Specter pointed out some inconsistencies" in Hill's testimony (Transcript, October 11, 1991, 225). Then he continued, "Because all we have heard for 103 days is about a most remarkable man, and nobody has come forward, and they scoured his every shred of life, and nobody but you and another witness . . . has come forward. And so maybe, maybe, it seems to me you didn't really intend to kill him, but you might have. And that is pretty heavy . . . to know that 43 or 35 years of your life or 60 years of your life, where no one has corroborated what is a devastating charge, kind of a singular torpedo blow below the water line and he sinks" (226). After Simpson finished, Senator Paul Simon cautioned, "One of the things we have to do in this committee, and my colleagues in the Senate have to do, is to make an evaluation, who is telling the truth?" (Transcript, October 11, 1991, 229). But he ended his brief questioning of Anita Hill with seeming approval, "I think you have performed a great public service" (230). Over and over again, the subtext of politics surfaced through the judicial text, radically altering and distorting the meaning of the text.

That evening, Chairman Biden attempted to remind everyone of the committee's proper role. After Anita Hill ended her testimony, he stated, "Now, let me just say, Professor Hill, we have heard in a sense the half of this story today, all of your story, and we have not heard all of Judge Thomas' story. . . . I view myself again here as a finder of fact and we have yet to hear the whole story from Judge Thomas" (Transcript, October 11, 1991, 244–45). But then he continued, complimenting her honesty and straightforwardness in coming forward, telling her that he admired her and admired the way in which she handled the matter (246–47). In this way, he too varied from his perceived role as neutral fact finder. The tone had now been set for chaotic role changes throughout the remainder of the hearings.

After the dinner recess, Clarence Thomas again testified, providing Senator Hatch with another opportunity to attack Anita Hill's credibility in his powerful role of "fact finder." Senator Hatch asserted, "I have to say, cumulatively, these charges, even though they were made on all kinds of occasions, I mean they are unbelievable that anybody could be that perverted. I am sure there are people like that but they are generally in insane asylums" (Transcript, October 11, 1991, 289). The next morning, October 12, Judge Thomas again testified. Again, Senator Hatch stepped out of his role as fact finder, commenting, "Judge, there are a lot of things that just don't make sense to me in Anita Hill's testimony. . . . it bothers me because it just doesn't square with what I think is—some of it doesn't square with what I think is common experience, and just basic sense, common sense" (Transcript, October 12, 1991, 20).

It is during this period of the hearings that Senator Hatch began his role as witness. As Clarence Thomas sat mute, Senator Hatch himself testified, offering his own evidence concerning Anita Hill's credibility. He introduced a case that he implied had given her the idea for her charges against Thomas; he referred to her "slick lawyers," who may have helped her fabricate her testimony; he implied that she copied part of her testimony from a popular novel; and he stated that smart, highly paid public interest attorneys (presumably like hers) are "ruining our country" (Transcript, October 12, 1991, 31–37). At this point, Senator Hatch had completely cast aside any pretense of neutrality, he was clearly indignant, and he even dropped his studied use of legal/judicial terminology. He appeared to be an emotional, outraged witness. Chairman Biden declined to enforce the rules that he had imposed the previous day.

That afternoon, Senator Specter had an opportunity to question Clarence Thomas. He began his questioning with a speech designed to demonstrate his role as a fact finder. He asserted, "I do not view this as an adversary proceeding, and I do not represent anyone in this proceeding except the people . . . who elected me" (Transcript, October 12, 1991, 81). He said he attempted "to be scrupulously polite and professional and non-argumentative" with both Anita Hill and Clarence Thomas (82). He explained how difficult it had been to weigh the testimony and assess the credibility of Anita Hill (although he did not refer to Thomas's credibility). Then, he addressed Thomas: "And what I want to examine with you for the next few minutes is an extremely serious question as to whether Professor Hill's testimony in the morning was or was not perjury" (83). After dropping this bombshell, he continued as he had before, with Thomas sitting mute while Senator Specter testified on his behalf. He concluded, "It is my legal judgment, having had some experience in perjury prosecutions, that the testimony of Professor Hill in the morning was flat-out perjury" (88–89). His language now was heavily laden with judicial references: "In searching for credibility, let me add that I am not representing that it is conclusive or determinative, but it certainly is very probative and very weighty" (89).

Later that morning, Senator Hatch again demonstrated that he had no intention of maintaining the pretext of neutrality. He told Clarence Thomas, "Well, Judge, I hope next Tuesday you make it . . . I believe you should. And I believe it is important for every American that you do. . . . And I am proud of you. I am proud of you for not backing down" (Transcript, October 12, 1991, 142). Senator Simpson then reminded Thomas that early on Simpson had predicted that Hill's charges would "be destructive of her and some said, well, isn't that terrible of Simpson, a menacing threat. It was not menacing. It is true. That she would come forward and she would be destroyed. She will, just as you have been destroyed" (147). Simpson thereby made it clear that he had no need to hear the evidence, to maintain neutrality, or to withhold judgment, for he had already judged even before the hearings began.

Once again, the committee chair attempted to inject neutrality into the hearings. He told Clarence Thomas, "My job is not to defend you or to prosecute you. It is to see to it that you get a fair shot in a system that is imperfect but it is a good system" (Transcript, October 12, 1991, 178).

On Sunday, October 13, four witnesses appeared on behalf of Anita Hill to testify that she told them about the harassment, three of them at the time it was occurring. After their statements, Senator Simpson appeared to be struggling for his proper role as he questioned them. Simpson stated, "We are, you know, trying our best. We really are not open-minded, but trying, because we have had a vote here already. . . . we are not here as judges . . . and it becomes ever more clear every day. But we are doing our best. . . . Something terribly, something terribly bad has happened here. I don't know that we will ever find it" (Transcript, October 13, 1991, 76–77). These comments indicate that the witnesses may have forced Simpson to rethink his earlier rigid position against Anita Hill. Later Senator Ted Kennedy, apparently encouraged by the testimony of these witnesses, stated, "I hope . . . that after this panel we are not going to hear any more comments, unworthy, unsubstantiated comments, unjustified comments about Professor Hill and perjury, as we heard in this room yesterday. . . . I hope we are not going to hear more about politics" (Transcript, October 13, 1991, 91–92).

When Senator Specter questioned these witnesses, his tone was also less argumentative. Now, he seemed to be asking viewers qua jurors to remain neutral. He asked each of the witnesses, "If you had to vote yes or no on Judge Thomas, what would it be?" (Transcript, October 13, 1991, 124). He also asked them more pointedly, "Would you want to hear the rest of the testimony?" (125). His questioning was certainly disingenuous, given his earlier performance.

Later that day, Senator Simpson again commented on the unusual process:

> So, I think just for the purposes of the record—and when you get to thinking about it, and all of us, as lawyers, have you ever seen a hearing in your life like this, where the opponents of the nominee and, in particular, a single witness, or almost on a par, and a status with the nominee, is all out of balance—and that's fine, I have no problem with that, but let us all realize what is happening here. This is about Clarence Thomas . . . not Anita Hill, and it seems to have tilted off in that extraordinary way. (Transcript, October 13, 1991, 322–23)

He then placed into the record a letter from someone who had listened to Anita Hill's testimony, decided to contradict it, and so wrote a letter to Simpson, which he read into the record.

The interchanges during these three days demonstrate the confusion of roles that contributed to the confusion of process. Those committee members opposed to Clarence Thomas's nomination attempted to honor their roles as fact finders but, at several points throughout the hearings, served as advocates for Anita Hill. Those committee members supporting the nomination were less inclined to play the role that the committee chair had assigned to them, particularly during the testimony of the nominee and Anita Hill. During these moments, although clinging to judicial/legal text, they served more as prosecutors against Hill and defense attorneys and witnesses for Thomas.

Hearsay: Someone Said This about That

> Hearsay: "Evidence not proceeding from the personal knowledge of the witness, but from the mere repetition of what he has heard others say."
> *Black's Law Dictionary*, 1951

Nearly everyone in our country has an instinctive notion of what constitutes "hearsay." We know that its value is less than if witnesses/speakers tell us something they experienced firsthand. The hearsay rule in our legal system has a long history and is incorporated in Rule 801 of the Federal Rules of Evidence. The rule attempts to exclude testimony that is unreliable: "The very nature of the evidence shows its weakness, and it is admitted only in specified cases from necessity. . . . Literally, it is what the witness says he heard another person say. . . . The term [hearsay] is sometimes used synonymously with 'report' . . . and with 'rumor'" (*Black's Law Dictionary*, 1951, 852).

The hearsay rule is designed to ensure that evidence used to establish the truth of any fact or issue should be the most reliable available and should be subject to cross-examination by the party disputing that fact or issue. Suppose, for example, that two cars collide at an intersection. Both drivers are killed; there are no passengers. One eyewitness standing at the street corner has the only firsthand knowledge of the facts in dispute. The surviving children of one driver bring a lawsuit against the estate of the other driver. The sole eyewitness should be subpoenaed to testify, so that both attorneys have an opportunity to question her, to ensure that her testimony is reliable and that she is a credible witness.

In criminal cases, the right to confront witnesses directly is protected by the Sixth Amendment of the U.S. Constitution.[9] In civil cases, it is protected by the hearsay rule. But what if that sole eyewitness does not testify at trial? Instead, suppose that several of her friends are called to testify. They intend to relate what the eyewitness told them about the accident. This is hearsay. It is far less reliable; more important, it cannot be subjected to cross-examination. Faced with rigorous questions about the vision of the eyewitness, whether she had been drinking alcoholic beverages or ingesting drugs prior to the accident, whether she was distracted at the time of impact, and other questions about the reliability of her story, the friends can only provide the story that has been given to them. They have no personal knowledge about the accident itself.

Suppose that the friends of the eyewitness are not subpoenaed to testify either. Instead they send notes to one of the parties explaining what happened. Or, at the extreme, one of the parties receives anonymous notes from persons who have no direct knowledge of the accident, but they have heard from other unnamed sources about what really happened. Although the hearsay rule has numerous exceptions, it is unthinkable that any court in this country would allow this kind of "evidence" to be heard, much less introduced into the record. All lawyers know better.

The most obvious disparity between a judicial proceeding and the Senate hearings took place in this crucial area of hearsay evidence. Here, as in other areas, the senators cloaked their actions in judicial/legal text to impress viewers with their legal expertise while at the same time advancing their political subtexts. Once it became clear to the committee that the hearsay door had opened, committee members rushed through, carrying in their arms loads of materials to offer the viewing public. In this respect, if in no other, any resemblance to a court hearing, even a "fact-finding" hearing, was quickly lost.

The order of the first day of hearings was as follows: Clarence Thomas read his statement. He was asked no questions at that time, with the understanding that he would return after Anita Hill had testified. Anita Hill read her statement. The committee questioned her extensively. Immediately after Thomas read his statement, Senator Hatch raised the right of confrontation and insisted that it be honored. His comment was a response to Senator Biden's statement that the committee was "not at liberty to publicly discuss what is in the FBI report" (Transcript, October 11, 1991, 29). Senator Hatch objected: "The heck we're not. . . . I think it is time to be fair to the nominee. . . . he has a right to face the accuser and everything the accuser says, and if he does not, then I am going to resign from this committee today. I am telling you, I don't want to be on it" (29). He thus made it clear that accusations should be met head-on with the accuser appearing in person.

Although Clarence Thomas would be asked to respond to Anita Hill's testimony, she was asked to respond to a variety of accusations from a variety of sources. For example, in his first question to her, Senator Specter asked her about a conversation she had had with someone she had met earlier that year (Transcript, October 11, 1991, 65). Then he questioned her about a statement he had from one of her former colleagues (67), about a statement made in a newspaper by a friend of hers (79), and about a former coworker's accusation in the *New York Times* that Hill was disappointed and frustrated that Thomas "did not show any sexual interest in her" (119). Specter read from another statement by the former dean of a law school where Hill had taught, who believed her allegations to be "the product of fantasy," and Specter asked her, "Would you care to comment on that?" (124). He then handed Hill a statement from John Doggett (a man she barely knew and had not spoken to in ten years) so that he could question her about the allegations in it (120).

This was the last straw for Senator Patrick Leahy. He attempted to curb what he viewed as an abuse of the process, noting that the committee members had agreed to certain "ground rules." He added, "And we have all had to develop whatever we were going to do within those ground rules. This [the Doggett statement] would go outside them, and as one who has been designated to ask questions, I would find it very difficult to do any kind of a follow up on this not having been able to at least delve into a statement of somebody who is not going to be a witness, but used almost as though they had been" (Transcript, October 11, 1991, 151). In response, Senator Hatch denied knowing about the ground rules. Somewhat disingenuously, he asserted, "I have not heard of this that you can't ask a witness questions. Now, admittedly we may decide that we do not call this man as a witness, but it is a verified statement, as I understand it. . . . It is relevant to the proceedings" (152). After further wrangling, Anita Hill agreed to respond to the statement. The chair attempted to reestablish the ground rules: "From now on, though, as I said, no document will be put in place until every member has had time" (155).

Just minutes later, Senator Specter referred to (but did not provide) an affidavit from yet another stranger to the proceedings. This provoked a response from Senator Howard Metzenbaum, who asserted that the rules were again being violated: "What we have now, within the last 15 minutes we were presented five pieces of paper, some of which are notarized, some of which aren't, various people making certain statements. . . . now we find that this lady is being called upon to respond to these statements" (Transcript, October 11,

1991, 163). After additional heated debate, the chair ruled that such statements could not be used to replace live witnesses, declaring that "this is another way of getting in two, five, seven, ten, twenty witnesses without their being able to be cross-examined representing what they said" (170). This determination would have ended the problem in a legal proceeding.

But later in Anita Hill's testimony, Senator Simpson raised a question: "Mr. Chairman, there are two additional documents here, and I am asking and take your advice, from the two FBI agents who are—if this has been furnished for over two hours under the rules—the affidavits from the two FBI agents indicating the inconsistencies as expressed by Professor Hill this morning. Is that not appropriate?" Astonishingly, Senator Biden responded, "It is appropriate. . . . At some point maybe we should read it. I think it may be helpful for you to read the entire thing in the record." Simpson then summarized the affidavit, which Anita Hill had had no opportunity to read (Transcript, October 11, 1991, 221–23).

Thomas supporters were not the only ones to breach the hearsay rule. When Clarence Thomas returned to answer questions, Senator Heflin raised another allegation that he had seen on a recent television show having to do with Thomas's failure to promptly fire a known sexual harasser in the EEOC. The only other hearsay introduced during Thomas's questioning came from Senator Hatch, who repeated Senator Joseph Lieberman's statement in support of Thomas (Transcript, October 11, 1991, 269–70).

The next day brought a new round of hearsay evidence. During the questioning of Clarence Thomas, Senator Hatch took over the testimony, reading from another case involving sexual harassment to prove that Anita Hill had fabricated her testimony. He then referred to an article in the *Washington Post* and summarized its attack on Hill (Transcript, October 12, 1991, 31–36). Senator Biden also referred to a newspaper article about Thomas, but very deferentially: "Now, as I am sure, if you don't know, I am sure it was pointed out to you, we all know that everything that is reported isn't true, not because it is intentionally meant to mislead, but sometimes there is a miscommunication. It was reported in the *New York Times* . . . that 'Judge Thomas told the investigators . . . that he had asked the woman out a few times. . . .' I assume that is a misunderstanding?" Clarence Thomas, of course, agreed that it was (Transcript, October 12, 1991, 58).

Later, Senator Strom Thurmond related for Clarence Thomas various reasons that might have motivated Anita Hill to fabricate her charges. He gathered the list from "talking with several people, some of them the press, and other people," and he asked Thomas to comment on them. He recounted the speculations, one after another, noting that one came from "several people" and another from "someone." Wisely, Thomas declined to speculate (Transcript, October 12, 1991, 80–81).

Senator Heflin was more careful in observing the committee's ground rules when he asked Thomas about Angela Wright, a woman who had been questioned by the FBI concerning her assertion that Thomas had sexually harassed her. He began by asking Thomas, "All right, have you seen the deposition of Angela Wright that has been taken in this case?" Thomas responded, "No, senator." Heflin countered, "Well, then I will wait on that. That has some reference in your relationship with Juan Williams. I suppose she is going to testify and the proper place would be to ask then" (Transcript, October 12, 1991, 112). That was the end of it.

Perhaps the best that can be said of much of this hearsay testimony is that Anita Hill and Clarence Thomas were confronted with it while they were still testifying; they could at least dispute it. The same cannot be said for some of the later hearsay testimony.

For example, while Clarence Thomas was testifying, Senator Hatch read long excerpts from an article in that day's *Washington Post,* written by Juan Williams, an ardent supporter of the Thomas nomination. In his article, which Hatch read aloud, Williams attacked those who opposed the nomination, referring to their actions as a "slimy exercise orchestrated in the form of leaks." After reading the article, Hatch asked Thomas to describe what it feels like to be "unjustly accused of sexual harassment" (Transcript, October 12, 1991, 136–40).

Senator Simpson joined the fray, announcing, "And now, I really am getting stuff over the transom about Professor Hill. I have got letters hanging out of my pockets. I have got FAXES. I have got statements from her former law professors, statements from people that know her, statements from Tulsa, Oklahoma saying, watch out for this woman. But nobody has got the guts to say that because it gets all tangled up in this sexual harassment crap" (Transcript, October 12, 1991, 146). No one on the committee objected to this comment. Simpson then referred to Angela Wright, whose name Senator Heflin had briefly raised earlier, but he insisted on characterizing her, in case she was called to testify: "Angela Wright will soon be with us, we think, but now we are told that Angela Wright has what we used to call in the legal trade, cold feet. Now, if Angela Wright doesn't show up to tell her tale of your horrors, what are we to determine about Angela Wright?" Then Simpson and Thomas speculated why she might have motivation to lie, Simpson finally referring to her as "a totally discredited and, we had just as well get to the nub of things here, a totally discredited witness who does have cold feet" (148–49). It is no wonder that Wright eventually decided not to appear at this proceeding.[10]

The next day, the matter of hearsay came up again, again in the context of Angela Wright's testimony. Senator Biden indicated that she might yet be willing to testify. Senator Thurmond emphasized that if she did, the committee had a right to cross-examine her. Biden replied, "That is absolutely correct." Thurmond responded, "But we object to any statement by her, or affidavit, being put in the record without cross-examination." Biden again replied, "That is absolutely correct" (Transcript, October 13, 1991, 158). No mention was made about the numerous times that Thomas's supporters had introduced hearsay into the record.

A few hours later, the news media learned that Anita Hill had taken and passed a polygraph examination. This information was not introduced into evidence, but Senator Hatch raised it nevertheless, claiming to be "highly offended" because such evidence "wouldn't even be admissible in a court of law" (Transcript, October 13, 1991, 238). Of course, neither would his comments. The senators began to quibble about the weight, if any, that the polygraph examination should carry, when Senator Hatch again raised objections. He asserted that introducing such evidence "as though it is real, legitimate evidence is highly offensive . . . and highly political, and again, too pat, too slick, exactly what a two-bit slick lawyer would try to do in the middle of something as important as this" (252–53). When Senator Metzenbaum attempted to place into the record the credentials and qualifications of the polygraph examiner, the chair refused (255). But he allowed both Senators Hatch and Specter to testify that the polygraph is unreliable and that it can yield any result, depending on the qualifications of the examiner (252, 254).

Senator Simpson joined in, introducing into the record a statement by a former U.S. attorney about the "total unreliability of a polygraph test" (Transcript, October 13, 1991, 260). Without objection, he read from the statement that "'if a person suffers from a delusional disorder he or she may pass a polygraph test. Therefore, a polygraph examination in this context has absolutely no bearing on whether the events at issue are true or untrue'" (264). Again, no one questioned the admissibility of this "evidence."

Toward the end of the hearings, Senator Leahy also was compelled to bring in a newspaper article to rebut the testimony of one of the Thomas witnesses. Charles Kothe, former dean of the Oral Roberts Law School, had testified that Clarence Thomas would never even think about pornographic movies. Senator Leahy then asked him if he was aware that one of Thomas's supporters was quoted in the *New York Times* as saying that Thomas talked about pornographic movies while a law student (Transcript, October 13, 1991, 436). Clearly, at this point in the proceedings, no one was inclined to object.

Conclusion

In the first hour of the Senate Judiciary Committee hearings on October 11, the committee chair imposed on the proceedings a text that he hoped would guide committee members for the next three days. The text, supposedly fashioned by committee agreement, employed a quasi-judicial framework designed to determine the truth and ensure fairness for all the participants. Within hours, the subtext of politics prevailed.

Unfortunately for Anita Hill, and fortunately for Clarence Thomas, the subtexts were most often employed by Thomas's supporters, particularly Senators Hatch, Simpson, and Specter. Early in the hearings, they rejected the chair's textual framework with its accompanying rules.

As with any game, once the rules were set aside, no safeguards were available to prevent abuse of the process. The players continued to play the game, from time to time feigning adherence to the text but more often inventing their own rules to promote political subtexts. In the end, the voices of those who adhered most closely to the text were drowned out by the din of those who viewed these hearings as no more than just another political battle.

NOTES

Professor Wiegand accompanied Professor Anita Hill to Washington in October 1991 for the Senate Judiciary Committee hearings.

   1. Present were Senators Joseph Biden, Hank Brown, Dennis DeConcini,

Charles Grassley, Orrin Hatch, Howell Heflin, Ted Kennedy, Herb Kohl, Patrick Leahy, Howard Metzenbaum, Paul Simon, Alan Simpson, Arlen Specter, and Strom Thurmond.

2. Ten members of the fourteen-member committee held law degrees. Only Senators Grassley, Kohl, Simon, and Thurmond did not.

3. Obviously, the point would be moot if they were not pulled from the water in a timely fashion.

4. In criminal trials, courts employ rules of *criminal* procedure, some of which are indistinguishable from the civil rules.

5. Obviously, the scales are not always perfectly balanced. When one party has substantially more money than the other, that party can hire several of the most experienced attorneys and can afford to pay those attorneys for far more hours of work than the poorer party. Some parties can afford to delay the litigation more than others can. In some cases, the parties may have few financial resources but can summon the power of public opinion to tip the scales in their favor. The rules in these cases will not provide sufficient influence to equalize the parties' positions.

6. Members of the Senate Judiciary Committee are still confused about their roles. In the controversy over the nomination of the law professor Lani Guinier, Senator Carol Moseley-Braun (Democrat from Illinois) was criticized for her lack of vocal support for the nominee. Both women are African Americans. Moseley-Braun's press secretary defended her boss, claiming that "the senator has a policy of not commenting on nominees until there is a confirmation hearing, because she sees her role on the Judiciary Committee as similar to that of a judge." (Branan, 1993, 56).

7. Quotations throughout this essay are taken from the transcript of proceedings prepared by the Miller Reporting Company, Inc., Washington, D.C. References are made to the date of the hearing. Occasionally, for clarity, I have corrected in my text obvious typographical errors without indicating such correction.

8. Obviously, Senator Hatch was well aware of how his behavior would play to television viewers and how it would benefit Clarence Thomas. He apparently did not agree with the role that Senator Biden had assigned to the committee.

9. The Sixth Amendment reads in part, "In all criminal prosecutions, the accused shall enjoy the right to a speedy and public trial . . . and . . . to be confronted with the witnesses against him. . . ."

10. Apparently the decision to release Angela Wright from her subpoena was the result of an agreement between Senator Biden's office and Wright. Her deposition was entered into the Congressional Record, however. See Mayer and Abramson, 1994, 343–44.

REFERENCES

Black's law dictionary. (1951). 4th ed. St. Paul, Minn.: West Publishing.

Branan, K. (1993, September–October). Lani Guinier: The anatomy of a betrayal. *Ms.*, 51–56.

Fiss, O. M. (1984). Against settlement. *Yale Law Journal*, 93: 1073–90.

Gifis, S. H. (1975). *Law dictionary*. Woodbury, N.Y.: Barron's Educational Series.

Mayer, J., and Abramson, J. (1994). *Strange justice: The selling of Clarence Thomas*. New York: Houghton Mifflin.

Wigmore, J. H. (1983). *Evidence in trials and common law*. Vol. 1. 4th ed. (Tiller's revision). Boston: Little, Brown.

The tortured tale has all the elements of a classic case of sexual harassment. The male boss indignantly swears he did nothing wrong. The female employee insists he did. There are no other witnesses. The aggrieved woman waits years before coming forward. And other men seem perfectly willing to ignore the matter.

S. GARLAND AND T. SEGAL, *Business Week*, OCTOBER 21, 1991

2

The Doing of Gender through Cross-Examination

CHRISTINA S. BECK, SANDRA L. RAGAN,
AND LYNDA LEE KAID

In early October 1991, after weeks of investigation, interrogation, and speculation, the U.S. Senate seemed set to vote on the confirmation of Clarence Thomas, a black conservative from the South, to the U.S. Supreme Court.[1] In fact, when word of Anita Hill's allegations of sexual harassment by Thomas spread on the eve of the confirmation vote, "it took a national uproar and unusual pressure in the Capital to change the dynamic" (Borger, Walsh, Thornton, and Gest, 1991, 36).

The ensuing Senate Judiciary Committee hearings on the allegations by Hill, a tenured law professor from the University of Oklahoma, thrust two unwilling witnesses (and equally unwilling members of the committee) and the very issue of sexual harassment into living rooms and boardrooms across the country. As Lewis Lapham (1991, 10) details, the Nielson ratings of the hearings confirmed there was widespread attraction to an unusual peek at politics in progress. The American people understood precisely what they were looking at and why, and their appreciation of the rarity of the October hearings showed up in the Nielson ratings. On the Friday evening Judge Thomas delivered his philippic against Anita Hill and the premises of democratic government, the two networks that broadcast the proceedings (ABC and NBC) received a 40 percent share of the audience. A championship baseball game appearing simultaneously on CBS received only 19 percent (Lapham, 1991, 10).

Regardless of their reasons for watching or their perceptions of Hill's or Thomas's honesty, Americans witnessed the colorful clash of gender, race, and politics encompassed in this case.[2] According to Gloria Borger and Kenneth Walsh (1991), "Once Hill's charges of sexual harassment against him [Thomas] leaked into public view, the fight escalated into a drama with all the intensity of the last days of a political campaign" (34). Moreover, as James Wall (1991) argues, "these unprecedented public hearings have taken public debate in the political arena to a new level of exposure" (955).

Using a microanalytic approach based on ethnomethodology, this essay explores one central dimension of these politically and socially significant hearings: the accomplishment and consequence of gender. Specifically, this examination of the Hill-Thomas hearings pursues, first, the patterns of language behavior that differ according to the gender of the key participants and, second, a preliminary explanation for the subsequent treatment of sexual harassment as a societal and political issue.

Ethnomethodological Foundation

Expanding on the works of Harold Garfinkel (1967), ethnomethodologists argue that social actors accomplish activities (such as the "doing" of "gender") only through interaction. As those social actors present themselves to others, they must necessarily make their activities available to others "accountably," that is, in a way that those others will recognize that activity as such.[3] For example, Garfinkel (1967) discusses the case study of "Agnes," a transsexual, who faced the challenge of learning how to present herself convincingly as a "woman" to others in this society (116–85).

In turn, based on their common sense understanding, social actors engage in the ongoing process of determining whether, for example, a certain display "counts as" an instance of "doing a gender" or "being a credible witness" (see, especially, Garfinkel, 1967, 78). The interactional treatment provides the means through which the particular identity is created and perpetuated.

In the case of the Clarence Thomas and Anita Hill hearings, the microlanguage behavior enables participants to present themselves as a particular "type" of person, given their self-presentation and their treatment of others. Analyzing this case thus involves more than simply comparing the content of what "he said" and "she said." Because the issue of gender played an integral part in the hearings, this microanalysis offers a valid way to describe and analyze the ways in which the participants presented themselves to each other and to the millions of television viewers.

Methods

Videotapes of the CNN coverage of the Hill-Thomas hearings in early October 1991 served as the data for this study. Excerpts of interactions between Hill and the Senate questioners and between Thomas and the Senate questioners were transcribed using conversation analytic conventions developed by Gail Jefferson (Atkinson and Heritage, 1984). All interactions that included instances of potential conflict (e.g., interruptions, disagreements, challenges) were transcribed. Nonconsequential descriptions (such as detailing job descriptions or personal or work history) were not included in this sample. These transcripts were then examined to determine patterns of language behavior regarding the nature of questions and responses by the various key participants.

Results

As this real-life drama unfolded in the Senate hearing room, Anita Hill stood alone, as the sole female participant, facing all-male committee members and a male counterpart, Judge Thomas. Although Senator Arlen Specter claimed at the beginning of his questioning of Anita Hill that he did not consider the hearings to consist of "adversarial relationships," the participants' interaction was clearly the interaction of opponents.[4] According to Gloria Borger, Ted

Gest, and Jeannye Thornton (1992), "By the time Thomas and Hill had given their opening statements, the nation was locked in a fierce and irreconcilable he-said, she-said battle" (33).

As the following discussion indicates, the way in which the participants made their gender apparently relevant to these hearings consists of more than the content of the diverse testimony by Hill and Thomas regarding the allegations. Of particular significance for simultaneous and subsequent debate about gender differences in the perception and treatment of sexual harassment charges, the male participants' confrontational and potentially threatening style contrasted sharply with Hill's nonconfrontational, nonthreatening manner of responding to questions.

Confrontational Nature of Male Participants

As Republican senators on the Senate Judiciary Committee questioned Anita Hill and as Clarence Thomas responded to committee members' inquiries about the allegations, they recurrently did so in a confrontational, potentially face-threatening manner. Extending from Erving Goffman's (1955) conception of face and Penelope Brown and Stephen Levinson's (1987) theory of politeness, face threats include verbal and nonverbal behavior that may hurt, embarrass, or humiliate another person, resulting in a loss of "face" for that person. In this case, the primary male participants in the hearings engaged in such face-threatening behavior through, first, directly challenging the beliefs of others; second, directly accusing and insulting others; and third, directly defining acceptable/unacceptable procedures, actions, and words.

Directly Challenging the Beliefs of Others

As excerpts one and two exemplify, members of the Senate Judiciary Committee repeatedly challenged Anita Hill's testimony in a direct and face-threatening manner. Although these questions and comments by Senator Arlen Specter fall short of directly accusing Anita Hill of lying, they do question the validity of her beliefs and the accuracy of her testimony, given her previous comments. (See the appendix at the end of this volume for an explanation of the symbol system used in the excerpts.)

Excerpt One

1	Specter:	did yo:u (.2) ca:ll (.) the: (.) »telephone log«
2		i:ssue (.) garbage (.1) unquote=
3	Hill:	=I believe »that the« issue i:z garbage (.1) when you
4		look a:t (.) hhh (.) what (.) you:re (.) u:h (.) what
5		se:ems »to be« impli:ed by (.) fro:m (.) »the
6		telephone« (.) log (.) yes (.) that i:z garbage (.5)
7	Specter:	»have you« se:en (.) the (.) records (.2) »ov
8		the« telephone lo:gs (.) »Pro⌈fessor Hill«⌉
9	Hill:	⌊»yes I« ⌋ have (.7)
10	Specter:	»do you« den:y the a.ccuracy (.) »ov these«
11		telephone lo:gs=
12	Hill:	= n:o (.) »I do« no:t (.)
13	Specter:	»then you« (.) no:w conce:de (.) »that you« had
14		ca:lled (.2) »Judge Thomas« (.1) eleven ti:mes (.1)
15	Hill:	I »do not« den:y the a:ccuracy »ov these« lo:gs (.1)
16		hhh I (.) I (.) cannot den:y »that theyre« accurate
17		(.) hhh um (.) »and I« will conce:de that (.) those
18		»phone calls« were made (.) yes (.)
19	Specter:	so (.) »theyre not« garbage (.)
20	Hill:	well (.1) senator (.) what I said (.) waz (.) the
21		i:ssue (.) iz garbage (.) those (.) telephone
22		me:ssages (.) hhh do not i:ndicate (.1) hhh tha:t
23		(.1) uh (.) which (.) theyre being u:sed (.) »to
24		indicate« (.1) that iz that (.) somehow (.) »I waz«
25		pursu:ing hhh something mo:re (.) »than a« co:rdial
26		(.1) relationship (.) professional relationship (.1)
27		each »ov those« ca:lls were ma:de (.) »in a«
28		professional co:ntect (.) text (.) so:me »ov those«
29		ca:lls (.) hhh revolved around (.) o:ne incident (.)
30		se:veral »ov those« ca:lls »in fact« (.) thre:e
31		involved (.1) hhh involved (.) one incident (.)
32		»where I« waz (.) tr:ying to (.) hhh »act on« behalf
33		(.) ov (.) another grou:p (.1) hhh so (.2) the (.)
34		i:ssue (.) »that iz« being crea-.ted »by the«
35		telepho:ne (.) calls (.) yes (.) indeed (.) iz garbage

In this excerpt, Specter leads a line of questioning regarding records that indicate Anita Hill attempted to call Judge Thomas eleven times over a period of nine years. In lines 1 and 2, Specter asks Hill about the *Washington Post* report that she called the telephone log issue "garbage." Hill responds to the inquiry by explaining why she believes that the issue is "garbage" in lines 3 through 6. She emphasizes the implications that may be drawn from the telephone log constitute "garbage"; she did not call the actual log "garbage."

However, Specter responds to Hill's explanation by directing a series of questions in lines 7–8, 10–11, 13–14, and 19 that serve as an exploration of Hill's position on the accuracy of the telephone log. In lines 7 and 8, Specter asks Hill if she has "<u>se:en</u>" the records and then, in lines 10 and 11, if she denied "the a:ccuracy (.) »ov these« telephone lo:gs." After Hill acknowledges that she has, indeed, examined the logs (line 9) and that she does not deny the accuracy of the logs (line 12), Specter verbalizes the implication of Hill's acknowledgement that the logs are valid by asking Hill whether she "no:w conce:de[s] (.) »that you« had ca:lled (.2) »Judge Thomas« (.1) 11 ti:mes" (lines 13–14).

Given Hill's concession in lines 15 through 18 that the logs are "accurate," Specter challenges Hill by stating "so (.) »theyre not« garbage" (line 19). Hill responds to Specter's suggestion that her beliefs lack foundation by reexplaining that the implications from the log, not the log itself, are "garbage" (lines 20–35). Specter's line of questioning presents a possible threat to Hill as a credible, honest, logical person by offering a line of reasoning that makes her claim appear invalid and unsubstantiated. As excerpt two indicates, Specter also lodged even more direct challenges to Hill's testimony.

Excerpt Two

1	Specter:	you (.) did no:t (.) te:ll (.) the FBI: (.2) that
2		(.) Judge Thomas (.) »waz guilty« (.) »ov sexual«
3		harassment (.2) did you (.2)
4	Hill:	I:don't (.) reca:ll »telling them« »that he waz«
5		guilty (.) »ov sexual« harassment (.1) no (.) I=
6	Specter:	=well you didn't characterize his co:nduct (.)
7		»ov sexual« harassment (.2)
8	Hill:	I'm (.) I (.) <u>di:d</u> (.) »or did« <u>no:t</u>=
9	Specter:	=you (.) did no:t (.) characteri:ze (.2) Judge
10		Thomas's condu:ct (.) »az sexual« harassment (.1)
11		»when you« <u>ga:ve</u> »tha statement« (.1) to the FBI (.2)
12		correct (.1)
13	Hill:	well (.2) senator (.) I <u>gue:ss</u> (.) »I m not« making

14		myself clea:r (.2) hhh (.) I wa:z no:t (.) ra:ising
15		(.) a le:gal (.) clai:m (.) in ei:ther (.) »ov my«
16		stateme:nts (.2)
17	Specter:	hmm (.)
18	Hill:	I »waz not« raising »a legal« claim (.1) hhh I waz
19		(.) »attempting ta« (.) to info:rm (.) hhh about =
20		co:nduct (.1)
21	Specter:	bu (.1) but (.) you di:d (.) rai:se (.) »a legal«
22		clai:m (.) in your intervie:w (.) »on Octob:r«
23		se:venth (.)
24	Hill:	no: (.) I »did not« rai:se »a legal« claim the:n (.1)
25	Specter:	well (.) I will (.) produce »the transcript« (.)
26		which sa:ys (.1) hhh that »it waz« (.) »sexual
27		harassment« (.)
28	Hill:	well (.) I would ss (.) suggest that call (.) saying
29		»that it iz« sexual hara:ssment (.1) and rai:sing
30		»a legal« clai:m (.) »are two« different thi:ngs (.)
31		hhh what I: waz trying »to do« (.1) hhh »when I«
32		provided informa:tion (.) »to you« (.) hhh waz no:t
33		(.) to yo:u (.) hhh I am clai:ming (.) »that
34		this«ma:n (.) sexually hara:ssed me (.1) »what I«
35		waz sa:ying (.) and »what I «say (.) state (.) state
36		no:w (.1) i:z (.) hhh that (.) this condu:ct (.2) »uh
37		took« place (.1) you have »your own« legal staff (.1)
38		»and many« (.) »are lawyers« (.) yourselves (.1) you
39		ca:n (.) investigate (.1) and (.) determine (.)
40		whether »or not« (.1) it (.) iz (.) sexual harassment
41		(.1) »and thatz« one »ov tha« things »that I« wanta
42		»get away« from (.1) hhh were I fi:ling (.) a clai:m
43		(.1) »if I« were filing »uh complaint« (.) in cou:rt
44		(.1) hhh this »would be« do:ne (.) very differently
45		(.2)»but this« does not co:nstitute (.1) a le:gal
46		complaint (.2)
47	Specter:	so: (.) tha:t (.) you (.) are (.) not (.) no:w (.2)
48		dra:wing (.) »uh conclusion« (.) »that Judge« (.)
49		Thomas »sexually harassed« you
50	Hill:	yes (.) I a:m (.) drawing that conclusion (.)
51		[that iz m:y
52	Specter:	[well then I] don't understand (.)
53	Hill:	pardon me (.1)

54	Specter:	»then I« don t understand (.2)
55	Hill:	we:ll (.) le:t me (.1) »try to« (.) explai:n again
56		(.2) I: (.2) »brought this« (.) information (.)
57		forward (.2) <u>fo:r</u> (.1) »the committee« (.) »to make«
58		(.) »their own« decisions (.2) I (.) did <u>no:t</u> (.)
59		bring »the information« forward (.2) to: »try to«
60		establish (.1) »a legal« claim (.) »ov sexual«
61		harassment (.1) I »brought it« forward (.) »so that«
62		the (.) commi:ttee (.) could determine (.) the
63		veracity »ov it« (.1) the <u>truth</u> »ov it« (.) and (.)
64		» from there« <u>o:n</u> (.) <u>yo:u</u> could evaluate (.1) the
65		information (.1) uh »az to« (.) »az to« whe:ther »or
66		not« it constituted (.) sexual harassment (.1) hhh or
67		(.1) whether (.) »or not« (.) it (.) went (.1) to
68		(.1) hiz (.1) ability (.2) hhh to conduct (.2) »uh
69		job« (.) »az tha« (.) »az an« (.) associate justice
70		(.) »ov tha« Supreme Court. . . .

In this series of questions, Senator Specter engages Professor Hill in a discussion of the nature of her allegations against Thomas. Specter points out, through his questions in lines 1–3, 6–7, and 9–12, that Hill "did no:t (.) characteri:ze (.2) Judge Thomas's condu:ct (.) »az sexual« harassment" (lines 9–10) when she spoke to the FBI. Hill responds by explaining that she "wa:z no:t (.) r:aising (.) a le:gal (.) claim (.) in <u>ei:</u>ther (.) »ov my« state<u>me:nts</u>" (lines 14–16). After Specter reacts only with a quick "hmm," Hill rephrases her explanation for not calling the behavior "sexual harassment" (lines 18–20).

Specter directly counters Hill's testimony by referring to a statement on October 7 (before the hearings yet after the FBI report) by stating "bu (.1) but (.) you <u>di:d</u> (.) rai:se (.) »a legal« clai:m (.) in your intervie:w" (lines 21–22). After Hill briefly denies that she did so (line 24), Specter further challenges the validity of Hill's testimony by offering to present documentation that Hill did call the behavior "sexual harassment" (lines 25–27). Through his statements (notably, *not* questions) in lines 21–23 and lines 25–27, Specter implies that Hill's testimony is inconsistent with her statements to the FBI and that Hill strengthened her allegations between the FBI report and the October 7 interview, thus posing a threat to Hill's credibility and honesty. Hill responds to this threat by explaining that she simply wanted Thomas's conduct examined, that she did not want to file a legal claim, and that the senators could determine for themselves whether the behavior constituted sexual harassment (lines 28–46).

Specter reacts to Hill's explanation by suggesting that Hill no longer draws "»uh conclusion« (.) »that Judge« (.) Thomas »sexually harassed«" her (lines 47–49). Through this reaction, Specter, again, lodges a potential face threat by implying that Hill's assessment of what transpired between Thomas and her had changed. Hill reiterates that she is "drawing that conclusion" (line 50), and Specter states that he does not understand (lines 52 and 54). Hill then attempts to "explai:n again" (line 55) that she considers the conduct to constitute sexual harassment but that she did not choose to label the behavior as such in her FBI report because she did not want to file a legal claim of sexual harassment.

In both excerpts one and two, Specter's manner of cross-examination exemplifies that of other Republican senators as they interrogated Professor Hill. They recurrently used face-threatening questions and statements that subtly and overtly challenged the validity of her beliefs. The male participants also continually incorporated accusations and insults into their questions and responses during the hearings.

Directly Accusing and Insulting Others

Throughout the hearings, tempers flared as the senators argued about hearing procedures and accused each other of leaking the information that had prompted the public hearings. Although the transcripts provide many examples of such interactions between the male senators, Clarence Thomas lodged vehement attacks on the "lies" and on the Senate Judiciary Committee's "validation" of those "lies," which made the senators' interactions with each other and with Hill appear restrained.

Excerpt Three

1	Thomas:	I think that (.1) this (.) to<u>da:y</u> (.1) »iz a«
2		travesty (.2) I think that »it iz« (.) disgu:sting
3		(.2) I (.) think (.) that <u>thi:s</u> (.1) hearing (.4)
4		should never (.1) occu:r (.1) »in America« (.2) this
5		»iz uh« <u>ca:se</u> (.) »in which« this <u>slea:ze</u> (.2) this
6		<u>di:rt</u> (.2) waz <u>sea:rched</u> fo:r (.) by (.) <u>sta:ffers</u>
7		(.) »ov members« (.) »ov this« commi:ttee (.2) »waz
8		then« (.) <u>leaked</u> (.1) »to tha« media (.1) »and <u>this</u>«

9	committee (.1) »and this« body (.2) validated it (.2)
10	and displa:yed it (.2) »on prime« ti:me (.2) over our
11	enti:re nation (.1) »how would« a:ny member (.2) »on
12	this« committee (.2) a:ny person (.1) »in this« room
13	(.1) or a:ny person (.) »in this« country (.1) would
14	like slea:ze (.) said about (.1) him »or her« (.1)
15	»in this« fashion (.2) »or this« di:rt (.1) dredged
16	up (.1) »and this« go:ssip (.1) hhh »and these« li:es
17	(.) displa:yed (.) »in this« manner (.1) »how would«
18	a:ny person (.) like it (.2) the Supre:me Court (.)
19	»iz not« (.) »worth it« (.2) no jo:b (.) iz »worth
20	it« (.1) »I'm not« he:re »for that« (.1) I'm here (.)
21	for m:y name (.1) my fa:mily (.1) my li:fe (.1)
22	»and my« integrity (.2) I think something iz
23	dreadfully wro:ng (.) »with this« country (.) when
24	a:ny person (.1) a:ny person (.1) »in this« free
25	country (.1) »could be« subjected »to this« (.1) this
26	»iz not«(.) »uh closed« ro:om (.2) there »waz an«
27	FBI: investigation (.2) »this iz« no:t (.1) an
28	opportunity (.1) »to talk« about (.) difficult (.2)
29	matters (.) privately (.1) or »in uh« closed
30	environment (.) this »iz uh« circus (.) this »iz
31	uh« na:tional disgrace (.2) »and from« m:y sta:ndpoint
32	(.2) »az uh« Black American (.1) az »far az« I m
33	conce:rned (.1) it »iz uh hi:gh tech ly:nching (.1)
34	for uppity bla:cks (.1) who in a:ny wa:y (.) deign
35	»to think« (.) for themselves (.1) to do: (.) »for
36	thimselves« (.1) » to have« (.) different ideas (.)
37	and »it iz uh« me:ssage (.1) that »unless you« co:w
38	to:w (.) »to an« old order (.1) thi:s (.) »iz what«
39	will ha:ppen »to you« (.2) you »will be« ly:nched
40	(.1) destro:yed (.1) ca:ricatured (.4) by (.) a (.)
41	commi:ttee (.l) »ov tha« US (.) »US« Senate (.1)
42	rather than hung »from a« tree

In excerpt three, Clarence Thomas responds to Anita Hill's earlier testimony to the committee when he returns to the witness table at about 9 P.M. He calls the hearings "disgu:sting" (line 2) and says they were contaminated with "slea:ze" (line 5), "di:rt" (line 15), and "go:ssip" (line 16). However, Thomas goes beyond such descriptors of the hearings' content to assess blame.

Thomas makes the accusation that "this »iz uh« ca:se (.) »in which« this slea:ze (.2) this di:rt (.2) waz sea:rched fo:r (.) by (.) sta:ffers (.) »ov members« (.) »ov this« commi:ttee (.2) »waz then« (.) leaked (.1) »to tha« media (.1) »and this« committee (.1) »and this« body (.2) validated it (.2) and displa:yed it (.2) »on prime« ti:me" (lines 5–10).

After calling the hearings a "circus" (line 30) and "uh« na:tional disgrace" (line 31), Thomas accuses the Senate Judiciary Committee of conducting a "hi:gh tech ly:nching" (line 33). In short, Thomas clearly accuses the Senate Judiciary Committee, the U.S. Senate, and the entire process of lacking ethics, fairness, and credibility (in that they would facilitate the spreading of these "lies"). Throughout his entire testimony during the hearings, Thomas responded to committee members' statements and questions with similar attacks and accusations.

Excerpt Four

1	Heflin:	»you didn't« (.) uh (.4) listen »to her« testimony
2		(.) »at all=
3	Thomas:	=no (.) I didn't (.2)
4	Heflin:	on television=
5	Thomas:	=no (.) I didn't (.1) I've heard enough li:es (.4)
6		toda:y (.1) iz no:t (.2) a da:y (.1) that (.1) in m:y
7		opinion (.1) iz hi:gh among tha da:yz (.) »in our«
8		country (.) this »iz a« tra:vesty (.2) you spent (.)
9		»the enti:re da:y (.1) destro:ying (.1) what »it haz«
10		taken me (.) fo:rty three years »to build« (.1) and
11		providing »a forum« (.) »for that«

Excerpt four occurred after Senator Howell Heflin refers to Hill's earlier testimony, and Thomas notes that he did not opt to view her testimony. When Heflin questions that assertion (lines 1–2 and line 4), Thomas strongly states that he has "heard enough li:es" (line 5). Further, he reiterates his accusation that the Senate provided a "forum" for "destro:ying (.1) what »it haz« taken me (.) fo:rty three years »to build«" (lines 9–10). Interestingly, in line 8 he says that "you" did this, as opposed to the more general and less personal "the Senate." This attack on the fairness and judgment of the Senate (and, especially, this personal reference to "you") constitutes a face threat to Heflin and to his colleagues who participated in providing such a forum. As excerpt five indicates, Thomas reacts even more vehemently when his own character and judgment are threatened by a senator's question.

Excerpt Five

1	Thomas:	it i:z (.) no:t tru:e (.2) so (.) tha fa:cts (.) can
2		cha:nge (.1) but (.) m:y deni:al (.) does no:t (.1)
3		Miss Hi:ll (.) waz treated (.) »in uh« wa:y (.1) that
4		a:ll (.) my special assistants »were treated« (.1)
5		cordial (.) professional (.) respectful (.7)
6	Heflin:	Ju:dge (.5) if you're »on tha« be:nch (.5) and you
7		approach (.2) a ca:se (.4) where you appear »to have«
8		uh clo:sed mi:nd (.3) »and that« (.1) you (.2) are
9		o:nly right (.3) »doesn't it« rai:se issues (.) »ov
10		judicial« temperament (.2)
11	Thomas:	Senator (.3) senator (.1) therez uh bi:g difference
12		(.) between approaching »a case«o:bjectively (.1)
13		»and watching« yourself (.) being lynched (.1) »there
14		iz« no: comparison (.1) whatsoever

Heflin, in lines 6 through 10, accuses Thomas of lacking adequate judicial temperament (i.e., not having an open mind). Thomas refutes that accusation in lines 11 through 14 by noting that Heflin's reference to a hypothetical case bears no resemblance to "watching« yourself (.) being lynched." By reiterating the lynching metaphor, Thomas also meets Heflin's accusation with a counter accusation: you and your colleagues are in the process of conducting a "lynching." The primary male participants in these hearings engaged in face-threatening behavior as they directly asserted what other participants could or could not do or believe during the hearings and by directly accusing others of engaging in inappropriate behavior either prior to or during the hearings.

Directly Defining Acceptable/Unacceptable Behavior

Given their stature as committee members, the senators who posed questions legitimately possessed the right to direct the lines of questioning. As excerpt six exemplifies, senators perpetuated that status through the nature of their interaction.

Excerpt Six

1	Specter:	we:ll(.) waz »Mister Single«to:n (.1)»on tha«
2		premise:s (.1) »for uh« bout (.) fou:r we:ek (.) in
3		adva:nce (.1) ov (.2) Judge Thomas's (.1) depa:rture

4		(.) az (.) the ⎡assis ⎤
5	Hill:	⎣I don't =⎦
6	Specter:	=»may I« finish »tha ques«tion (.)
7	Hill:	I don't (.) »oh I'm« sorry (.)
8	Specter:	»may I« finish »tha ques«tion (.)
9	Hill:	I'm sorry

In this exchange, Specter begins a question that Hill attempts to answer before he completes it. Specter asks to complete the question in line 6, and Hill, realizing her interactional error, apologizes in line 7. Interestingly, Specter responds to her apology with yet another request to complete his question (line 8). Following a second apology from Hill, Specter goes on to complete the question. In short, Specter interactionally reaffirms his right to direct the interaction, and in so doing, he potentially threatens Hill by overtly marking her interactional error and by soliciting two apologies for it.

Whereas such interactional assertions of what may and may not occur appear throughout the transcript during the senator's questioning of Hill or during interaction between the senators, Thomas, as a witness and a nominee, does not accept the senators' authority to dictate the hearings. Excerpt seven exemplifies how he voices his own "ground rules" for what may and may not occur during the hearings.

Excerpt Seven

1	Thomas:	I »will not« provi:de »the rope« (.1) »for my« own
2		lynching (.2) »or for« further humiliation (.4) I »am
3		not« (.) »going to« enga:ge »in dis«cussio:ns (.2)
4		nor »will I« submit (.) »to probing« questions (.2)
5		»ov what« goes o:n (.) »in tha« most intimate parts
6		»ov my« private life (.1) »or tha« sanctity (.) »ov
7		my« bedroom (.3) these »are tha« mo:st intimate
8		pa:rts »ov my« privacy (.) »and they« will remai:n
9		just that (.1) private

Through this strong statement about what he will and will not respond to during the hearings, Thomas subtly challenges the power that the senators possess to direct the hearings. Further, he undermines the Senate Judiciary Committee's power to confirm him to the Supreme Court by informing them that his sole purpose was to "defend my name" and that "no job is worth this." In short, he implies that he no longer cares whether they confirm him. Thomas's downplaying of these two types of power that the committee organizationally and politically "held" over him constituted potential threats to the committee's authority, stature, and credibility.

Primary Female Participant

In sharp contrast to the nature of the male participants' interaction in the hearings, Anita Hill, the primary female participant, did not engage in confrontational, potentially face-threatening behavior. As numerous newspaper articles pointed out at the time of the hearings, Anita Hill remained calm, deliberate, and polite during her testimony, despite face-threatening questioning by Senate Republicans.[5]

This analysis reveals that Anita Hill's responses to questioners were explanatory and not face threatening. As in excerpts one and two, excerpt eight exemplifies how Hill opted to provide detailed explanations in response to questions that challenged her character, integrity, and honesty.

Excerpt Eight

1	Specter:	the (.3) questi:on (.) which (.) I ha:ve for ya
2		(.2) i:z (.2) how reli̲:able (.3) »is your« te:stimony
3		(.1) hhh »in October« (.) »ov nineteen« (.) »ninety
4		one« (.2) on eve:nts (.) that occurred (.) eight (.)
5		ten (.) years ago (.2) whe:n (.2) yo:u (.) are
6		a:dding »new factors« (.2) explai:ning them »by
7		saying« (.) »you have« repre:ssed »a lot« (.3) and
8		»in tha« fedral la:w (.1) hhh »iz very« fi:rm (.1)
9		»on a« (.) six month (.) period »ov limit«ati:on (.2)
10		how su:re (.1) can yo:u (.) expe:ct this committee
11		to be: (.1) »on tha« a:ccuracy (.2) »ov your«
12		statements (.1)
13	Hill:	well (.) I (.1) I think (.) »if you« (.) sta:rt »to
14		look« (.) »at each« (.1) hhh individual (.)
15		pro:blem (.) »with tha« statement (.1) the:n (.) then
16		you're no:t (.) going »to be« satisfied (.) that itz
17		true (.2) »but I« think (.) tha statement ha:z »to
18		be« taken (.) »az uh« who:le (.2) there iz no:thing
19		»in tha« sta:tement (.) tha:t (.) u::h (.) »or uh«

20	(.) »nothing in my« <u>ba:ck</u>ground (.) »nothing in my«
21	<u>sta:te</u>ment (.) »there iz« <u>no:</u> mot<u>iva:</u>tion (.) that
22	(.) would <u>sho:w</u> (.) »that I« wou:ld (.) <u>ma:ke</u> up (.1)
23	something (.) <u>li:ke</u> thi:s (.2) <u>a:nd</u> hhh (.3) I guess
24	(.) one rea:lly <u>doe:z</u> »have to« under<u>sta:nd</u> (.)
25	something »about tha« <u>na:</u>ture (.) ov sexual harassment
26	(.1) wa uh ih (.) it iz (.) ve:ry <u>di:ffi</u>cult (.) for
27	people »to come« <u>fo:r</u>ward »with these« things (.2)
28	these <u>ki:nds</u> (.) »ov things« (.1) <u>a:nd</u> (.1) it wazn't
29	»az though« I <u>ru:shed</u> forward (.) »with this«
30	information (.3) I can<u>no:t</u> (.1) I »can only« (.) show
31	<u>te:ll</u> you (.) what happened (.) »in the« (.) to »to
32	tha« <u>be:st</u> »ov my« recollection (.) what occurred
33	(.1) <u>a:nd</u> (.) »and ask« you to »take that« into
34	<u>accou:nt</u> (.2) no:w (.) you »have to« make your <u>o:wn</u>
35	judgements (.) »about it« (.) from here on (.1) but
36	I <u>do:</u> want you »to take« (.) »into account« (.) tha
37	<u>who:le</u> thing

Specter in lines 1 through 12 questions how the committee can believe her statements, given the long period of time between the alleged behavior and her disclosure of that behavior. Hill briefly hesitates and then launches into an analytical, logical explanation of why her statements should be considered accurate. She informs Specter that if he examines each statement in isolation, then "you're <u>no:t</u> (.) going »to be« satisfied" (line 16). Instead, she suggests that the statement needs to be read holistically. She offers collaborating evidence for the accuracy of her claim by asserting that she has no motivation to make this up and that her previous behavior does not indicate that she would "<u>ma:ke</u> up (.1) something (.) <u>li:ke</u> thi:s" (lines 22–23). Further, she notes that her behavior is consistent with the behavior of other victims of sexual harassment and that those familiar with the nature of sexual harassment would understand.

Hill offers Specter two "outs" for not immediately understanding her behavior when she notes that examining individual statements instead of looking at her whole statement could yield a different picture and when she explained that "one rea:lly <u>doe:z</u> »have to« under<u>sta:nd</u> (.) something» about tha« na:ture (.) ov sexual harassment" (line 24–25). By offering Specter a reason for not automatically accepting her version of events, she engages in *face-preserving*, not *face-*

threatening, behavior. Further, the explanatory nature of her comments in lines 13 through 37 constitute the logical presentation of "facts," as opposed to confrontational, interactional behaviors, such as challenging or accusing others in the interaction. Unlike the face-threatening manner that pervades the primary male participant's interaction, this particular manner of interacting enables both parties in the interaction to retain their face.

Politicalization of Sexual Harassment

Unlike stereotypes of women under pressure, Hill remained cool and rational, even when she faced being called a virtual liar. The very nature of Hill's demeanor likely contributed to the public's immediate reaction to her. As Carol Sanger (1991) suggests, the public "found Hill too somber and stoic" (1412).

Moreover, as she interacted with the senators, she simply did not fit into stereotypical categories for gender, race, profession, or marital status. Her violations of those stereotypes severely limited her credibility in the eyes of traditional white males because her status as a professional, black single woman and experience with sexual harassment were well beyond the senators' experiences as privileged white males (see Associated Press, 1992). As Hill explains, "Since (my) experience did not fit their reality, they had to reconstruct it" (Associated Press, 1992). The male senators thus attempted to categorize Anita Hill for the American public and for each other. For example, some senators called Anita Hill, in essence, a "spurned woman" (Crenshaw, 1992; Lawrence, 1992.)

Despite the fact that Hill did not fit gender stereotypes, the interaction between the participants during the Hill-Thomas hearings served as a catalyst for the perpetuation of perceived gender differences. Specifically, the senators' treatment of Hill (and Hill's reaction to that treatment) exemplified a classic case of sexual harassment. The senators attacked Hill's character and expressed sympathy for Thomas (Reinhardt, 1992, 1433). As Stephen Reinhardt (1992) suggests, every panelist sympathized with Thomas about his ordeal (thus giving the impression that they presumed him innocent) while exhibiting far less concern about the trauma Anita Hill underwent.

Ironically, the senators' approach to the cross-examination of Anita Hill infuriated women across the country, who maintained that the all-male panel of senators could not and would not understand the essential nature of sexual harassment. Stephanie Riger's (1991) article on gender differences in perceiving and treating sexual harassment offers an empirical foundation to the outcry during these hearings that men "just don't get it." In short, despite Hill's violation of gender stereotypes regarding women's reactions to pressure, her presentation of herself as a victim (i.e., not immediately coming forward, maintaining contact with Thomas, not discussing her problem with others) and the senators' attacks on the victim, not the accused, perpetuated the perceived gender differences regarding the issue of sexual harassment.

This case drew attention to the issue of sexual harassment, and the character assassinations of the victim have resulted in the politicalization of sexual harassment. R. W. Apple (1992) notes the link between the senators' treatment of Anita Hill and the increased number of women running for public office. Further, the subsequent emphasis on the importance of sexual harassment as an issue that requires immediate attention may account for the shift in public opinion polls in favor of Anita Hill. After the hearings ended, only 24 percent of those polled believed Anita Hill. A year later, 44 percent of those polled believe Hill (as opposed to 34 percent who believe Thomas). Thus, Anita Hill may be regaining the credibility she lost at the hands of the white male Senate Judiciary Committee as the more diverse American becomes increasingly educated about the issue and implications of sexual harassment.

NOTES

1. For coverage of this, see, for example, Biskupic, 1991; Borger, Walsh, Thornton, and Gest, 1991; Kramer, 1991; and Kuntz, 1991a, 1991b.

2. For discussion of the clash of gender, race, and politics, see, for example, Alston and Donovan, 1991; Borger, Gest, and Thornton, 1992; Borger and Walsh, 1991; Kaplan et al., 1991; Kramer, 1991; Lapham, 1991; and Wall, 1991.

3. See, for example, Beck, 1992; Beck and Ragan, 1992; Garfinkel, 1967, 1976; Wieder, 1974; and Wieder and Pratt, 1990.

4. For descriptions, see Borger and Walsh, 1991; Biskupic, 1991, Borger, Walsh, Thornton, and Gest, 1991; Clymer, 1991; Dowd, 1991a, 1991b, 1991c, 1991d; Fineman, 1991; Jenkins, 1991; Kaplan et al., 1991; McDaniel, 1991; Pollak 1991a, 1991b; Rosenthal, 1991a, 1991b; Smith 1992; Smolowe, 1991; and Sowell, 1991.

5. See, for example, Dowd, 1991a, 1991b, 1991c, 1991d; Kaplan et al., 1991; Lapham, 1991; and Smolowe, 1991.

REFERENCES

Alston, C., and Donovan, B. (1991, October 12). Gender gulf on Capitol Hill. *Congressional Quarterly Weekly Report*, 49: 2951.

Apple, R. W. (1992, May 24). Steady local gains by women fuel more runs for high office. *New York Times*, section 4: 1, 5.

Atkinson, J. and Heritage, J. (eds.). (1984). *Structures of social action: Studies in conversation analysis.* Cambridge: Cambridge University Press.

Associated Press. (1992, October 18). Hill levels criticism at Senate committee. *Norman Transcript* (Norman, Okla.).

Beck, C. (1992). The co-creation of joint television viewing as a social activity. Ph.D. diss., University of Oklahoma.

Beck, C., and Ragan, S. (1992). The co-creation of roles in the gynecologic exam. Paper presented at the annual meeting of the Western Speech Communication Association, Boise, Idaho.

Biskupic, J. (1991, October 12). Thomas drama engulfs nation; anguished Senate faces vote. *Congressional Quarterly Weekly Report*, 49: 2948–57.

Borger, G., and Walsh, K. (1991, October 28). The swearing never stops. *U.S. News and World Report*, 34–35.

Borger, G., Gest, T., and Thornton, J. (1992, October 12). The untold story. *U.S. News and World Report*, 28–37.

Borger, G., Walsh, K., Thornton, J., and Gest, T. (1991, October 21). Judging Thomas. *U.S. News and World Report*, 33–36.

Brown, P., and Levinson, S. (1987). *Politeness: Some universals in language use.* Cambridge: Cambridge University Press.

Clymer, A. (1991, October 16). Senate's futile search for safe ground. *New York Times*, 20.

Crenshaw, K. (1992). Race, gender, and sexual harassment. *Southern California Law Review*, 65 (3): 1467–76.

Dowd, M. (1991a, October 8). The Senate and sexism: Panel's handling of harassment allegation renews questions about mostly male club. *New York Times*, A1.

———. (1991b, October 9). Congresswomen march to Senate to demand delay in Thomas vote. *New York Times*, A1.

———. (1991c, October 10). Facing issue of harassment, Washington slings the mud. *New York Times*, B1.

———. (1991d, October 16). Image more than reality became issue, losers say. *New York Times*, A1.

Fineman, H. (1991, October 28). Playing white male politics. *Newsweek*, 27–28.

Garfinkel, H. (1967). *Studies in ethnomethodology.* New York: Prentice-Hall.

———. (1976). A manual for the studies of naturally organized ordinary activities: Volume 1. Unpublished manuscript.

Garland, S., and Segal, T. (1991, October 21). Thomas vs. Hill: The lessons for corporate America. *Business Week,* 32.

Goffman, E. (1955). On facework. *Psychiatry,* 18: 213–31.

Jenkins, K. (1991, October 16). Area senators split in wrenching debate. *Washington Post,* A11.

Kaplin, D., Cohn, B., McDaniel, A., and Annin, P. (1991, October 21). The moment of truth. *Newsweek,* 24.

Kramer, M. (1991, October 21). Shame on them all. *Time,* 46–47.

Kuntz, P. (1991a, October 12). Senate scrambled to delay vote. *Congressional Quarterly Weekly Report,* 49: 2955.

———. (1991b, October 12). Tracking the unknown leader. *Congressional Quarterly Weekly Report,* 49: 2956.

Lapham, L. (1991, December). More light. *Harper's,* 10–15.

Lawrence, C. R., III. (1992). Cringing at myths of black sexuality. *Southern California Law Review,* 65 (3): 1357–60.

McDaniel, A. (1991, October 28). The attack of the Bush men. *Newsweek,* 26.

Pollak, R. (1991a, October 28). Judging Thomas. *Nation,* 501, 503.

———. (1991b, November 11). Presumed innocent. *Nation,* 573, 593.

Reinhardt, S. (1992). The end of the age of ignorance. *Southern California Law Review,* 65 (3): 1431–40.

Riger, S. (1991, May). Gender dilemmas in sexual harassment policies and procedures. *American Psychologist,* 497–505.

Rosenthal, A. (1991a, October 14). White House role in Thomas defense. *New York Times,* A11.

———. (1991b, October 15). Gains for Republicans by going nasty early. *New York Times,* A1.

Sanger, C. (1992). The reasonable woman and the ordinary man. *Southern California Law Review,* 65 (3): 1411–18.

Smith, B. (1992, January–February). Ain't gonna let nobody turn me around. *Ms.,* 37–39.

Smolowe, J. (1991, October 21). She said, he said. *Time,* 36–37.

Sowell, T. (1991, November 11). Of ends and means. *Forbes,* 56.

Wall, J. (1991, October 23). Sexual harassment and conflicting perspectives. *Christian Century,* 955–56.

Wieder, D. L. (1974). *Language and social reality: The case of telling the convict code.* The Hague: Mouton.

Wieder, D. L., and Pratt, S. (1990). On being a recognizable Indian among Indians. In D. Carbaugh (ed.), *Cultural communication and intercultural contact*, 45–64. Hillsdale, N.J.: Erlbaum.

3

Sex, Race, and Politics: An Intercultural Communication Approach to the Hill–Thomas Hearings

CYNTHIA S. ROPER, MIKE CHANSLOR, AND DIANNE G. BYSTROM

In the aftermath of the October 1991 Senate Judiciary Committee hearings on Anita Hill's allegations that the Supreme Court Justice nominee Clarence Thomas had sexually harassed her when she worked for him at the U.S. Department of Education and the Equal Employment Opportunity Commission (EEOC), few paid attention at first to the issue of race in the hearings (Bikel, 1992; Brooks, 1992; Dervin, 1992; Duke, 1992a, 1992b; Fraser, 1992). Initially, many may have ignored race as an issue in the hearings because they involved a black woman's charges against a black man (Bikel, 1992).

But from the beginning—with President George Bush's announcement that race was not a factor in his nomination of Thomas—race was, indeed, the issue. As Eleanor Holmes Norton (1992) put it, "Race had been responsible for the nomination and only race could undo it. . . . Not surprisingly, with a nomination of a black man to the Supreme Court at stake, race trumped sex" (43).

This essay examines the interlocking and overlapping roles that race, gender, and politics played in the Hill-Thomas hearings. Using a model proposed by William Gudykunst and Young Kim (1992) for studying communication between strangers, the essay focuses on the similarities and differences among four of the key participants in the hearings—Hill, Thomas, Senator Arlen Specter, and Senator Orrin Hatch—and analyzes the decoding/encoding behaviors involved in their interactions.

Description of the Case: A Communication Perspective

On October 11, 12, and 13, 1991, 80 percent of the television viewing audience tuned in to view the modern American melodrama (Beck, Ragan, and Kaid, 1992). That the hearings were even held was a product of the communication process. Although rumors that Thomas had sexually harassed Hill were known in political and media circles as early as July 1991 (Phelps and Winternitz, 1992), it was not until October 6, when the media "leaked" her charges—and the failure of the Senate Judiciary Committee to take them seriously—that Hill's story became the focus of public discourse. Responding to this disclosure and the mounting public outrage that the Senate would ignore Hill's claims, the Senate voted on October 8 to delay the scheduled confirmation vote on Thomas until October 15 and to hold public hearings on the charges beginning October 11 (Phelps and Winternitz, 1992).

An Intercultural Model

According to the Gudykunst-Kim model, communication is influenced by a number of conceptual filters that screen all incoming messages—cultural, sociocultural, psychocultural, and environmental. Cultural influences include such things as values and norms; high context communication (typified by indirect or restricted codes) or low context communication (characterized by the use of explicit, elaborated codes); and individualism or collectivism. Socio-cultural influences include membership in social groups, how people categorize themselves (e.g., male-female, black-white, professional-nonprofessional), how people view members of outgroups, and whether those individuals communicate with members of outgroups on an intergroup or interpersonal basis. Psychocultural influences include individual expectations, consisting of stereotypes and intergroup attitudes, ethnocentrism, and prejudice. Finally, environmental influences include the physical and psychological environments (Gudykunst and Kim, 1992). An examination of the hearings reveals how these conceptual filters served to create an intercultural interaction among the participants.

Everyone is aware of belonging to various membership groups. Gudykunst and Kim (1992) point out that "as part of our socialization into our membership groups, we are taught we should avoid interacting with certain . . . [outgroups] because of their ethnic heritage, race, social class, color, religion, or occupation" (66). At the sociocultural level, communication patterns are largely determined by how people view members of outgroups—as individuals, leading to more interpersonal communication patterns, or as representatives of their groups, leading to more intergroup communication patterns. If their communication is primarily intergroup, people tend to rely on their stereotypes and intergroup attitudes to predict and explain the behavior of outgroup members (Gudykunst and Kim, 1992).

Because this case study focuses on the interactive effect of race, gender, and politics on the communication process during the hearings and the public discourse that continues, the exchanges between Professor Hill and Senator Specter and between Judge Thomas and Senator Hatch are analyzed. These interactions provide examples of how two white male Republican senators communicated with two African Americans of different genders and political persuasions. Close readings of these interactions reveal them to be fruitful ground for examining the hearings from an intercultural communication perspective.

Description of Key Participants

All four participants in the interaction were attorneys; three—Hill, Thomas, and Specter—graduated from Yale Law School. Specter, a former prosecutor, and Hatch were white U.S. senators from Pennsylvania and Utah, respectively. Thomas and Hill were black. Thomas had worked in state and federal government since graduation from law school; Hill had worked in private law practice, for the federal government, and at Oral Roberts University before accepting her position as a law professor at the University of Oklahoma (Phelps and Winternitz, 1992).

Hatch, Specter, and Thomas were Republicans, whereas Hill was a Democrat, who had been known for keeping her views on politics and women's rights quiet (Phelps and Winternitz, 1992). Although Hatch and Thomas were politically conservative, Specter was moderate to liberal, pro-choice, and supportive of women's rights. At least three of the participants—Hatch, Hill, and Thomas—came from modest family roots. Hatch was born in poverty in Pennsylvania; Hill and Thomas were raised in the South. Their early upbringing differed, however.

The youngest of thirteen children from a rural Oklahoma farming family, Hill attended segregated grade schools until she was fourteen; an integrated junior high and high school, where she was valedictorian of her senior class; and Oklahoma State University as a National Merit Scholar. In high school, college, and throughout her career, Hill fit in easily with blacks and whites (Phelps and Winternitz, 1992).

Thomas was the son of a teenaged mother who had been abandoned by Thomas's father, and Thomas and his brother were raised in Georgia by their grandfather. An honors student, Thomas attended private all-black Catholic schools and later an all-white Catholic seminary. As a youth, he did not fit in with whites or blacks. Thomas "embraced black militancy" as an undergraduate at Holy Cross but "grew increasingly conservative" at Yale (Phelps and Winternitz, 1992, 50–51).

Hill was raised as a Baptist, whereas Thomas moved from the Baptist Church, to Catholicism, to Protestant fundamentalism (Phelps and Winternitz, 1992). Hatch was a lay minister in the Mormon church. Both Hatch and Specter were married. Thomas had a child from his first marriage to a black woman and had then married a white woman. Hill never married.

At first glance, all four participants appear to be representatives of the upwardly mobile dominant U.S. culture, a culture whose values include rugged individualism, materialism, success, work and activity, progress, rationality, democracy, and humanitarianism (Gudykunst and Kim, 1992). Three—Hill, Thomas, and Hatch—had demonstrated many of these values by their success in overcoming adversity and realizing "the American dream." As white male senators, Specter and Hatch were representatives of one of this culture's most powerful sociocultural membership groups. Although both Hill and Thomas were black, the issue of race impacted each differently. Hill, of course, was the only female. The intergroup nature of the communication becomes apparent by focusing on the race and gender of each of the four participants: white male, black male, and black female. To fully understand how race and gender interacted to create these membership groups, it is important to examine the historical context in which they developed.

Emergence of Membership Groups

As has been mentioned, stereotypes are one of the primary psychocultural influences affecting communication with others (Gudykunst and Kim, 1992). Historically, black men and black women have been subject to sexual stereotypes that grew out of the slave culture and have continued to oppress blacks. Belief in a part of this stereotype led to mass lynchings of black men. During the first thirty years following the Civil War, Ida B. Wells estimated that over ten thousand lynchings of blacks occurred (Davis, 1981). Though few of these cases actually involved charges of rape, the myth of the black rapist and his "assaults on white Southern womanhood" became the justification for continued violence against blacks (Davis, 1981, 185).

Black women also have been victimized by negative sexual stereotypes. According to Patricia Collins (1991), the image of the sexually aggressive "Jezebel . . . lie[s] at the heart of Black women's oppression" by the dominant culture (77). Linda Williams (1986) explores the idea that adverse treatment of black women is acceptable. In work on black women and rape, Williams argues that black females may be seen as legitimate victims of rape because of three sexual stereotypes rooted in slavery: (a) a denial of responsibility, in which the attacker actually becomes the victim because he was provoked by a stereotypical black female with a questionable sexual nature and low morals; (b) a denial of any possible injury to a sexually assaulted black female because of her constant desire for sex and her previous experience with black men, who, as the stereotype goes, possess larger genitals than do their white counterparts; and (c) a denial that the black woman can possibly be seen as a victim if she provoked the attack and already brings to the encounter a bad character.

In conjunction with the image of the Jezebel is the black matriarch, symbol of the "bad Black mother . . . who emasculates Black men because she will not permit them to assume roles as Black patriarchs" (Collins, 1991, 72, 78). Black matriarchs have been held responsible for black men's low educational achievements, inability to earn a living for their families, personality disorders, and delinquency (King, 1973). More recently, aspects of the domineering black matriarch have been channeled into newer stereotypes of career-oriented black women. They often are viewed "as egotistical career climbers, better paid, better educated and more socially mobile than [their] male counterparts" (Ransby, 1992, 169–70). As a black female, Hill was subject to these stereotypes.

In addition to cultural, sociocultural, and psychocultural influences, the communication between these participants was influenced by the environment of the hearings. Held in the Senate Caucus Room—a familiar place for Specter, Hatch, and even Thomas but unfamiliar for Hill—the hearings were a political process, not a judicial one. As Senator Joseph Biden, the committee chair, noted, "The rules of evidence that apply in courtrooms will not apply here today. Thus, evidence and questions that would not be permitted in a court of law must, under Senate rules, be allowed here" (Hearings, October 11, 1991).[1]

What transpired was a hearing in which members of two political parties played by two different sets of rules: "Democrats wanted to be fair; the Republicans wanted to win" (Phelps and Winternitz, 1992, 393). Thus, Specter and Hatch acted as defense attorneys for Thomas, prosecutors of Hill, and jurors; Democrats had no one to defend Hill or prosecute Thomas.

She Said/They Said: Encoding/Decoding Behaviors

An analysis of the encoding/decoding behaviors involved in Senator Specter's questioning of Hill and Senator Hatch's questioning of Thomas reveals the reconstruction of the story of a black woman into the context of white or black male experiences. Attesting to the intergroup nature of the hearings, Hill has noted that "because I and my reality did not comport with what they accepted as their reality, I and my reality had to be reconstructed by the Senate committee members with assistance from the press and others" (Barringer, 1992, 6). This reconstruction of Hill's testimony—and attribution of possible motives for her actions—by the white male senators who questioned her and by the black man about whom she testified effectively served to silence her story during the hearings.

In His Own Words: Specter Reconstructs Hill's Testimony

As the Republican's chief interrogator of Hill, Specter constrained her narrative by the type of questions he asked and continually reconstructed her responses in his own words. In a number of ways, he attempted to cast doubt on Hill's testimony. Specter began this reconstruction by dwelling on what he viewed as inconsistencies in her story—for instance, why she did not tell colleagues about Thomas's alleged sexual harassment of her in recent conversations about his nomination or the FBI investigators about every incident of harassment she later described at the hearing. Nineteen times he compared the FBI report with her written statement and oral testimony and pointed out alleged inconsistencies. Although Hill gave credible reasons for these alleged inconsistencies—for example, she was more "comfortable" speaking with the FBI agents in generalities rather than specifics—and although it was finally revealed that the FBI report consisted only of a summary, not a transcript, of her interview with FBI investigators, Specter questioned "how sure" the committee could be about the accuracy of testimony about events that happened eight to ten years ago (Hearings, October 11, 1991).

A second way in which Specter questioned Hill's testimony was by challenging her credibility as a reliable witness. First, he juxtaposed her testimony against statements from a variety of males—Carlton Stewart, John Doggett, Dean Charles Kothe, and Harry Singleton. Of these men, only Kothe, the former Oral Roberts University law dean, and Doggett, a black Texas lawyer who had been acquainted with Hill in Washington, actually appeared at the hearings. Hill again gave credible answers—for example, she "did not want to insult or argue" with her friends who supported Thomas, or the men in question did not know her well enough to speak on her behalf. Next, Specter questioned her credibility by citing stories in the popular press—the *New York Times, U.S. Today,* the *Kansas City Star,* and the *Washington Post*—as though they represented expert, reliable, and authoritative sources. Not only did he use this line of questioning to cast doubt on her believability, he also seemed to place the responsibility for these stories at her door. Finally, through a long series of questions about the telephone logs, he attempted to undermine her credibility by implying that these records constituted absolute proof of her continued efforts to pursue Thomas, a pursuit that was first seen when she followed him from the Department of Education to the EEOC. Finally, Specter attributed various stereotypical motives for her actions by asking such questions as was she a jilted woman disappointed and frustrated by Thomas's lack of sexual interest in her or simply "fantasizing" about Thomas? Asserting that she had an "active social life" at the time of the alleged incidents, Hill maintained that she was "not given to fantasy. This is not something that I would have come forward with if I were not absolutely sure about what it is I am saying" (Hearings, October 11, 1991).

Noting that she had "nothing in [her] background, no motivation to make this up," Hill told Specter and the other senators that they needed to "understand the nature of sexual harassment" (Hearings, October 11, 1991). However, Specter's next line of questioning demonstrated that he did not understand the nature of sexual harassment—at least from Hill's perspective.

Throughout the hearing, Specter created and narrowly defined the roles Hill was expected to play, then allowed no deviation from them. Sometimes he accomplished this by restating her responses in his own words; at other times he simply ignored her answers; often he repeated the same question a number of times, as if she had not yet given an answer. This tendency to reconstruct Hill's responses became especially apparent in his closing statement, where he reiterated many of his arguments and virtually ignored the answers she had provided.

By constructing various roles for Hill—legal expert and victim of sexual harassment—Specter attempted to show how, in his view, her behavior violated the expectations for these roles (Darwin, 1992). For example, Specter asked Hill—whom he described as a law professor and experienced attorney versed in sexual harassment—why she did not take notes as "evidence" of the harassment at the time it supposedly occurred and why she was bringing these charges after the statute of limitations for such claims had expired. Hill responded that she was not interested in filing a claim of sexual harassment then or now; rather, she was describing conduct that the committee could investigate and evaluate "on its own" as "unfitting to a member of the court" (Hearings, October 11, 1991).

When it suited his purposes, Specter defined her as a legal expert on laws regarding sexual harassment. One way that Specter accomplished this was by repeatedly (nine times) citing her interest in and experience with civil rights law. Through his questions, he narrowly defined civil rights law as it relates to women's rights, specifically those regarding sexual harassment in the work-place. Specter was thus able to redefine Hill's identity in two ways. First, he created her role as a legal expert on sexual harassment; second, by stressing how civil rights law has provided protection for women regarding sexual ha-rassment, he obliquely succeeded in robbing her of her racial status as a black female.

Throughout the hearings, Specter demonstrated his intergroup attitudes and his ethnocentric stance toward Hill. One example of this emerged dur-ing his line of questioning regarding her move to the EEOC. In this series of questions, Specter compared her actions and behavior at the time of the events with what he described as being the only appropriate, responsible, and, there-fore, acceptable actions—that is, what any rational, middle-aged, white male, national political figure would do. To do this, Specter drew on the "legal ex-pert" image he had created for Hill and completely ignored her personal iden-tity at the time the events occurred—a twenty-five-year-old black female ex-periencing sexual harassment by a black male superior. This interaction served the purpose of casting doubt on her intelligence, her rationality, her veracity, and her motives.

Specter, after declaring he had experience and "some sensitivity" about sexual harassment as a former district attorney, also questioned Hill's behav-ior as an alleged victim of sexual harassment. No experts on sexual harass-ment were consulted by the Senate Judiciary Committee or allowed to testi-fy. Instead, Specter set the parameters of what it means to be a victim of sexual harassment through the questions he asked Hill—why, for instance, did she follow Thomas from one job to another and keep in contact with him by tele-phone? Although Hill asserted that her actions were "not atypical" of victims of sexual harassment (Hearings, October 11, 1991), she was not allowed to explain the logic of her responses. By not permitting her the opportunity to explain, Specter left viewers with the impression, once again, that Hill must be lying.

Race Trumps Sex: The Hatch-Thomas Interactions

Close examination of the Hatch-Thomas interactions provides further evi-dence that the hearings represent an intercultural exchange in which mem-bers of different groups were influenced by their conceptual filters to shape the meaning and direction of the communication. Of all the factors that contributed to the communication process during the hearings, race was the most evident and dominant. Indeed, for many black Americans, race and racism were the main issues of the hearings (Brooks, 1992). A survey conducted by the Joint Center for Political Studies found that almost 45 percent of black Americans polled believed racism was involved (Brooks, 1992).

Although racial issues were alluded to in the Specter-Hill interactions, Thomas brought race front and center in his interactions with Hatch. According to Congresswoman Eleanor Holmes Norton (1992), Hill "declined to use her race . . . to enhance her charges while Thomas made race his central, indeed his only defense" (43). Norton also noted that "to many blacks the Committee looked like nothing so much as an all-white jury" (43). Thomas appealed to this jury, and perhaps just as important to black public opinion, by claiming to be the victim of black male sexual stereotypes.

Thomas first raised the race issue in his second statement, when he accused the committee of using the hearings as a "high-tech lynching" for "uppity blacks" (Hearings, October 11, 1991). He reintroduced the topic during Hatch's second round of questioning, when the senator was asking questions about whether Thomas asked Hill for dates and if that was the kind of language he would use if he were trying to do so. Following up on Thomas's introduction of black stereotypes, Hatch gave the judge an opportunity to expound on the subject by claiming not to understand what he meant by "stereotyped language." Thomas responded, "Throughout the history of this country and certainly throughout my life, language about the sexual prowess of black men, language about the sex organs of black men and the sizes, etc., that kind of language has been used about black men as long as I've been on the face of this earth . . . and this plays into the most bigoted racist stereotypes that any black man will face" (Hearings, October 12, 1991).

Further, Thomas reasserted that such sexual stereotyping was associated with the lynching of black males: "that is the point that I'm trying to make and that is the point that I was making last night, that this is a high-tech lynching. I cannot shake off these accusations, because they play to the worst stereotypes we have about black men in this country" (Hearings, October 12, 1991).

By evoking the powerful lynching metaphor, Thomas effectively divided the discourse in the hearings—and the reactions of the U.S. Senate and the public to Hill's testimony—along racial lines. Although Hill also is black, she did not have a similar metaphor to evoke and did not fit easily into often-used stereotypes because of her education, demeanor, and marital status (Barringer, 1992; Duke, 1992b).

In fact, as Dan Dervin (1992) contends, Thomas's denial of the charges, accompanied by the lynching metaphor, effectively served to make him the victim in the situation. With the judge cast as the helpless victim of a vicious lynch mob, Hill became the ruthless inciter of that mob. Metaphor thus served as a vehicle for "transforming the issue from one of gender to one of race . . . in which Hill was either invisible, insane, or calculatingly evil" (Preston, 1992, 187–88). Once race was introduced as the central issue, the Democratic senators on the panel, also white males, were effectively blocked from pressing Thomas to respond to their questions for fear of appearing racist.

Thomas's careful use of such phrases as "uppity black" and "high-tech lynching" also represents the employment of restricted verbal codes, which rely heavily on hidden, implicit cues that are embedded in the social contexts of various membership groups (Gudykunst and Kim, 1992). Because of their reliance on social context, these phrases communicated much more to the black community than to the white community. Although not apparent to the dominant culture group, these phrases stood in stark contrast against the backdrop of low context, elaborated verbal codes—typical of the dominant U.S. culture—which other participants had used throughout the hearings. Thomas's use of black stereotypes in his defense might have been seen as somewhat paradoxical given his recent conservative political history, but without a doubt it was a rhetorical stroke of genius that served to mobilize black public opinion in his favor.

One of the great ironies of the hearings was that Thomas's use of the lynching metaphor was inaccurate in this context. Although he claimed to be suffering a symbolic lynching at the hands of the all-white committee for sexually threatening a black woman, there is no historical evidence that either a black or white man was ever lynched for sexual crimes against African American women (Allen, 1992).

Though it was almost certainly unintentional, Hatch himself undermined Thomas's case as a victim of stereotypes. After Thomas reintroduced the lynching metaphor, Hatch methodically worked his way through the list of Hill's allegations, asking Thomas if they represented black stereotypes. This exchange uncovered only two clear instances of stereotypes (size of black sexual organs and sexual prowess) and one partial stereotype (promiscuity, which relates to sexual prowess). This lack of evidence for such stereotypes did not, however, prevent Hatch from later characterizing Thomas as a victim of a "bunch" of black stereotypes.

This example illustrates Hatch's consistent championing of Thomas's cause. It began even before Thomas's opening statement, when the senator from Utah plainly stated he believed the judge was telling the truth. In his opening round of questioning addressing Hill's allegations, Hatch was almost apologetic to Thomas when he told him that "I hate to go into this, but I want to go into it, because I have to" (Hearings, October 11, 1991). This politeness and concern for the witness sharply contrasted with Specter's treatment of Hill, but it was perfectly understandable when viewing the hearings as a partisan battle among Senate Judiciary Committee members. Partisanship represented one of the strongest sociocultural influences on the hearings and resulted in their being not so much a quest for truth as a political and ideological battle. Such battles were apparent in Hatch's comment, during his "questioning" of Thomas, that he knew the reports of Democratic Senate staffers trying to dig up dirt on Thomas were true.

The presence or absence of patrons on the Senate Judiciary Committee also contributed to the politics of the hearings. As sponsors, patrons are able to pave the way for members of outgroups to join the ingroup. Thomas entered the hearings with numerous patrons on the panel. Hill did not have a patron, nor had she at any time pursued such a relationship in a city where patronage is important (Duke, 1992b). Hatch served as one of Thomas's chief political patrons on the committee, telling him at one point, "You've been a champion in many ways for a lot of us. . . . I've been outraged over the way this committee has treated you" (Hearings, October 12, 1991).

Like Specter before him, Hatch spent much of his time talking for the witness; however, whereas Hatch was trying to help Thomas, Specter clearly wanted to discredit Hill. One of the main strategies Hatch used was to paint Thomas as the victim of a nomination process corrupted by a leak from the Democratic side. This leak and its resulting media attention had produced a very public physical and psychological environment for the hearings. This environmental influence undoubtedly had a tremendous impact on the communication process. References Hatch and the other senators made to the leak seemed to be an effort on their part to distance themselves from the hearings and any responsibility or guilt associated with them.

The placement of various persons as backdrops for the witnesses also contributed to the manipulation of the physical and psychological environment. Hill's backdrop was her legal team. Thomas had his wife and Senator John Danforth behind him, a backdrop that served to identify him with the dominant culture group and kindle sympathy for his cause. Given the knowledge that many viewed Thomas as too unemotional, this staging was particularly effective for the television audience.

By portraying Thomas as the helpless target of a dominant political group—the Democrats—and powerful special interests that wanted the nomination derailed, Hatch was able to frame the hearings as intergroup conflict in which a powerful ingroup victimizes an outgroup representative. As with many of his other points, Hatch established Thomas's status as a victim by using much of his time to make speeches rather than ask questions. One technique was to interrupt the flow of his own rhetoric to remind the audience of the leak: "In a four page statement that she issued, which was of course leaked to the press by somebody on this committee, in violation of law, in violation of Senate ethics, in violation of the stringent rule formulated because these FBI reports contain raw data" (Hearings, October 12, 1991).

Later Hatch made a more overt attack on special interest groups that he believed "found" some of Hill's allegations in *The Exorcist* and in a sexual harassment case from the U.S. Court of Appeals for the Tenth Circuit: "And there's a lot of slick lawyers in those groups. Slick lawyers! The worst kind. There's some great ones too. And it may have been a great one that found the reference to Long Dong Silver" (Hearings, October 12, 1991). Ironically, in this particular tirade, Hatch accused the special interest groups of using slick lawyers when it was obvious he must have employed similar techniques to find this "evidence" refuting Hill's testimony.

Thomas was an obligingly indignant victim, who was able to come up with adequately descriptive language to portray his feelings about the process. In response to Hatch's passage about slick lawyers Thomas replied, "Senator, I would have preferred an assassin's bullet to this kind of living hell that they have put me and my family through!" (Hearings, October 12, 1991). Later Thomas suggested that he was a patriotic martyr as well as a victim when he stated, "And if by going through this another nominee in the future or another American won't have to go through it then so be it" (Hearings, October 12, 1991).

Espousing dominant patriotic values, both Hatch and Thomas even went so far as to imply that the proceedings had been destructive to the basic American value system:

> I'm not talking about liberal and conservative politics. I'm talking about decency. I'm talking about our country, America. . . . (Hatch, Hearings, October 12, 1991)

> I think I've died a thousand deaths . . . but I had a faith that at the least this system was working in some fashion though imperfectly. I don't think this is right . . . I think it's wrong for the country. . . . And I think it's hurt the country. (Thomas, Hearings, October 12, 1991)

The Hatch-Thomas interaction was as significant for what was said or implied about Hill as for what was said about Thomas. Hatch was careful not to attack Hill directly, describing her as "impressive . . . an intelligent woman . . . and a lovely human being" and claiming that he had a lot of "sympathy" for her. Nevertheless, he did attack the veracity of her testimony, and, in a particularly good example of doublespeak, Hatch told Thomas, "Now I've known you almost 11 years. And the person that the good professor described is not the person I've known" (Hearings, October 11, 1991).

One of the more insidious stereotypes the Hatch-Thomas interaction brought to the forefront about Hill was that of the sexually aggressive black Jezebel. To create this imagery, Hatch asked Thomas to verify whether it was true that Hill on occasion had asked Thomas for rides home and had invited him in to continue their discussion. Hatch stated, "You never thought of any of this as anything more than normal for a friendly or professional conversation with a colleague. Am I correct on that or am I wrong?" (Hearings, October 11, 1991). Hatch's inquiry, coupled with Thomas's confirmation that Hatch was correct, contributed to the impression that Hill was actively pursuing a romantic relationship with Thomas. In addition to this, Hatch seemed to take every possible opportunity to reread the most graphic portions of Hill's testimony, all the while expressing his own disgust and assuring himself that Thomas would never stoop to the use of this type of language. By the process of elimination, Hatch implied that Hill herself must have been the source of this "gross" and "terrible" language. As Charles Lawrence (1992) writes, "When [Hatch] reads the most lurid language in her account over and over again, all the while protesting his disgust, he is conjuring up these same racist images of the wanton black woman" (137).

Conclusion

An intercultural approach has made it possible to examine many of the underlying racial and gender biases and the ways in which the two interacted to effectively reconstruct both the identity and the testimony of a black woman. The focus on various levels of conceptual filters, provided by Gudykunst and Kim's model, helps to reveal specific examples of such things as ethnocentrism, stereotypes, and intergroup attitudes that together impacted the communication process of the hearings for both the participants and the viewing audience.

Hill believes that her race—and the assumptions and perceptions it evoked—undercut her credibility with the senators and, ultimately, the American public. "Whether to believe me . . . was the bottom line for the hearings," she has said. "And in making that assessment, what they were doing—the public as well as the Senate—was making an assessment about whether to believe an African-American female when she claimed she had been sexually harassed" (quoted in Duke, 1992a, 10A).

The dynamics of race—combined with gender—infused the communication process during the hearings and have since dominated the public discourse. The historic hearings divided the black community, some of whom felt forced to choose between loyalty to their race and loyalty to their gender (Duke, 1992b). However, as Emma Coleman Jordan, a Georgetown University law professor, has observed, there is no real choice for black women because these identities cannot be separated (Duke, 1992b). Historically, both black men and black women have been the "targets of harmful stereotypes about their sexuality," Jordan notes. "To complain about the sexual harassment of an African-American man raises the specter of rejuvenating these negative stereotypes. But at the same time, to fail to complain about it requires that one must choose between race and gender and subordinate gender to the racial components of one's being, when they can't be separated" (quoted in Duke, 1992a, 10A).

Hill, who did not choose between her gender and race, thus entered the hearings as a member of two low-status outgroups, women and blacks. She faced a committee made up of members of the two most powerful ingroups, men and whites. Treating her as an member of an outgroup, the senators created their own narratives—based on their cultural beliefs, stereotypes, and experiences as white males—to explain away her allegations (Duke, 1992b).

Since the hearings, Hill has indicated that she has come to "understand how images based on stereotypes and myths are often substitutes for analysis and careful thought" (quoted in Duke, 1992b, 7A). According to Hill, "What the Senate Judiciary Committee did not count on was that their exhibition of abuse and power in the hearings . . . would become a metaphor for the sexual and gender abuses suffered by women" (quoted in Duke, 1992b, 7A). This metaphor—often called the Anita Hill effect—helped elect four new women to the U.S. Senate, tripling the number of women who serve there, and contributed to a 68 percent increase—from 28 to 47—in women in the House of Representatives ("From Anita Hill to Capitol Hill," 1992; "Women Break," 1992–93).

George E. Curry noted shortly after the hearings, "Our dirty little secret is finally out in the public—that black men are at least as sexist as white men, probably more so, and this really hasn't been discussed freely" (quoted in Brooks, 1992, 9). Hill suggests that blacks should talk more openly about blacks' sexual harassment of other blacks. Or as the journalist Lynne Duke puts it, "Hill maintains that one might even argue that our credibility as a community on issues of racism will turn on our willingness to denounce sexism within and outside our community" (Duke, 1992b, 7A).

NOTE

1. All quotations from the hearings are taken from the authors' videotaped recording of the nationally televised hearings before the Committee on the Judiciary on the nomination of Judge Clarence Thomas to serve as an associate justice of the Supreme Court of the United States, October 11, 12, and 13, 1991.

REFERENCES

Allen, E., Jr. (1992). Race and gender stereotyping in the Thomas confirmation hearings. In Chrisman and Allen (eds.), *Court of Appeal,* 25–28.

Barringer, F. (1992, October 17). One year later, Anita Hill interprets Thomas hearings. *New York Times,* 6.

Beck, C. S., Ragan, S. L., and Kaid, L. L. (1992, October). He said-she said: The doing of gender through cross examination. Paper presented at the Speech Communication Association annual meeting, Chicago.

Bikel, O. (1992). Public hearing, private pain. *Frontline,* television program.

Brooks, D. W. (1992, October). The search for harmony: African-American discourse on the Anita Hill–Clarence Thomas controversy. Paper presented at the Speech Communication Association annual meeting, Chicago.

Chrisman, R., and Allen, R. L. (eds.), *Court of Appeal: The black community speaks out on the racial and sexual politics of Clarence Thomas vs. Anita Hill.* New York: Ballantine Books.

Collins, P. H. (1991). *Black feminist thought: Knowledge, consciousness, and the politics of empowerment.* New York: Routledge.

Darwin, T. J. (1992, October). Silencing Anita Hill: Constructing credibility in the Thomas-Hill Hearings. Paper presented at the Speech Communication Association annual meeting, Chicago.

Davis, A. Y. (1981). *Women, race, and class.* New York: Random House.

Dervin, D. (1992). Testimony of silence: A psychohistorical perspective on the Thomas-Hill Hearings. *Journal of Psychohistory,* 19: 257–68.

Duke, L. (1992, October 16). Hill says racial perceptions undercut her credibility. *Washington Post,* 10A.

———. (1992, October 17). Hill says she was overwhelmed by negative reactions. *Washington Post,* 7A.

Fraser, N. (1992). Sex, lies, and the public sphere: Some reflections on the confirmation of Clarence Thomas. *Critical Inquiry,* 18: 595–612.

From Anita Hill to Capitol Hill. (1992, November 16). *Time,* 21.

Gudykunst, W. B., and Kim, Y. Y. (1992). *Readings on communicating with strangers: An approach to intercultural communication.* New York: McGraw-Hill.

King, M. C. (1973). The politics of sexual stereotypes. *Black Scholar,* 4 (6–7): 12–23.

Lawrence, C. R., III. (1992). Cringing at myths of black sexuality. In Chrisman and Allen (eds.), *Court of Appeal,* 136–38.

Norton, E. H. (1992, January–February). . . . and the language is race. *Ms.,* 43–45.

Phelps, T. M., and Winternitz, H. (1992). *Capitol games: Clarence Thomas, Anita Hill, and the story of a Supreme Court nomination.* New York: Hyperion.

Preston, C. T., Jr. (1992). Characterizing the issue: Metaphor and contemporary impromptu discussions of gender. *Argumentation and Advocacy,* 28: 185–91.

Ransby, B. (1992). The gang rape of Anita Hill and the assault upon all women of African descent. In Chrisman and Allen (eds.), *Court of Appeal,* 169–75.

Williams, L. M. (1986). *Race and rape: The black woman as legitimate victim.* Eric Document Reproduction No. ED 294970. Durham: Family Violence Research Laboratory, University of New Hampshire.

Women break all congressional election records. (1992–93, Winter). *Women's Political Times,* 1, 3.

4

Who Is Anita Hill? A Discourse-Centered Inquiry into the Concept of Self in American Folk Psychology

ERICA VERRILLO

This essay explores the means by which the multiple depictions of Anita Hill's "self" in the Hill-Thomas hearings served to reflect and maintain power relationships through a variety of culturally potent social images. These images—also known as personae, archetypes, roles, and personality types—constitute a part of what can be called American folk psychology, and appeals to it have a powerfully persuasive, yet hidden, effect. I suggest that the public dissection of Hill's character has hidden within it the forms of self-defining discourse that serve to establish who may—and who may not—have credibility in contemporary American culture. Viewing the hearings in this light gives us some insight into the socially constructed nature of the self and explains the importance placed on defining the characters of Hill and Thomas in the hearings. This essay presents some aspects of the discourse that was employed to divide and conquer Anita Hill and to forge an indivisible identity for Clarence Thomas. It concludes with some observations about how we may understand a contested public self in the context of individual psychology, collective discourse, and institutional power.

The Self and Social Context

"Who am I?" constitutes perhaps one of the oldest questions that humans have asked themselves. It is a question that is dependent on and in turn stimulates self-reflection. One cannot ask the question unless one has self-consciousness to start with, and one cannot answer it without considerable self-reflection about the nature of that consciousness. This gives the question an elusive, Escher-like quality as the self must perform the simultaneous functions of subject, object, and means of inquiry to arrive at an answer (Lewis, 1982). The question "Who am I?" in its various permutations—"What is the self?" "What is a person?" and "What is a human?"— has plagued and tantalized philosophers through the ages, perhaps because of its very elusiveness. But none, with the possible exception of Descartes, has come up with a "bottom line" definition. For Descartes, thinking sufficed. For other philosophers, even thinking has not offered enough evidence of existence. "I think, therefore I am" seems to beg the question of "Who is thinking?" Hume, Hobbes, Locke, Kant, Nietzsche, Heidegger, Derrida, and a host of other philosophers have struggled with notions of the self and reflexivity without coming to a satisfactory conclusion about its nature (Lawson, 1985).

Psychologists have investigated the matter with equal fervor and determination and with equally uncertain results.[1] Inquiries about the nature, function, and development of the self have generated as little consensus in psychology as they have in philosophy. While psychologists take the individual as their main unit of analysis, they—unlike many philosophers—do not regard the self as a unified entity. Freud's influence predicated whole lines of study on bipolar distinctions (unconscious/conscious, ego/id, and the like) within the individual organism. Subsequent social psychological schools of thought, while rejecting many Freudian conceptualizations of the individual, have also developed "dichotomous" or "divided" self categorizations, such as "public" and "private" (Baumeister, 1986), "ideal" and "actual" (Baumeister and Tice, 1986), and "competent" and "moral" (Vallacher, 1980). Selves may be motivational, intentional, or emotional, and they may be developed through processes that are cognitive, biological, or situational (Mischel, 1977; Young-Eisendrath and Hall, 1987; Wegner and Vallacher, 1980). Running through this plethora of interpretations is the idea that the self, while defying definition, is basically a social phenomenon, something that is developed, sustained, and revised in a social context.

That the self is social in nature is also the perspective some sociologists have adopted (Kotarba and Fontana, 1984). Erving Goffman has been highly influential in this regard. Goffman's social self is an actor, an individual who both intentionally and unintentionally "gives" and "gives off" expressions (Goffman, 1959, 2). The self, for Goffman, is an interactive and profoundly social entity. This is also the perspective that contemporary sociologists take when they speak of a "victimized self," (Johnson and Ferraro, 1984), a "media self" (Altheide, 1984), a "homosexual self" (Messinger and Warren, 1984), or a "competent self" (Patrick and Bignall, 1984). The existence of all of these selves is contingent on experience with other people. Stanford Lyman summarizes this position when he states, "Asked, 'Who am I?,' the individual is likely to respond categorically: I am a black, an American, a professor, a homosexual, a cripple, etc. The 'I' seems to require a reference *group* that owes its own claim to recognizable existence to the social constitution of collectivities" (Lyman, 1984, x). It appears that the individual nature of "I" is dependent on a socially defined "we" or, perhaps, "you."

The "social self" concept to which most sociologists adhere when they consider the self at all resonates with the "cultural self" that informs the anthropological perspective. While sociologists tend to define the self in terms of social roles, anthropologists see the self in relation to culture. Different cultures have different requirements for what constitutes a self (Kavolis, 1984; Lee, 1976). For the anthropologist, the principle of cultural relativity implies that there can be no universal definition of the self and that there theoretically may exist as many categorizations and definitions of the self as different cultures allow. The group definition of the self, however, carries within it all of the complications inherent to societies such as our own, in which hierarchies, competition, and even open conflict between ambiguously defined groups are the norm. How I define myself may not coincide with how others

define me. In addition, these identities may vary radically given different circumstances creating self-definitions that clash. In Hill's case, her conflict with
a black man subsumed her sexual identity as a (feminist) woman within her
social identity as a (black) woman. Her professional status as a lawyer and
professor sometimes overshadowed her identity as a black woman. At one time
or another, all of these identities competed with the "type of person" Hill was.
Yet Hill managed to speak as all of these people—and more.

So where does this leave us in our search for the answer to the question
"Who am I?" Scholars simply cannot reach a consensus. While philosophers
and certain psychologists seek out universals, anthropologists and sociologists
point to the particular; and, as if disagreements among these specialists were
not sufficient, there are also priests, poets, judges, and a multitude of other
"experts" who can define the "self" for us in ways that differ, sometimes rather
dramatically, from the definitions the academic community employs. The
"true" nature of the self seems to be an unsolvable mystery, yet we all have
some kind of theory, or we would not be able to address the issue at all.

An alternative, but as yet not thoroughly explored, approach has been most
eloquently expressed by Jerome Bruner, one of the founders of cognitive
psychology. Bruner, in his book *Acts of Meaning* (1990), argues that the crucial criteria for a culturally sensitive treatment of the self are meaning and
practice. As he succinctly expresses it, "Saying and doing represent a func-
tionally inseparable unit in a culturally oriented psychology" (19). Bruner
suggests that "folk" psychology, as opposed to psychology as conceived of by
specialists, is what provides the framework for most people's behavior. By folk
psychology, Bruner means the "system of organizing experience" that members of a given culture share to satisfactorily explain what makes people "tick"
(35). He points out that "we learn our culture's folk psychology early, learn it
as we learn to use the very language we acquire and to conduct the interpersonal transactions required in communal life" (35). Bruner puts forth the idea
that to understand the concept of personhood in any given culture (including our own), we must look to what people commonly say and do in a natural
setting. Like many anthropologists, Bruner proposes anchoring the notion of
the self deep within cultural practice—a practice that remains largely uncon-
scious and is quintessentially group oriented.

This essay describes the self as it is currently interpreted in American culture.[2] It does not define the nature of the self in terms of how the self ab-
stractly functions, behaves, or is developed. Nor does it rely too heavily on

what specialists have said about the structure of the self. The questions this study raises are simply, What are our quotidian beliefs about the self, and how do we enact them in common behavior? Getting at how the self is culturally conceived is not a straightforward task since the true nature of the self is not a typical topic in daily conversation. Rather than look for a "metalanguage" of selves talking about selves, I have taken an interactional approach; that is, I investigate how selves are required to perform in response to social interactional demands. If the self is formed in a cultural and social context, what better way to examine it than investigating the ways in which selves perform in interaction, and what better place to look for it than in common discourse. The Hill-Thomas hearings provide an exceptionally rich setting for both performance of and discourse about the self in a natural environment. Government officials, media managers, witnesses, and, of course, Hill and Thomas themselves all demonstrated the intricate and varied ways that the self can be portrayed, enacted, constructed, and contested.

A Discourse-Centered Approach

The analysis of what people say to each other and how they say it has been the primary focus of discourse analysis. One of the leading members of the field, John Gumperz, has stated, "The analyst's task is to make an in depth study of selected instances of verbal interaction, observe whether or not actors understand each other, elicit participants' interpretations of what goes on and then (a) deduce the social assumptions that people have made in order to act as they do, and (b) determine empirically how linguistic signs communicate in the interaction process" (Gumperz, 1982, 35). In this description of the task of the ideal discourse analyst, spoken discourse between people provides the subject matter and serves as an analytical tool. Gumperz, in the tradition of many anthropologists, includes how people interpret their own discourse as an important element in his analysis. He also indicates that by comparing observation and "native" interpretation, one can "deduce" social assumptions. Gumperz indicates that the means for arriving at underlying social assumptions is language.

Gumperz's approach to the study of discourse dovetails nicely with Bruner's perspective. Gumperz's search for social assumptions mirrors Bruner's quest for "folk psychology." Though Bruner tends to limit his discourse to narrative, it is clear that he, along with Gumperz, thinks that spoken interaction of all kinds provides the means by which social assumptions/folk psychology may be discovered. Each values the importance of "native" interpretation in arriving at social or cultural assumptions. Each also highlights the social significance of what people commonly say.

There are many other spokespersons for this position. In sociolinguistics there is an explicit premise that social status, ethnic group, gender, professional role, and, in sum, any social or cultural phenomenon will be manifested in language "as spoken by ordinary people in their everyday lives" (Trudgill, 1983, 33). Although sociolinguists tend to focus on the linguistic means by which such social classificatory phenomena as status, gender, age, and the like are manifested, Bruner is interested in the ways in which personally felt experience relates to such diffuse cultural phenomena as conceptions of self.

This study is based on the view that the individual's subjective experiences of self are culturally contextualized by and manifested in discourse. Following Gumperz's recommendation to "make an in depth study of selected instances of verbal interaction," I show how the different interactional demands of common discourse are instrumental in formulating a cultural notion of the self. To put it another way, the question "Who am I?" might be rephrased in the context of discourse as "How are you requiring me to manipulate, reveal, portray, modify, maintain and defend my 'self' through questions, demands, requests, statements, suggestions, inferences, and insinuations?" To demonstrate this perspective, I draw on public discourse in an event that was observed and interpreted by millions of Americans—the Hill-Thomas hearings.

Although a nationally televised political forum might not constitute an "everyday" setting, the types of discourse strategies the participants employed were not out of the ordinary. The yes/no questions and requests to "tell the story," describe feelings, and explain actions are common in everyday discourse. With the exception of Senator Arlen Specter, members of the committee were also at pains to keep syntax and lexicon as colloquial as possible. Since the hearings were largely directed to issues concerning character and personality (Thomas's character, Hill's personality), they offer an unprecedented opportunity to examine sustained public discourse focusing on the nature and practice of self. For the purpose of this study, I concentrate on the types of discourse employed in questioning Anita Hill and, strictly as a source of comparison, those used in questioning Clarence Thomas. This analysis of the type of discourse that specifically elicits conceptions of the self can serve as a means of uncovering the culturally relevant concepts of the self that depend on our own folk psychology.

The Hill-Thomas Hearings

The Thomas confirmation hearings constituted the second major media event of 1991, competing only with the Gulf War. It was one of those events that "everybody" knew about and that held most people who watched it spellbound. As networks cleared their airtime to show the hearings in their entirety, viewers sat riveted to their screens, captivated by this "real life drama." What so enthralled audiences was not just the topic—any sexual scandal is considered a "juicy" topic for lively speculation in the United States—but also the mystery. Two very believable people told two very different stories, stories that in themselves were each quite believable. Who was lying?

The notions of "truth" and "credibility" were the two central issues around which the members of the Senate Judiciary Committee based their investigation. Each had its representation on the committee. Senator Howell Heflin asked "Who's telling the truth?" almost as often as Senator Specter asked "Who is credible?" The two questions, though related, are essentially quite different. The first seeks to arrive at a judgment based on observable events— truth as a "real," objective state, independent of the impressions we may have of actors. The other seeks to establish the believability of the actors; the truth value of "events" hinges on the actors' credibility. Though each approach generates its own distinct method of questioning, each of these concepts relates intimately to the portrayal of the "character" of the person under investigation. While a seeker of truth may look for a motive and try to establish a narrative sequence of events and behaviors, as Senator Heflin and Senator Joseph Biden did, the seeker of credibility looks for logical consistency and attempts to divorce behavior from sequential context, as did Senator Specter and Senator Alan Simpson. The factor that either makes the motive plausible or demonstrates inconsistency is the person's character, hence, the importance placed on character witnesses.

Character, in the way it is employed in the legal process, functions as another gloss for the self. When lawyers try to build or destroy credibility through character portrayals, they are treating character as though it were an immutable part of the self. Character may be invoked as a justification for behavior. A person's character may both cause and explain certain actions. When lawyers ask such character questions as "Why do you think . . . ?" "How well do you know X?" or "Is X the kind of person who would . . . ?" they are essentially asking witnesses to identify the selves. Because the Thomas hearings focused primarily on such matters as character and credibility, considerable attention was devoted to this type of questioning. The interchanges that resulted constitute an excellent source of information on how the self is handled in dialogue. The following sections describe some of the ways in which dialogue was used to establish Hill's self. The first two focus on categorization strategies and the committee's efforts to establish a temporally consistent image of Hill. The third deals primarily with Hill's battle to substitute the committee's portrayals for her own.

Categorizations: Archetype, Persona, and Address

Perhaps no other dialogue sequence during the hearings demonstrates the use of cultural categories better than the following interchange between Senator Heflin and Anita Hill:[3]

> Sen. Heflin: Are you a scorned woman?
> Prof. Hill: [murmuring] No.
> Sen. Heflin: Are you a zealot civil rights believer that progress will be turned back if Clarence Thomas goes on the court?
> Prof. Hill: No [pause] I have my opinion [pause].
> Sen. Heflin: Do you have a militant attitude relative to the area of civil rights? Do you have a martyr complex?
> Prof. Hill: [laughing] No, I don't.
> Sen. Heflin: Well, do you see that you can be the hero in the civil rights movement?
> Prof. Hill: Even if I liked attention I would not lie to get attention.

What stands out in this rather dramatic line of questioning is Heflin's use of archetypes. The "scorned woman," "zealot," "militant," "martyr," and "hero" figures that Senator Heflin called up are not individualized but categorical models. The archetypical figure represents a generic prototype that may be filled by an individual—George Washington was a "hero," Christ a "martyr," and Malcolm X a "militant"—but that is not dependent on any single individual for its characterization. The archetype represents some cluster of traits and behaviors that are perceived as transcending the individual person, and in that sense archetypes are impersonal. Archetypes, as culturally "fictionalized" people, are predictable. Their behaviors, as well as their social function, fit into a pattern. Martyrs are sacrificed for a cause, scorned women seek revenge, and zealots show no moderation.

What was Senator Heflin trying to accomplish by invoking this set of archetypes? How was he asking Anita Hill to respond? Before launching into his set of questions, Senator Heflin explained that he was trying to "determine motivation for the one who is not telling the truth." In evoking archetypical categories, Senator Heflin was attempting to "type" Hill's motivations in the context of an impersonal self. The motives for each of the archetypes he suggested need little elaboration, since motive is predetermined by the archetype.

It is important to note that Senator Heflin was not actually asserting that Anita Hill was any of these. He was asking her. His discourse strategy was to set up a set of images for Anita Hill to reject.[4] Hill, in responding to the questions "Who are you?" and "Are you any of these?" needed to share the archetype and to understand the full implications of identifying with or rejecting any of them. In rejecting the archetypes offered and saying "I am not any of these," she was affirming her individual nature, a nature that she also affirmed by stating, "I would not lie to get attention." This final statement attests to her individual makeup, not to a categorical trait, and is made all the stronger by her repeated rejections of earlier unacceptable identifications.

A second type of person with whom Anita Hill was asked to identify is a social persona. Social personae typify professional categories that entail certain specific modes of behavior. They are generalized, or ideal, people whose behavior or "personality" is predicated on a profession or social position.[5] Mothers as personae are supposed to be nurturing. Judges are supposed to be fair and impartial. Both Senators Heflin and Specter invited Hill to "speak as" a persona on a number of occasions. In the context of discussing the issue of fantasy, Senator Heflin asked, "As a psychology major what elements of human nature seem to go into that type of situation?" to which Hill replied, "I felt he was using his power and authority over me." In the course of this particular line of questioning, Hill was asked to evaluate her own personality from the perspective of an "expert" and to give authoritative testimony. To accomplish this, she must speak in two voices and as two selves. By calling up the personae, Heflin was requiring that the professional persona "self" of the "psychologist Hill" make a respected evaluation of Hill's "real" personality. In other words, Heflin asked Hill to split herself into professional and nonprofessional selves.

Senator Specter also asked Anita Hill to speak as a persona to evaluate, negatively, her own actions. In the following interchange he called up Hill's lawyer persona.

> Sen. Specter: As an experienced attorney didn't it cross your mind that your evidentiary position would be much stronger if you took some notes?
> Prof. Hill: I don't know why it didn't cross my mind.
> Sen. Specter: The law of evidence is that notes are very important.
> Prof. Hill: I'm not a person [pause] I was not interested in any litigation.

Lawyers write things down; therefore, as a lawyer, Anita Hill should have written things down. By repeatedly calling on Hill to identify and evaluate herself as a lawyer ("You're an expert in the field," he said later), he cast doubt on her actions. If lawyers are supposed to behave in a certain way and if Hill, a lawyer, does not behave according to the persona, then an inconsistency arises. But the inconsistency stems from a conflict in persona behavior rather than personal behavior. Hill attempted to address the difference when she started her second reply, "I'm not a person. . . ." It seems Hill was starting to say she was not a person who sought conflict. While this may be viewed as a personal character trait, it is not a "lawyer persona" trait. Hill contrasted the two by stating that she "was not interested" in any litigation. In so doing, she stressed her primary identification as a person, that is, as "Anita Hill," rather than as the persona of lawyer.[6]

A third means of identifying the self is address, or the names by which we call ourselves and are called by others. Titles of address bear social information. Addressing a woman as "Mrs." or "Miss" reveals her marital status, as "Professor" or "Doctor" does her professional status. Anita Hill opened her initial statement with the words, "My name is Anita F. Hill," giving her legal name. This was the only form of self-address she used during the hearings. The terms by which others addressed her or referred to her varied. She was directly addressed as "Professor Hill" on most occasions, emphasizing her professional status. However, in indirect reference she was referred to as "Anita Hill," "Professor Hill," "Mrs. Hill," "Miss Hill," "Ms. Hill," "Anita F. Hill," or simply "Anita." All of these forms of address carry their own implications. Addressing someone by first name implies familiarity; by full name, distance; by title, respect; by civil status, a woman's marital relationship. Some of the senators could not decide exactly how best to refer to Anita Hill. In asking if Clarence Thomas knew her, Senator Heflin began by referring to her as "Mrs.," changed the error to "Ms.," then changed the title to "Professor," and finally, in exasperation, settled on "Anita F. Hill." Senator Biden also, erroneously, called her "Judge" and "Miss Thomas" on more than one occasion.[7]

All three of these forms of identification represent strategies on the part of the participants in the dialogue. When Anita Hill was asked to reveal a possible motive by identifying herself as an archetype, she resisted, thereby avoiding a predetermined behavioral "story." When her professional persona was addressed, she responded by speaking as that persona, although during interchanges in which the professional persona weakened her explanation, she rejected the persona in favor of the individual. The strategies her questioners employed in asking her to respond as various "selves" were matched by the types of responses Hill used to portray herself. Although she consistently took active steps to enhance positive and authoritative identifications, the committee apparently still found it difficult to identify her. Perhaps the multiple references and forms of address used to identify Hill were symptomatic of the committee's ambiguous feelings about Hill. For some members, it must have been quite complicated to show respect for her position even as they questioned her credibility. For her supporters, having more than one identification at play was probably equally difficult. The potential conflict between Hill's professional personae and her presentation of herself as a simple Baptist woman from rural Oklahoma may have made it difficult for them to aid her in establishing credibility.

The Process of Identification: Continuity in Narrative

The problem of identifying an individual, of determining who someone is, is complex. The self requires not only a name of some sort but also continuous identification with that name. If the self who went under the name of Clarence Thomas in 1982 is not recognizably the same self as the Clarence Thomas being accused of sexual harassment, then can one even consider the possibility of holding him accountable for his actions of ten years ago? By the same token, the Anita Hill of ten years ago must be the same person who has accused Clarence Thomas or she would not be able to make a complaint of damage done to her person. Common sense might dictate that if the person resides in the same body, it must be the same person. The legal issue of continuity of the self is not as straightforward as the common sense explanation, however. In cases in which an individual has a split personality, one personality may not be held accountable for what another personality does. A minor is not held as accountable as an adult even if the crime is the same. In everyday life, individuals may be reborn, go through mid-life crises, or undergo any number of personal transformations, in which case a former self may no longer be recognizable. In the legal arena, establishing a consistent self is crucial for determining credibility, because people recognized as consistent in their feelings and behaviors are generally considered truthful. Courtroom questioning frequently involves the telling of a narrative to establish continuity (Bennett, 1979). Asking whether Anita Hill gave consistent narratives was one of the principle lines of questioning Senator Specter and Senator Patrick Leahy employed. The following exchanges exemplify the attempts to provide a consistent narrative:

> Sen. Leahy: Tell us in your own words [pause]. How did you feel (when Clarence Thomas described pornographic films to you)?
> Prof. Hill: I was embarrassed. It was [pause] I made the point that it was offensive. The nature of the conversation was disgusting, embarrassing, degrading.

> Sen. Leahy: How did you feel at the time?
> Prof. Hill: I was very depressed. I was embarrassed.
> Sen Leahy: How do you feel today?
> Prof. Hill: Today I feel more angry. It was irresponsible for a person in a position of authority.

To answer Senator Leahy's questions, Anita Hill was required to project herself back in time, express her feelings, and compare her past feelings with her present feelings. This is a psychologically complicated maneuver. Hill might not have put her feelings into words when the incidents occurred, but she must now re-create and then formalize past feelings into a present context to make them intelligible to her questioner. Being asked to evaluate past feelings in the light of her present interaction meant that Hill had to identify herself consistently over time and demonstrate this continuity to her interlocutors. Anita Hill was also asked to consider a development in her feelings over time. When Hill was asked to compare her past and present feelings, she stated that "today" she was more angry. She indicated that her "embarrassed" feelings have evolved to include anger. While a consistent portrayal of past feelings projected into the future is important, it is equally important to note any change. Changing emotions can be considered to be quite natural and expected in people. If Hill were lying, she would have had the task of not only "making up" the events of the past but also inventing a "natural" evolution of feelings from a fictitious past to the present.

By constructing continuities and changes in feelings over time, Hill was contextualizing her emotions into a story. She was powerfully aided in that task by Senators Biden and Leahy when they asked, "Can you lay out the sequence of events that brought you forward?" or when they requested that she "walk through" the events. Narrative provides a convincing format for explaining events and feelings. It also gives the temporal continuity a listener needs to perceive the logic behind a person's actions (Bennett and Edelman, 1985; Hollihan and Riley, 1987; Kirkwood, 1983). Leahy's request to have her tell her own story gave Hill an excellent opportunity to convey the sense of her actions to the committee. The narrative also helped her convey a self who had unwillingly come forward with a painful story. This was a story meant to counter opposition stories that she had been duped or persuaded to come forward by special interest groups. The logic of the story gave continuity over time to Anita Hill's self, which augmented her credibility and provided a context for her feelings, motivations, and behaviors.

Senator Specter attempted to dismantle this logic by asking Hill to take her actions out of context. Specter repeatedly made the statement that "following" Thomas to the Equal Employment Opportunity Commission (EEOC) did not make any sense to him. Why, he asked, should she *follow* a man who had done *that* to her?[8] The implication was that Anita Hill "followed" Thomas because he never, in fact, did anything to her. Hill, in response to Specter's attempts to destroy the logic of her story, tried to reestablish the validity of her narrative when she responded to him by saying, "The statement has to be taken as a whole."

The "story" provides the basis for which one's actions can be judged as consistent or logical. Behaviors that follow sequentially according to a comprehensible pattern can also explain inconsistencies and changes over time. Anita Hill, speaking now, is not the same person she was then. The experienced and respected professional of today might not be believable as a victim. The inexperienced and vulnerable young woman of ten years ago might be. Relating the two Anita Hills over time through a story contextualizes her actions and makes them understandable. Senator Leahy was cognizant of this fact when he asked her how old she was at the time the incidents took place. Senator Specter was equally cognizant when he asked her to evaluate herself "as an expert." While Leahy hoped to provide sense, Specter was aiming toward non-sense. Each played in different ways on temporally determined images of the self. Each, in turn, required Hill to do the same.

The fact that Hill, as a participant in the dialogue, was asked to manipulate herself in terms of these temporal identification strategies does not mean that she was a passive partner in establishing who she was. Even though each senator had a stake in having her present herself in a fashion that would either further or prevent Thomas's appointment, she also had a personal interest in how she portrayed herself. Regardless of whether Thomas was appointed, Hill wanted her story to be believed and her person respected. She pursued these ends in her own self-characterization.

Self-Portrayal

So far this discussion has highlighted the role that the members of the Senate Judiciary Committee played in determining the identity of Anita Hill, whether through pursuing direct "identification" strategies or through establishing narrative continuities and discontinuities of the self in direct questioning. Hill's questioners clearly occupied the more powerful position in the investigation. It was their right to ask her what they wished and her obligation to respond. The inequality in status and in power meant that control of information was largely in their hands. In spite of the imbalance, Anita Hill was still able to actively and effectively portray the self of her own choosing.

Hill portrayed herself primarily as a thinking person. After Specter suggested that she might be given to "fantasy" Hill replied, "I'm not given to fantasy. I weighed this carefully. I considered it carefully and I made a determination to come forward." Throughout her testimony, Hill used "thinking" verbs. She "weighed," "considered," and "determined." She was careful and deliberate. Hill expressed her past inaction against Thomas as a choice. Her failure to make a formal complaint ten years ago was a "judgment I made at the time."

Anita Hill also downplayed herself by avoiding self-reference. When the questions focused on her emotions, she rapidly shifted to events. For example, after stating that she was embarrassed in the above interchange with Senator Leahy, she continued with, "It was [pause]" and resumed a little later with "The nature of the conversation. . . ." She shifted the topic from her feelings to the situation. In a similar topic shift, when she stated that she felt angry, she immediately followed up with, "It was irresponsible for a person in a position of authority." In yet another exchange with Senator Specter, Hill made the statement, "It is difficult for people to come forth." Instead of directly expressing her own personal difficulty, she stated a generality.

The ways in which Anita Hill portrayed herself is an indication of who she would like to be, if not of who she was. The calm, rational individual who thinks carefully and makes free choices was Anita Hill's ideal Anita Hill. This is the projected person who will not fit herself into an archetype and even at times rejects the professional persona, who is deeply a part of her public presentation. Hill "weighs" and "considers," not as a lawyer in the face of a legal decision but as a person in the face of a moral decision. The ideal Hill was not an emotional Hill either. Her steady emphasis on thoughts, options, and choices indicates that Anita Hill was an independent and self-reliant person free to evaluate her own situation and act on her decisions. That this might not have been the best self-portrayal given the circumstances was probably not even a consideration for Anita Hill.[9] Her commitment to her own self-perception was probably even greater than her need to convince others of her victimization.

Self-Work and Strategic Selves: Hill and Thomas in Contrast

Who is Anita Hill? Anita Hill herself was asked to do a great deal to answer this question. She was required to recognize and respond to labels, personify social roles, and project her feelings, thoughts, and self-evaluations through time. Anita Hill was required to be a number of people. She simultaneously fulfilled the somewhat conflicting roles of reluctant witness and cooperative witness. She portrayed a professional high-status persona, even as she performed the low-status task of subjecting herself to questioning. Over and above what was asked of her in questioning, she needed to make her own portrayal of herself to be believed and, perhaps, to preserve integrity. In short, Anita Hill, in the course of her interactions with the senators on the committee, did an enormous amount of interactional work to define and maintain a self. The interactional work one does to portray a social self, or "self-work," is not quite the same as maintaining an impression. Impressions may not require the degree of self-identification inherent in a presentation of the self.[10]

It is tempting to stop at this point and speculate about the self-work that is characteristically required in interactions. However, since all of the interactions discussed so far have focused on one person's self-work, it might be beneficial to take a brief look at data generated from another participant in these interchanges—Clarence Thomas.

Comparing identification strategies reveals that Thomas was addressed and referred to as "Clarence Thomas" and as "Judge Thomas" only. He was never addressed according to his civil status as "Mr.," nor was he addressed informally as "Clarence." Thomas was asked to speak in the role of judge and mentor on one occasion by Senator Biden, but other than that one instance he was not asked to take up a secondary persona. This gave the impression that Clarence Thomas's persona of judge was also who Clarence Thomas was.

Like Anita Hill, Thomas was asked to project himself back in time in order to assess his actions. Rather than comply by evaluating himself, however, Thomas chose to focus on processes instead. When asked how he would have adjudicated a sexual harassment charge ten years earlier, he described the process in some detail, leaving his own possible actions and opinions out of the description entirely. By avoiding an explanation of how he felt about sexual harassment at a former time, Thomas was free to present his current self (the type of person who did not tolerate harassment) as representative of his past self.

In contrast to Anita Hill's self-portrayal, Thomas chose to identify himself with a group—the black male. He also portrayed himself through metaphor by describing his office as a family and himself as a father.[11] These abstract identifications provided for Thomas a "story." On the one hand, as a black male, he could convincingly tell the story of racism, stereotyping, and "high-tech lynching." The racism story that Thomas clearly articulated is one in which whites prevent "uppity" blacks from succeeding in life. On the other hand, the image of father provided an emotional and behavioral framework for his "real" self. Fathers are supposed to be supportive and caring with their children, as Thomas said he was with Hill. Another part of this story is that children (Anita Hill) are at times ungrateful and can even betray their parents. Thomas's statements that he did "everything" to help Hill (and *this* was how she repaid him) were an evocation of the ungrateful child story.

Although the committee did not ask Thomas to speak as an archetype or as a secondary persona (only as his primary persona of "judge"), he took these abstract identifications upon himself. Thomas was in control of both the quantity and types of self-image being used to identify him. Limiting self-portrayals to just a few options, all of which Thomas controlled, lent consistency to his presentation. This was buttressed by the constancy of Thomas's observable emotional state.[12] Thomas spoke of his anger and pain, as did Hill, but the difference between them was that, unlike Hill, Thomas also showed his anger.

What does this comparison reveal about the self and how it is enacted? In each of these presentations of the self, what stands out is the interactive nature of self-definition. In each case, both participants in an interaction either cooperated or competed in forming a coherent picture of the self. In Thomas's case he garnered cooperation that manifested itself in consistency of address and reference as well as in the senators' direct statements, such as "I've known you for 11 years" (Senator Hatch). Thomas was aided in forming a cohesive and coherent self-presentation. Hill, however, was hindered in her efforts to establish a coherent self. She was presented with multiple images of herself, which she could either choose from, let stand, or reject in favor of her own portrayal. The selves with which Hill was invited to identify were largely dissociated from her central narrative self—a woman wronged.

Presented in this fashion, the self is transformed from an inherent state of being to a strategy. If people are believed on the basis of their believability, the definition of the self becomes less a metaphysical question than a rhetorical one. People who strive to convince others of the truth on the basis of their self-presentation necessarily must adapt their presentation to their audiences. Defining the self in terms of rhetorical impact perhaps is an indication that selves might be best evaluated in terms of their success.

In the short run at least, Thomas's rhetorical self strategy was more successful. One of the popular perceptions of Hill was that she was holding something back. Many perceived her as duplicitous. It is quite possible that this perception was based on Anita Hill's multiple selves. Thomas, by contrast, in portraying a more limited number of selves, may have been perceived as more genuine. The responses to Hill and Thomas seem to indicate that in spite of the fact that each was asked to enact, and indeed did portray, more than one self, there is a popular notion that the self is unitary, that is, that there is a true self. Senator Hatch called up Clarence Thomas's true self when he said that all of these (accusations) were "inconsistent with the real Clarence Thomas." The real Clarence Thomas was a judge, an honorable man, a father to his staff. Even when Senator Leahy asked him to "step out of the role for a moment of being a Supreme Court Nominee and go back to being head of EEOC for a moment," his self-image was not substantially altered. He had the same authority, the same persona. We recognized him. The real Anita Hill was harder to identify. Was she a "nice person," "Yale graduate," "good lawyer," "fantasizer," "scorned woman," "zealot," "hero," "arrogant selfseeker," "martyr," or an "example to us all"? Although numerous self-portrayals may not work to one's advantage, multiple selves may be unavoidable when there is social inequity.

Conclusion

Examining the discourse people commonly engage in when they portray themselves, or are portrayed by others, can serve multiple purposes. In terms of Bruner's idea of a cultural psychology, the ways that the self is performed may provide information on what the interactional limitations of the self are composed of in a given culture. This addresses the question of what the self does in a given culture. It seems that in ours at least, the self is integrally related to concepts of truth and credibility. This may not be the case in cultures in which credibility may be subsumed in behavioral codes or relegated to the world of the supernatural instead of being established through individualized self-identification.[13] Cultural labels, such as archetypes, personae, and forms of address, also provide information on the available repertoire of selves. Anita Hill's portrayal of self might have been more limited in a culture in which women occupy a very circumscribed social niche. The degree to which different members of a society employ self may also lead to cultural information about the distribution of available selves. The Thomas hearings seem to indicate that a multiplicity of selves may result from ambiguity in social position. Do lower-status individuals (women and blacks, for instance) in our culture occupy more ambiguous positions that necessitate developing more selves? Do different social groups in a culture practice the self in different ways? Questions of this nature are raised in examining the different ways that selves are expressed by different social groups. A last issue that emerges by examining this particular piece of discourse is that of power. Perhaps the management and control of limited selves in our culture is a behavior that both reflects and constitutes authority. Those with more authority may have more right to determine and limit their repertoire of selves. Authority may also be bestowed by maintaining limitations—as appears to have been the case with Judge Thomas.

This essay has uncovered some of the notions of self that are particular to our own culture. Although the Hill-Thomas hearings do not provide the quantity of data needed to make a broad generalization about American culture, they do provide material for interesting questions about social relations. The differentiation between the types and amounts of self-work required by Thomas and Hill opens up the possibility that there may not be a coherent cultural pattern on how all members of a cultural group conceptualize or are required to perform selves. The disparity may indicate that people in positions of power may attain and maintain their power by controlling their self-image. Conversely, people in positions that do not entail power, though they may have authority (as Anita Hill did), do not have the same control over self-definition. The control over self-definition for one's self and for others may be one of the identifying features of power in our society. Given this interpretation, it may behoove us to look deeper into the notion of the "true" or "real" self that characterizes one aspect of our folk psychology. If we do indeed hold a cultural notion of a unitary true self, how does this belief correlate with the practice of multiple selves? Those who are not in positions of power may find that portraying multiple selves (both those they desire and those foisted on them by people with power) decreases their credibility. But if multiple selves are inherent to people without power, they will never be able to achieve credibility, whereas people who exercise a limiting self-control will always be believed. This presents a certain cultural dilemma. How does one uniformly judge sincerity, honesty, or truth in a given culture if these traits are ultimately determined by how much control of self-definition (power) a person has? If the answer to this question is to be found in politics rather than personality, perhaps this is the juncture at which a folk psychology of the self parts ways with a folk ideology of the self.

NOTES

1. For a very useful and concise synopsis of the main models of self used in current social psychology, see Potter and Wetherell, 1987.

2. I am using the term *American culture* very loosely here to facilitate discussion. I do not mean to make an a priori assumption that there is a unified American culture to which all Americans adhere.

3. All quotations from the hearings are taken from the author's videotaped recording of the nationally televised hearings before the Committee on the Judiciary on the nomination of Judge Clarence Thomas to serve as an associate justice of the Supreme Court of the United States, October 11, 12, and 13, 1991.

4. Senator Orrin Hatch employs a similar strategy with Clarence Thomas when asking him, in rapid succession, if he spoke to Anita Hill about Long Dong Silver, mentioned oral sex, et cetera. The string of denials has a rhetorical effect that is cumulative; that is, the series of denials is stronger than each one taken by itself.

5. The term *persona* used to describe an aspect of social character differs from Jung's psychological application of the concept. Here *persona* is related to the rhetorical and literary notion of the persona as a "fictive being" (Black, 1970; Campbell, 1975). The social persona that defines the character of the self is in some ways as fictive and artificial as the personae in drama and in political rhetoric.

6. Hill's reformulation of her reply from "I'm not a person who" to "I was not interested in litigation" may represent a translation of her personal behavior into "lawyerese." Since she on earlier occasions stated that she "did not know why" she did not keep written accounts of what had occurred, she probably was not thinking in terms of a suit at the time. In that case, telling Specter that she was not interested in litigation represents an assessment adjusted to the kind of legal language Specter used in his questioning.

7. Senator Biden's errors in address might have been because he was attempting to establish parity in a situation in which there was no formal title for a lawyer but there was for a judge.

8. It is worth noting that Senator Specter's emphasis on "following" the man rather then the job promoted the impression that Hill's relationship with Thomas was more important to her than her job.

9. Hill's decision to maintain a calm, rational exterior, while crucial to maintaining her own self-image, might have ultimately done her more harm than good. The stereotype of the hysterical woman, while abhorrent to Hill, would have better matched the cultural expectations of how a violated woman is supposed to behave. Had Hill broken down and sobbed at any point during the hearings, she would have gained instant credibility as a woman suffering from the pain and humiliation of sexual harassment.

10. I am making a differentiation between *self-work* and Goffman's term *face-work* as well. *Face-work* is an interactive strategy that pertains to social ritual. The

difference between the two lies in the lasting quality of an identifying "self" as opposed to circumstantial "face."

11. The metaphorical self is not the same as a persona. Thomas really is a judge and a black man. He is not, and was not, Anita Hill's father. The metaphor of the father Thomas evoked carries with it certain behavioral implications that are incompatible with Anita Hill's charges. Fathers do not try to seduce their daughters or talk about sexual matters with them. Evoking the powerful metaphor of the father was an attempt to undercut Hill's claims. A father simply could not do such things; therefore, Hill's claims were false.

12. In her analysis of popular expressions of relationship styles in the 1960s, Virginia Kidd (1975) notes, "'Being your real self', 'self-fulfillment', 'being more yourself' were cue words for wise alive behavior. Often the 'self' was equated with an individual's feeling" (36). Those who were the most convinced by Thomas's show of anger were probably adherents to this popular philosophy of the self, which raises the question of historicity. If the sixties and seventies generation was unduly influenced by emotional presentation, perhaps the previous generation was not. Given the rapidity with which these perceptions may change, it might be impossible to derive cultural norms of self-perception that fail to take historical factors into account.

13. Jonathan Potter and Margaret Wetherell (1987) discuss an alternative view of the self. In their discussion of Harre's work among the New Zealand Maori, they point out that the Maori concept of the self is so heavily invested in the supernatural that individual actions are less the result of the individual than the divine forces into which an individual is born. The possibility that the self may not represent the originator or even the experiencer of action is almost incomprehensible in Western thinking. Such a philosophy of the self would seriously undermine a legal system that depends on establishing blame and punishing the person responsible.

REFERENCES

Altheide, D. (1984). The media self. In Kotarba and Fontana (eds.), *The existential self in society*, 177–95.
Baumeister, R. F. (ed.). (1986). *Public self and private self*. New York: Springer-Verlag.
Baumeister, R., and Tice, D. (1986). Four selves, two motives, and a substitute process self-regulation model. In Baumeister (ed.), *Public self and private self*, 63–74.
Bennett, L. (1979). Rhetorical transformation of evidence in criminal trials: Creating grounds for legal judgment. *Quarterly Journal of Speech*, 65: 311–25.

Bennett, L., and Edelman, M. (1985). Toward a new political narrative. *Journal of Communication*, 35 (4): 156–71.

Black, E. (1970). The second persona. *Quarterly Journal of Speech*, 56: 109–19.

Bruner, J. (1990). *Acts of meaning*. Cambridge, Mass.: Harvard University Press.

Campbell, P. N. (1975). The personae of scientific discourse. *Quarterly Journal of Speech*, 61: 391–405.

Goffman, E. (1959). *The presentation of self in everyday life*. New York: Double-day Anchor Books.

Gumperz, J. (1982). *Discourse strategies*. Cambridge: Cambridge University Press.

Hollihan, T., and Riley, P. (1987). The rhetorical power of a compelling story: A critique of a "toughlove" parental support group. *Communication Quarterly*, 35: 13–25.

Johnson, J., and Ferraro, K. (1984). The victimized self: The case of battered women. In Kotarba and Fontana (eds.), *The existential self in society*, 119–30.

Kavolis, V. (ed.) (1984). *Designs of selfhood*. Rutherford, N.J.: Associated University Presses.

Kidd, V. (1975). Happily ever after and other relationship styles: Advice on interpersonal relations in popular magazines, 1951–1973. *Quarterly Journal of Speech*, 61: 31–39.

Kirkwood, W. (1983). Storytelling and self-confrontation: Parables as communication strategies. *Quarterly Journal of Speech*, 69: 58–74.

Kotarba, J., and Fontana, A. (eds.). (1984). *The existential self in society*. Chicago: University of Chicago Press.

Lawson, H. (1985). *Reflexivity: The post-modern predicament*. La Salle, Ill.: Open Court.

Lee, D. (1976). *Valuing the self*. Englewood Cliffs, N.J.: Prentice-Hall.

Lewis, H. (1982). *The elusive self*. London: Macmillan.

Lyman, S. (1984). Foreword. In Kotarba and Fontana, *The existential self in society*, vii–xii.

Messinger, S., and Warren, C. (1984). The homosexual self and the organization of experience: The case of Kate White. In Kotarba and Fontana (eds.), *The existential self in society*, 196–206.

Mischel, T. (ed.). (1977). *The self: Psychological and philosophical issues*. Totowa, N.J.: Rowman and Littlefield.

Patrick, D., and Bignall, J. (1984). Creating the competent self: The case of the wheelchair runner. In Kotarba and Fontana (eds.), *The existential self in society*, 207–21.

Potter, J., and Wetherell, M. (1987). *Beyond attitude and behavior*. London: Sage Publications.

Trudgill, P. (1983). *Sociolinguistics: An introduction to language and society*. London: Penguin.

Vallacher, R. (1980). An introduction to self theory. In Wegner and Vallacher (eds.), *The self in social psychology*.

Wegner, D., and Vallacher, R. (eds.). (1980). *The self in social psychology*. New York: Oxford University Press.

Young-Eisendrath, P., and Hall, J. (eds.). (1987). *The book of the self: Person, pretext and process*. New York: New York University Press.

We give lip service to the morality of speaking truth. But the television saga of Clarence Thomas and Anita Faye Hill both affirms and dramatizes how acceptable flat-out lying has become in society. Much of it through TV.

HOWARD ROSENBERG, *Los Angeles Times*, OCTOBER 16, 1991

5

Impression Management Mismatch on Capitol Hill: The Anita Hill–Clarence Thomas Confrontation

DALE G. LEATHERS

The hearings of the Senate Judiciary Committee on the nomination of Judge Clarence Thomas to be associate justice of the U.S. Supreme Court were hardly routine even before the fateful day of October 11, 1991. Witnesses by the score had appeared before the committee. Three volumes of well over 2,200 pages were already devoted to the hearings.

Clarence Thomas's nomination to the Supreme Court by President George Bush was controversial from the start, but the nature of the hearings changed dramatically on October 11, 1991, when Professor Anita Hill of the University of Oklahoma College of Law appeared before the Senate Judiciary Committee and read a prepared statement. Hill made a series of charges against Thomas that were both categorical and sensational in nature (Hill had worked under Thomas's supervision at the U.S. Department of Education's Office for Civil Rights in 1981–82 and at the Equal Employment Opportunity Commission from 1982 to 1983). From this moment forward the attention of many millions of Americans became riveted on the televised confrontation of Clarence Thomas and Anita Hill. As Patt Morrison (1992) wrote in the *Los Angeles Times,* "If you happened to be in a sensory-deprivation tank during the televised pajama-party-from-hell weekend last October, the sight of 14 white men, one black man and one black woman thrashing through the pain of centuries of sexual and racial politics became a Harper's Ferry for women, igniting anger over the whiteness and maleness of power and the trivializing of women's concerns" (BR2).

Impression Management Analysis

Once Anita Hill made her charges, the debate over Thomas's positions on legal and constitutional issues became a secondary matter. Thomas's previous testimony and the testimony of a seemingly endless list of witnesses had not become irrelevant, but they were of marginal relevance to the jury of American public opinion. Thomas's fate would be decided on the basis of the relative effectiveness with which he and Anita Hill exercised their skills of self-presentation. The image they were ultimately able to project to millions of viewers on national television became the paramount concern. Impression management suddenly took center stage.

Central Concepts

Impression management often has been studied as a static phenomenon, where the impressions made are primarily, if not exclusively, a function of the self-concept of the impression manager. Little attention has been given to the most powerful determinants of impressions: the communicative behaviors individuals display in interpersonal contexts (Leathers, 1988, 1990, 1992; Leathers and Ross, 1992). The dramatic testimony of Clarence Thomas and Anita Hill before the Senate Judiciary Committee and, more important, before the nation as a whole lends itself to an impression management analysis, because the judgments the public made about these two individuals were largely a function of their skills of self-presentation and the impression management skills of those who worked for and with them.

Development of a workable conceptualization of impression management can begin by drawing selectively on Barry Schlenker's insights. Schlenker (1980) in his innovative treatment of impression management contends that impression managers are most directly concerned with claiming images for themselves that are useful to them in achieving their own goals. Impression managers try to associate themselves with desirable "image qualities" while seeking dissociation from undesirable "image qualities." Schlenker refers to this as the "principle of association" (1980, 1985, 1986). Furthermore, impression managers—who are not constrained by ethical or pragmatic reasons from criticizing an opponent—may seek to associate their opponents with undesirable "image qualities" and to dissociate them from desirable "image qualities."

Republican image strategists, for example, have become famous, or infamous, for defining their candidate's opponent. Roger Ailes, who was George Bush's chief image analyst in the presidential campaign of 1988, was a master of this technique. One of his television ads "defined" presidential candidate Michael Dukakis as a hypocrite because he stressed environmental issues but allegedly allowed Boston Harbor to become polluted while he was governor of Massachusetts (Leathers, 1992).

The effective use of the principle of association is easily illustrated in the impression management activities of the defense attorney Roy Black in the William Kennedy Smith rape trial. The media and, to a lesser extent, the prosecution had associated William Kennedy Smith and his uncle Ted Kennedy with some highly undesirable "image qualities" before the rape trial began. For example, William Kennedy Smith was pictured as a cruel, violent, and unfeeling monster who in his alleged rape of Patricia Bowman was simply perpetuating the male Kennedys' reputations for debauchery, dissipation, and domination. Similarly, Ted Kennedy was frequently pictured as a heavy drinker and womanizer with poor judgment. Not surprisingly, Roy Black moved quickly and skillfully to dissociate William Kennedy Smith and Ted Kennedy from these negative images and to associate them with contrasting, positive images.

Impression management is defined by an individual's attempt to exercise conscious control over selected communicative behaviors and cues—particularly nonverbal cues—for purposes of making a desired impression. We may seek to manage the impressions we make on others, and we may also use other individuals to try to exercise an influence over the impressions we make. Politicians, for example, sometimes use surrogates to help them in their impression management efforts. The presidential press secretary is an example of a surrogate trying to manage the impressions others form of the president.

The impressions an individual makes are not categorical in nature. Their positivity or negativity is a matter of degree. For example, a person is rarely perceived to be either totally competent or incompetent. The impressions we make on others are therefore best defined not by categories but by image dimensions. The impressions we make are defined by three basic types of image dimensions: credibility, interpersonal attractiveness, and dominance (Leathers and Ross, 1992). How credible, interpersonally attractive, or dominant we are perceived to be in a given communicative context is a matter of degree and is largely controlled by the communicative behaviors we exhibit as an impression manager.

Credibility, which repeatedly has been found to be the most important image dimension, is in turn defined by competence and trustworthiness. Interpersonal attractiveness is defined by likability, interestingness, emotional expressivity, and sociability. Finally, dominance is defined by power and assertiveness.

Clarence Thomas's strategists decided very early that Thomas would have a perceived deficit on the credibility subdimension of competence. They therefore decided to try to divert attention from Thomas's competence, as reflected in his modest legal credentials, and to focus instead on his alleged trustworthiness, or character.

Objectives of Analysis

This analysis focuses on the efforts of Clarence Thomas, his image consultants, and the surrogates who performed on his behalf to deal with the impression management crisis he encountered on October 11, 1991. Thomas is the focus not because he is considered more important or skillful than Anita Hill but because Thomas and his closest supporters made a well-organized, systematic, and sustained effort to use the full potential of impression management to save Thomas's nomination.

To do a complete impression management analysis, the study examines the following: (1) the impression management team for Clarence Thomas; (2) the impression management strategy for Clarence Thomas—before and after

Anita Hill's charges; (3) the effort to destroy Anita Hill's image; (4) the effort to rehabilitate Clarence Thomas's image by both verbal and nonverbal means; and (5) impression management mismatch in retrospect—judgments of effectiveness and ethical propriety.

The Impression Management Team for Clarence Thomas

White House and Other Governmental Operatives

Well before the hearings on Clarence Thomas's nomination it became obvious that President Bush was assembling a formidable staff that would be directed by the White House. As early as July 3, 1991, the title of an article in the *Wall Street Journal,* "Duberstein to Play Role in Thomas Senate Hearings," was a tipoff of things to come. The article indicated that the White House would use Kenneth Duberstein, a former presidential chief of staff and marketing expert, to head up preparations for the hearings on Clarence Thomas's nomination to the Supreme Court.

Duberstein was expected to have a rough time selling Thomas to the Senate. "The job," according to Timothy Phelps and Helen Winternitz (1992), "was to create a positive image of the new nominee, to make Thomas a well-known and well-liked personality. Duberstein was an expert craftsman at this sort of political portraiture, as were many others in the capitol, where image vies with substance in importance. An effective lobbyist knows how to groom a political player for the Washington showing. Image-making is one of Washington's most important industries" (22).

The strategy team met two or three times a week in the office of Frederic McClure, the person in charge of liaison for Congress. These meetings were chaired by Duberstein. Senator John Danforth (a Republican from Missouri) was asked to "champion" the Thomas nomination. Danforth, an ordained clergy, became Thomas's mentor and front man. Since Thomas was to be sold on the presumed strength of his character, it would certainly not hurt to have a front man such as Danforth, who not only was an ordained clergyman but also seemed to communicate an image of stern rectitude.

Thomas's Senate Judiciary Committee Impression Management Team

The Republican members of the Senate Judiciary Committee were Strom Thurmond of South Carolina, Orrin Hatch of Utah, Alan Simpson of Wyoming, Charles Grassley of Iowa, Arlen Specter of Pennsylvania, and Hank Brown of Colorado. Two of these senators emerged as central figures in the Republicans' efforts to destroy Anita Hill's credibility and rehabilitate Clarence Thomas's image: Senator Specter and Senator Hatch. The Republicans were well-organized, leaving little to chance. Senator Specter was chosen by the Republican senators to be the official questioner of Anita Hill. Senator Hatch was to be the official questioner of Clarence Thomas. Other Republican senators yielded most of their time to Specter and Hatch so that they could concentrate on their duties.

Senator Specter, who got his law degree from Yale Law School, probably had the best combination of forensics and communicative skills on the Judiciary Committee. Senator Hatch was undoubtedly the most theatrically inclined of his Republican colleagues on the committee. Senator Hatch was referred to as "smarmy" or the "smarmy senator" by more than one member of the media, who watched and wrote about Hatch's impression management efforts while he questioned Thomas (Morrison, 1992; Watson, 1991). He was also described as affectedly and self-servingly earnest, which may be an accurate description of the senator's communication style.

After Anita Hill made her charges, Senator Danforth assumed another more important role. Every time the committee recessed for a few minutes, Danforth would emerge and address the television cameras. Displaying the extremely serious mien that one might expect from an undertaker, Danforth used the principle of association with great vigor. He would explain why the negative qualities Specter attributed to Hill were entirely believable, why Anita Hill's charges against Thomas were quite unbelievable, and so forth. In short, Senator Danforth became the Republicans' "spin doctor," who was in charge of damage control for Clarence Thomas.

Since Danforth was the only governmental official who pontificated regularly on television on the credibility of specific statements Hill and Thomas made, his own credibility was particularly important. Senator Danforth held several honorary divinity degrees and was an ordained deacon, priest, and rector in the Episcopal Church. In Washington, Danforth was known as Saint Jack because of his propensity for injecting morality into political arguments (Phelps and Winternitz, 1992).

The Republicans' impression management operatives on the Senate Judiciary Committee were a formidable team. They were well-organized and determined, and they possessed a complementary set of legal and communication skills. One could therefore anticipate that the attack on Anita Hill's image would be aggressive and sustained. One could also expect the impression management efforts of Senators Specter, Hatch, and Danforth to have an emotional and evangelical flavor, since all three men had a communication style that seemed to be grounded in a strong sense of self-righteousness.

The Impression Management Strategy for Clarence Thomas

Clarence Thomas's strategy team knew it would be difficult to get him confirmed even before it learned of Anita Hill's charges. Thomas had conservative views on such issues as abortion, affirmative action, and equal opportunity that were controversial, and serious questions had been raised about the strength of Thomas's legal credentials.

Before Hill's Charges

Thomas's strategy team therefore decided early on that it would be foolhardy to try to sell Clarence Thomas on the basis of his "competence." Since one's credibility is defined by competence and trustworthiness, the strategy decision was predictable. Clarence Thomas must be packaged and sold by diverting attention from his perceived competence and focusing on his perceived trustworthiness.

Ultimately, the strategy of Bush's White House had two parts, both of which were designed to divert public scrutiny away from Thomas's legal credentials and his competence. The strategy was designed to focus on Thomas's character (i.e., his trustworthiness) and on the claim that he had risen from poverty in Georgia. This strategy became known as the "Pin Point Strategy" since Clarence Thomas grew up in a small town in Georgia by the name of Pin Point. As Phelps and Winternitz (1992) observe, "From this point on [once the basic strategy had been set], the White House referred to Clarence Thomas as the man who had struggled against poverty, segregation, and adversity, and won. In the 'talking points' handed out to key supporters to guide them in their dealings with the press, this was the first point listed. The tone of the nomination had been set. Because he really didn't have much legal experience, Thomas was being sold on his character" (14).

A sustained effort was made to implement this strategy by putting Clarence Thomas through impression management "workouts" (Eaton, 1991, A1).

Thomas frequently "labored" on his performance in an office in the Justice Department until eight or nine at night. Thomas, Phelps and Winternitz (1992) report, "had a number of intense days in room 180 of the Old Executive Office Building, across from the White House, going through what some in the White House termed 'murder boards.' . . . He had been rehearsed for this drama with the Senate down to the movement of his hands and the tone of his voice" (170).

Thomas was to avoid assiduously taking a position on any controversial issue and to keep attention focused on the remarkable "character" qualities he had shown in his striking "rise from poverty" that had begun in Pin Point, Georgia. This second part of the strategy developed for Thomas—to avoid alienating senators on the committee by evading their attempt to get him to take positions on such controversial issues as abortion—had the effect of raising serious doubts about his trustworthiness, however.

To put it more bluntly, Thomas's strategy of evasiveness reinforced the impression that he was lying (Brock, 1993). Even David Brock, whose pro-Thomas book gives Thomas every benefit of the doubt, concludes that "Thomas was able to sidestep these snares, but in so doing he created the impression that his refusal to discuss his views on many Constitutional issues—particularly *Roe v. Wade*—amounted to lying" (87). Thomas's evasiveness in his responses, or nonresponses, to senators' questions subsequently led more than one person in the hearing room to believe that he was lying again when he was forced to respond to Anita Hill's allegations about sexual harassment.

After Hill's Charges

The impression management strategy that seemed well-conceived before Anita Hill's charges appeared to be untenable after those charges. The man the Republicans were trying to sell on the basis of his sterling character suddenly was being pilloried by members of the media for his lack of character.

The perception that Thomas was being evasive—if not actually lying—in his testimony even before Hill's charges was highlighted in the titles of newspaper articles that appeared at this time: "Senators Question Nominee's Character as He Appears to Be Changing Positions" (*Detroit News*), "T's in the News . . . A Sidestepping Thomas, a Punchy Tyson, and Tiptoeing Liz Taylor Puts My Brain in a Spin" (*Detroit News*), "Thomas Proved to Be Elusive Target" (*Amsterdam News*). Significantly, Herb Boyd, author of the last article, discussed the "vagueness and duplicity" of the Thomas's testimony before the Senate Judiciary Committee.

Worse yet, Clarence Thomas was savaged in cartoons in newspapers, which served to indict both his competence and trustworthiness. Paul Conrad (1991) depicted the statements and thoughts of Judge Clarence Thomas as a "blank slate" in an editorial cartoon in the *Los Angeles Times*. Mike Royko of the *Chicago Tribune* (1991) lampooned the whole Hill-Thomas affair by writing about the public's keen interest in locating a pornographic movie actor who played the part of Long Dong Silver. Finally, Jeff MacNelly of the *Chicago Tribune* (1991) went so far as to do an editorial cartoon that combined a visual depiction of the Pee Wee Herman disgrace and the Clarence Thomas spectacle.

From the perspective of impression management, Thomas and his strategy team were now confronted with a crisis of major proportions. Not surprisingly, they have not announced to the world how they decided to cope with this crisis. Nonetheless, the nature of the major decisions they made became apparent in studying the "post-charge" testimony and communication of Clarence Thomas and his surrogates.

The impression management strategy the Republicans devised after Anita Hill made her charges against Thomas seemed to be based on two premises: (1) the highest priority must be given to destroying Anita Hill's credibility; and (2) secondary attention must be given to rehabilitating Clarence Thomas's image.

The Effort to Destroy Anita Hill's Credibility

The Republicans moved quickly to try to destroy Anita Hill's credibility. In terms of political expediency, it was either destroy or be destroyed. Either Anita Hill's credibility had to be destroyed (or seriously damaged) or Clarence Thomas's own credibility would be destroyed. The latter would have been disastrous for the Republicans; the obvious result would be that Clarence Thomas would join the ranks of such failed Supreme Court nominees as Robert Bork.

A direct attack on Anita Hill's competence was not a viable option for the Republicans for several reasons. The most obvious was that Anita Hill had an impressive record of achievement that reflected very favorably on her competence. Anita Hill was an honor student during her undergraduate days at

Oklahoma State University; she was a graduate of Yale Law School, one of the most prestigious law schools in the country; and she was hired by a top law firm after graduation from Yale Law School—Ward, Hardrader and Ross of Washington, D.C.

The most discomforting news of all for the Republican impression management strategists was that Clarence Thomas himself had judged Anita Hill to be highly competent. Key Republican operatives on the Senate Judiciary Committee were therefore forced to acknowledge not only that Clarence Thomas had hired Hill for two important positions at the Department of Education and the Equal Employment Opportunity Commission (EEOC) but also that he was on record publicly as repeatedly praising the high quality of her work.

If one looks at it cynically, the only way to destroy Anita Hill's credibility would be to destroy her character or trustworthiness. This is precisely what the Republicans tried to do. In fact, Senator Specter's aggressive and insinuative interrogation of Anita Hill might appropriately be labeled "the attempted character assassination of Anita Hill."

A careful study of the transcript of the Hill-Thomas confrontation makes it quite clear that the Republican senators used the principle of association to try to assassinate Anita Hill's character. They focused on "redefining" Hill's public image so that she would be perceived as an untrustworthy person with a flawed character. Eight of the nine "negative image qualities" attributed to Anita Hill by Senator Specter—and his fellow Republican senators—were intended to damage her character. The other negative image the Republicans tried to establish was that she was marginally competent since she allegedly was fired by the first law firm that had hired her. This claim was later discredited as untrue.

The following are the eight major negative images—or image qualities—Republican members of the Senate Judiciary Committee claimed about Anita Hill that were designed to destroy her character: (1) Anita Hill was a spurned woman; (2) Anita Hill was a prudish woman who experienced "sexual fantasies" as a result of a mental disorder known as erotomania; (3) Anita Hill was a malevolently motivated, unfair person who was trying to harm Clarence Thomas because she was losing her power and influence with him; (4) Anita Hill was a malevolently motivated, unfair person who was trying to force Clarence Thomas to bear the unbearable burden of the black stereotype of the sexually well-endowed, active, and promiscuous black man; (5) Anita

Hill was a malevolently motivated, unfair person who was trying to take advantage of our legal system, because she waited for more than eight years after the statute of limitations on sexual harassment charges had run out before making her charges against Thomas; (6) Anita Hill was an evasive person who intentionally distorted reality and the nature of her relationship with Thomas; (7) Anita Hill was a liar who committed perjury in her testimony before the Senate Judiciary Committee; and (8) Anita Hill was the "front person" in a major conspiracy made up of left-wing and feminist interest groups that were using and manipulating her to discredit Clarence Thomas.

The "spurned woman" image that the Republican impression management team projected for Anita Hill was nothing if not inventive. The Republican image strategists tried to turn the tables on Anita Hill by claiming that it was Clarence Thomas who rejected Anita Hill rather than vice versa.

Without a doubt, the most vicious negative image her Republican tormentors presented was related to this "spurned woman" image. The spurned woman image was, of course, hardly complimentary to Anita Hill. But how much more damaging would it be if the Republicans could plausibly claim that Anita Hill was a prudish woman with serious sexual hang-ups about men, that these sexual hang-ups manifested themselves in Hill's "sexual fantasies" about men, and that Hill was an inept man chaser?

Senator Specter, and some of his fellow Republican senators, tried to make the "sexual fantasy image claim" a plausible one by relying on the testimony of two men: Charles Kothe, former dean of the Law School at Oral Roberts University, who subsequently was employed by Clarence Thomas; and John N. Doggett III, who was a graduate of Yale Law School, as was Anita Hill. Presumably, in an attempt to shore up John Doggett's incendiary and highly subjective "interpretations," Senator Specter praised Doggett's professional credentials profusely and in a curiously unqualified way: "Mr. Doggett, turning to your affidavit. . . . And permit me to comment, I found your testimony of your professional background extremely, enormously impressive" (Nomination, 1991, 554).

Doggett then read from his affidavit:

> It was my opinion at that time, and is my opinion now, that Ms. Hill's fantasies about my sexual interest in her were an indication of the fact that she was having a problem with being rejected by men she was attracted to. Her statements and actions in my presence during the time when she alleges that Clarence Thomas harassed her were totally inconsistent with her descrip-

tions and are, in my opinion, yet another example of her ability to fabricate the idea that someone was interested in her when in fact no such interest existed. (Nomination, 1991, 554)

The fact that John Doggett had no professional expertise as a psychiatrist, psychologist, or sex counselor that would justify such an "interpretation" of Anita Hill's alleged emotional and sexual problems was not lost on Senator Joseph Biden, who said to Doggett, "The fact, you believe Ms. Hill's fantasies about [your] sexual interest in [her] were an indication of the fact she was having a problem with being rejected by men she was attracted to. It seems to me that is a true leap in faith or ego, one of the two [Laughter]" (Nomination, 1991, 559).

The Republicans clearly wished to use a mystifying sleight-of-hand impression management tactic whereby Clarence Thomas would be transformed from the victimizer to the victim. Clarence Thomas as "victim" would be the foundation on which their attempts to rehabilitate Thomas's image would be built. To make this inherently implausible effort plausible, the Republicans sought to establish that Anita Hill was a malevolently motivated woman who was being grossly unfair to Thomas.

Clarence Thomas provided the basis for the charge that Anita Hill was motivated to harm him because she lost power and influence when she moved with him from the Department of Education to the EEOC. In his opening statement to the Senate Judiciary Committee Thomas said that "at EEOC our relationship was more distant. And our contacts less frequent, as a result of the increased size of my personal staff and the dramatic increase and diversity of my day-to-day responsibilities. Upon reflection, I recall that she seemed to have had some difficulty adjusting to this change in her role" (Nomination, 1991, 6).

The sharp-tongued Thomas assistant Phyllis Berry was quick to try to give credence to this negative image of Anita Hill:

Senator Heflin: What were the facts pertaining to that?
Ms. Berry: Just my observation of Anita wishing to have greater attention from the chairman. I think she was used to that at the Department of Education. Wanting to have direct access to the office, as though she had a right to have access to his office. (Nomination, 1991, 354)

In addition, the Republicans tried to establish that Anita Hill was a malevolently motivated, grossly unfair person because she tried to burden Clarence Thomas with what the Republicans claimed was the most unfair of all stereotypes—that of the sexually preoccupied and highly sexually active black man. Thomas is perhaps most responsible for articulating and pressing this negative image of Anita Hill.

Under Senator Hatch's leading and highly confused questioning, Clarence Thomas made it quite clear that Anita Hill had done something grossly unfair and deplorable by burdening him with the "most bigoted racist stereotype that any black man will face." He added:

> Senator, the language throughout the history of this country, and certainly throughout my life, language about the sexual prowess of black men, language about the sex organs of black men, and the sizes, et cetera, that kind of language has been used about black men as long as I have been on the face of this earth. These are charges that play into racist, bigoted stereotypes and these are the kind of charges that are impossible to wash off. . . . And this [Anita Hill's charges against Thomas] plays into the most bigoted, racist stereotypes that any black man will face. (Nomination, 1991, 202)

The Republicans then tried to show what a grossly unfair, malevolently motivated person Anita Hill was by turning to the statute of limitations on sexual harassment charges:

> Senator Specter: Professor Hill, as you know, the statute limitations for filing a case on sexual harassment is 180 days, right?
> Ms. Hill: Yes.
> Senator Specter: A very short statute of limitations because of the difficulty of someone defending against a charge of sexual harassment, right?
> Ms. Hill: Well, it is a short turnover time. (Nomination, 1991, 80)

In case anyone missed his point that Anita Hill was treating Clarence Thomas unfairly and victimizing him by waiting nearly a decade to make her charges against him, Senator Specter engaged Hill in the following manner:

> Senator Specter: Well in the context of the federal law limiting a sexual harassment claim to six months because of the grave difficulty of someone defending themselves in this context, what is your view of the fairness of asking Judge Thomas to reply eight, nine, ten years after the fact?
> Ms. Hill: I don't believe it is unfair. I think that is something that you have to take into account in evaluating his comments. (Nomination, 1991, 81)

The Republicans made little if any pretense that the first five negative images of Anita Hill that they projected had any basis in fact. These images were supported solely by personal opinion, and these opinions came from dedicated supporters of Clarence Thomas. By comparison, the Republicans tried to give the sixth and seventh negative images of Anita Hill—that she was an evasive person who intentionally distorted reality and that she was a liar—the veneer of what might be accepted as fact.

Not surprisingly, Senator Specter pounded away at his claim that Anita Hill's testimony was internally inconsistent. More specifically, Specter claimed that Hill told increasingly detailed stories as she moved from an interview with the FBI to her sworn written statement to the Senate Judiciary Committee to the details of her actual testimony in front of the committee. The clear implication was that she was making up details to make her untruthful story seem believable:

> Senator Specter: Well, in your statement to the FBI you did refer to the films but there is no reference to the physical characteristics you describe. I don't want to attach too much weight to it, but I had thought you said that the aspect of large breasts was the aspect that concerned you, and that was missing from the statement to the FBI.
> Ms. Hill: I have been misunderstood . . .
> Senator Specter: Professor Hill . . . in the last sentence in the first full paragraph, you again make in that statement a very serious allegation as to Judge Thomas, and I would ask you why you didn't tell the FBI about that when they interviewed you. (Nomination, 1991, 61)

Under the persistent questioning of Chairman Joseph Biden, Anita Hill made two allegations that the Republicans used to try to saddle her with the charge not only that her testimony was evasive and unreliable but also that she had simply made up significant portions—perhaps even all—of her charges against Clarence Thomas:

> Mr. Chairman: Of those incidents that occurred in places other than in the cafeteria, which ones occurred in his office?
> Ms. Hill: Well, I recall specifically the incident about the Coke can [where Clarence Thomas allegedly asked who put pubic hair on his Coke can] occurred in his office at the EEOC. (Nomination, 1991, 55)

An exchange then occurred that the Republicans tried to exploit repeatedly. They suggested Anita Hill's statements during this exchange provided convincing evidence that she not only was deeply perfidious but also might have fabricated all of her charges against Thomas:

The Chairman: Are there any other incidents that occurred in his office?

Ms. Hill: I recall at least one instance in his office at the EEOC where he discussed some pornographic material and he brought up the substance or the content of pornographic material.

The Chairman: Again, it is difficult, but for the record, what substance did he bring up in this instance at EEOC in his office? What was the content of what he said?

Ms. Hill: This was a reference to an individual who had a very large penis and he used the name that he had referred to in the pornographic material——

The Chairman: Do you recall what it was?

Ms. Hill: Yes; I do. The name that was referred to was Long Dong Silver. (Nomination, 1991, 56)

Senator Hatch jumped all over Anita Hill's last statement, not when she had a chance to respond personally while testifying but later when Clarence Thomas was on the stand:

Senator Hatch [addressing Clarence Thomas]: You said you never did say this, "Who has put pubic hair on my Coke?" You never did talk to her about "Long Dong Silver." *I submit, those things were found* [emphasis added]. On page 70 of this particular version of the *Exorcist*, "'Oh Burk,' sighed Sharon. In a guarded tone, she described an encounter between the senator and the director. Dennings had remarked to him, in passing, said Sharon, that there appeared to be 'an alien pubic hair floating around in my gin.'" Do you think that was spoken by happenstance? She would have us believe that you were saying these things, because you wanted to date her? What do you think about that, Judge?

Judge Thomas: Senator, I think this whole affair is sick. (Nomination, 1991, 206)

For the Republican impression management team it was only a small step from charging that Anita Hill was being evasive and was distorting—and even constructing—"reality" to charging that she had committed perjury—that she was a liar. Specter quickly moved to make this charge while he was questioning Clarence Thomas: "Judge Thomas . . . it is my legal judgment, having had some experience in perjury prosecutions, that the testimony of Professor Hill in the morning was flat-out perjury . . ." (Nomination, 1991, 230).

Aside from the lack of factual support for these negative images, the claims seemed to lack an internal coherence or logic that would tie them together.

To create the illusion that there was something tying these claims together, the Republicans turned to an old tactic they had used frequently over the years—a conspiracy theory. Specifically, they claimed that Clarence Thomas was the victim of a conspiracy.

Phelps and Winternitz (1992) make clear that Senator Hatch was trying to sell a conspiracy theory: "The implication, and a farfetched one, was that Hill had been somehow familiar with this particular case [where Long Dong Silver was mentioned] and had employed its material to slam Thomas. Hill had not participated in the case in any way and it had nothing to do with her specialty in commercial law. But Hatch suggested that liberal groups had fed Hill this information, colluding with her to make up the charge and using this case for embellishing details" (Nomination, 1991, 342).

Hatch pressed his conspiracy theory in the following way: "These interest groups have scratched through everything on earth to try and get something on you, all over the country, all over this town, all over your agency, all over everybody. And there are a lot of slick lawyers in those groups, slick lawyers, the worst kind. There are some great ones, too, and it may have been a great one who found the reference to 'Long Dong Silver,' which I find totally offensive" (Nomination, 1991, 205).

Even when being questioned by Chairman Biden, Clarence Thomas made it clear that he believed Anita Hill was deeply involved in a conspiracy designed to destroy him:

Chairman Biden: Let me make sure that I understand one thing. Do you believe that interest groups went out and got Professor Hill to make up or do you believe Professor Hill had a story, untrue from your perspective, that groups went out and found. Which do you believe?

Judge Thomas: Senator, I believe that someone, some interest group, I don't care who it is, in combination came up with this story and used this process to destroy me.

The Chairman: A group got Professor Hill to say or make up a story?

Judge Thomas: I believe that in combination this story was developed or concocted to destroy me.

The Chairman: With Professor Hill? I mean it is a critical question. Are you saying a group concocted a story with Professor Hill and then went out——

Judge Thomas: That's just my view, senator. (Nomination, 1991, 252)

The Effort to Rehabilitate Clarence Thomas's Image

Without question, the Republicans concentrated their energies on attempting to destroy Anita Hill's credibility with no less than nine negative claims about Anita Hill that were explicitly designed to destroy her character. By contrast, they made few attempts to rehabilitate Clarence Thomas's image directly. An analysis of the transcripts reveals that the Republican strategy team made only three positive claims of central importance about Clarence Thomas that were designed to rehabilitate his overall image: (1) Clarence Thomas was the *victim* of a left-wing conspiracy led by liberal and feminist interest groups; (2) Clarence Thomas had a record of dealing honorably and effectively with problems of sexual harassment when he encountered them; and (3) Clarence Thomas was Anita Hill's nobly motivated "mentor" rather than her "sexual harasser."

Verbal Efforts at Image Rehabilitation

Both Clarence Thomas and Senator Orrin Hatch worked hard to cultivate the image of Thomas as a victim. In his opening statement to the Senate Judiciary Committee, Thomas made it quite clear that he wished to be viewed as a victim: "Mr. Chairman, I am a victim of this process and my name has been harmed, my integrity has been harmed, my character has been harmed, my family has been harmed, my friends have been harmed. There is nothing this committee, this body or this country can do to give me my good name back, nothing" (Nomination, 1991, 9).

In case his point was missed, Thomas stressed that "I have never, in all my life, felt such hurt, such pain, such agony. My family and I have been done a grave and irreparable injustice. During the past two weeks, I lost the belief that if I did my best all would work out. I called upon the strength that helped me get here from Pin Point, and it was all sapped out of me. It was sapped out of me because Anita Hill was a person I considered a friend, whom I admired and thought I had treated fairly and with the utmost respect. Perhaps I would have better weathered this if it were from someone else, but here was someone I truly felt I had done my best with" (Nomination, 1991, 8).

Hatch pressed the claim that Clarence Thomas had been a vigorous opponent of sexual harassment. Although Senator Hatch surely did not intend to be humorous when he said that Clarence Thomas was "an expert in sexual harassment," he asserted repeatedly that Thomas had persistently sought to deal effectively with problems of sexual harassment when they arose. Thomas himself took pains to say that "during my tenure in the executive branch as a manager, as a policy maker, and as a person, I have adamantly condemned sex harassment. There is no member of this committee or this Senate who feels stronger about sex harassment than I do. As a manager, I made every effort to take swift and decisive action when sex harassment raised or reared its ugly head" (Nomination, 1991, 7).

Finally, Thomas and Hatch both repeatedly presented the positive image of Thomas as a nobly motivated person who was Anita Hill's selfless "mentor." In his opening statement to the Senate Judiciary Committee, Thomas said, referring to Anita Hill, "I find it particularly troubling that she never raised any hint that she was uncomfortable with me. . . . This is a person I have helped at every turn in the road, since we met. She seemed to appreciate the continued cordial relationship we had since day one. She sought my advice and counsel, as did virtually all of the members of my personal staff" (Nomination, 1991, 7).

Nonverbal Efforts at Image Rehabilitation

The Republican impression managers used nonverbal communication artfully to communicate implicit messages at the subconscious level. Their basic type of nonverbal persuasion was indirect suggestion. Recognizing that indirect suggestion requires the use of emotional rather than rational appeals, they focused on the controlled display of emotions, particularly by the two central players who proved to be most adept at nonverbal communication: Judge Clarence Thomas and Senator Orrin Hatch.

The effort to use nonverbal communication to rehabilitate Clarence Thomas's image began with a careful attempt to control the immediate environment in which Clarence Thomas, or his surrogates, communicated. Thomas's wife, Virginia, was always seated behind him and to his right. Her expressive face often seemed to mirror the precise emotions the Republican impression managers were attempting to communicate. To her immediate right sat Thomas's mentor and champion, Senator John Danforth, looking like a father attending his son's first disciplinary hearing.

Whenever there was a break in the televised coverage, Danforth would move purposefully outside the hearing room and give his latest "spin" on the testimony to the television cameras. His efforts to "interpret" the testimony and "help" the viewing public understand its implications were particularly important on Friday afternoon, October 11, 1991, because it was then that Anita Hill was testifying and making such a seemingly strong, positive impression.

During one break in the testimony on that Friday afternoon, Danforth—dressed in a dark gray suit and dark blue tie—addressed the television cameras with his visage of stern rectitude. Danforth suggested that in spite of appearances, everything was going to be alright. Danforth declared, "Well first of all a lot that has gone on this afternoon has been concerning what are inconsistencies in Anita Hill's various statements about Clarence Thomas. One thing about Clarence Thomas is that he has been totally consistent in what he has said from beginning to end. And he will continue to be very consistent . . ." (C-Span—all subsequent verbal and nonverbal communication of witnesses cited in this section is from television coverage by C-Span).

Clarence Thomas used his own nonverbal skills to communicate a set of emotions that were consistent with and served to reinforce his contention that he was innocent of the charges. Consider, for example, Thomas's reactions to Hatch's statements early in the testimony:

Senator Hatch: I know it outrages you, as it would anybody who is accused of these activities.
[Thomas nods his head up and down as if to signal agreement with Hatch that he is innocent of Anita Hill's charges.]

Senator Hatch: Hill says that he [Thomas] discussed oral sex between men and women.
[Thomas stops nodding his head up and down vertically and begins to shake his head horizontally from side to side as if to communicate denial.]

Senator Hatch: She then said in this statement—this is the second—after brief discussions about work he would turn the conversation to discussion about sexual interests.
[Thomas continues to shake his head from side to side seemingly to communicate denial and closes his eyes as if to suggest disgust.]

Senator Hatch: And you have denied each and every one of these allegations last night.
[Thomas sighs deeply as one often does when experiencing intense and troubling emotions, displays a discernible expression of facial anger, and shakes

his head up and down vigorously as if to affirm his denial of all of these charges.]

Senator Hatch: On several occasions, Thomas told me graphically of his own sexual prowess.

[Thomas begins shaking his head from side to side in denial at the precise moment that Hatch repeats Hill's charges, closes his eyes with an expression that might be described as agony, and finally flashes a facial expression of contempt.]

Senator Hatch: Don't worry, Judge, probably before the weekend's out they will find somebody who will say that.

The primary medium of nonverbal communication Thomas and Hatch used, however, was their voice, or vocal, cues. Verbal communication often assumes a central role in the formation and management of impression. Miron Zuckerman and Robert E. Driver (1989) emphasize the importance of vocalic communication in impression management when they write that "there is a large literature showing that both voice cues (e.g., pitch intensity, etc.) and speech cues (e.g., non-fluencies, speech rate, etc.) are rich sources of interpersonal impressions" (68).

More specifically, both Clarence Thomas and Senator Hatch proved adept at using their voices to communicate a given emotion or to make a desired impression. When Thomas used his face and hands to communicate a given emotion, such as disgust, he also used the pitch, volume, and intensity of his voice to reinforce that emotion.

Thomas probably reached a peak of effectiveness in using his voice to communicate emotions when he said, "Senator I would have preferred an assassin's bullet to this kind of living hell that they have put me and my family through." Thomas delivers each of these words with great vocal emphasis and intensity, and his eyes appear to "tear up" at the end. Thomas pounces on the words "me and my family" through enunciation, increased volume, and vocal intensity and emphasis. Similarly, when Thomas is talking about being unfairly stereotyped as a sexually well-endowed and sexually active black man, Thomas says, "And once you pin it on me, I can't get it off." As he utters these twelve words, Thomas slows his speaking rate way down to emphasize each word, and he thumps the table in front of him with his index finger each time he utters one of these words.

Senator Hatch also proved to be a master at using his voice for emotional effect. One of his most interesting techniques is to drastically increase the pitch of his voice at the end of a strategically important question. The rapid increase in pitch clearly communicates the idea that Hatch is incredulous and suggests that the expected answer to Hatch's question is no. This is one of techniques that Hatch used to "lead" Thomas through his questioning. Consider the following examples:

> Senator Hatch: People hearing yesterday's testimony are probably wondering could this quiet, you know retiring, woman know about something like "Long Dong Silver"? Did you tell her that?
> [As Hatch asks Thomas this question, there is a sharp increase in the pitch of Hatch's voice, as if to suggest "I am incredulous. Surely, a man of your character did not tell her that."]

> Senator Hatch: . . . if you wanted to seduce her, is this the kind of language you would use? Is this the kind of language a reasonable person would use, is this the kind of language that anybody would use who wanted a relationship?
> [As Hatch finishes this series of questions to Thomas, there is once again a sharp rise in the pitch of his voice as if to suggest that he can't believe this and expects Thomas to answer no.]

Impression Management Mismatch in Retrospect

There can be no doubt that the American public is fascinated by the spectacle of lying in public (Ekman, 1985; Lewis and Saarni, 1993). Nonetheless, this is one instance where we will probably never have sufficient information to determine definitively whether Clarence Thomas or Anita Hill was lying. The limited amount of evidence available, however, suggests that Thomas was lying. A recent study (Leathers et al., 1995) compared the nonverbal profiles of Thomas and Hill for their testimony before the Senate Judiciary Committee and concluded "that Clarence Thomas, and not Anita Hill, was being deceptive during the televised Senate Hearings" (15). Furthermore, only Anita Hill took a polygraph exam—a lie detector—and passed it. "She was asked about her allegations regarding Judge Thomas, and the test concluded that she was not lying" (Nomination, 1991, 389).

The Republican impression management strategy team was highly effective in achieving their immediate goals. They clearly damaged Anita Hill's credibility, and they rehabilitated Clarence Thomas's image partially if not totally—a majority of the members of the Senate Judiciary Committee ultimately voted to confirm Clarence Thomas (even though it appeared the vote might be negative immediately after Anita Hill testified), a majority of the entire Senate voted for him, and he currently is a member of the Supreme Court.

There seems to be little doubt that the impression management effort of the Republicans had a major, positive impact on American public opinion. Indeed, polls conducted at the time of the hearings showed over two-thirds of the Americans polled believed that Clarence Thomas, as opposed to Anita Hill, testified truthfully ("Most Back Thomas," 1991).

The ethics the Republican impression management team displayed was quite another matter. Even the casual observer seemed to sense that Anita Hill was treated unfairly. Clarence Thomas appeared to receive every break in a tactical sense. For example, he was allowed to make a detailed preemptive statement denying Hill's charges even before she appeared and to make a second statement after she appeared; Anita Hill never appeared on prime-time television, while Clarence Thomas and his supporters appeared almost exclusively during prime time; and the timid and character-scarred Democrats provided no coherent defense for Anita Hill. "The net result," as Phelps and Winternitz (1992) put it, "was that no senator in the Caucus Room defended Anita Hill. The role of judge was acted by Biden, that of the jury by the committee, and that of the prosecutor by the combination of Specter and Hatch" (395).

This was an impression management mismatch from the start because Anita Hill was left utterly alone. She was left at the witness table to turn and twist agonizingly in the searing heat and wind of condemnation generated by her highly aggressive Republican antagonists. Although her own public presentation was poised and credible, her opponent was given every advantage. If this had been a sporting event, it probably would been canceled as a grossly unfair mismatch even before it began.

Certainly many members of the media also condemned Senators Specter, Hatch, and Simpson for their unethical behavior. Media critics emphasized that the Republican impression management team used the medium of television masterfully to convey hidden and implied messages; to trigger a highly emotional response from many viewers; and to express a sense of moral righteousness, outrage, and condescension. While some noted media representatives recognized the effectiveness with which the Republicans exploited television, they also found much of what Republicans did to be ethically reprehensible.

Howard Rosenberg (1991) of the *Los Angeles Times* wrote, "Whatever your conclusion the above [the repetition of the unsubstantiated charge that Anita Hill had committed perjury] is a vivid example of how masterfully Thomas' supporters used the camera. While Hill's supporters seemed content to make legal points as if a jury would be examining the transcript, Thomas' side led by Sen. Orrin Hatch (R.—Utah), and Alan Simpson (R.—Wyoming) shrewdly made TV points. Their arguments seemed designed primarily to persuade through TV by tone and emotion better than anything else" (F1, F3).

In her review of the book *Capitol Games* for the *Los Angeles Times*, Patt Morrison makes clear that she found the Republican effort to be unethical. In view of what the Republicans did, writes Morrison, the book she reviewed might more appropriately have been titled *The Unsurprising Triumph of Political Tactics over Truth*. Morrison reveals her own contempt for the Republicans' unethical behavior in the words she uses to describe their efforts: "They [the authors of *Capitol Games*] take the Republicans to task for their smarmy ruthlessness, for their willingness to use race to their advantage with Thomas as they had with Willie Horton" (BR9).

Similarly, Morrison condemns the Democrats on the Senate Judiciary Committee for their failure to challenge the ad hominem, the innuendo, and the irrelevant emotional appeals the Republicans used in their attempt to discredit Anita Hill. It is certainly justifiable, writes Morrison, that the Democrats are "pilloried for their fumbling hesitancy and personal vulnerabilities. (There sat Teddy Kennedy, a potted plant on the panel, hamstrung by his personal scandals.)" (BR9).

Specter's treatment of Hill was strongly condemned in an editorial in the *New York Times* titled "Mr. Specter's Deserved Discomfort." This editorial stated pointedly that "whether the senator wins or loses in this close race, he deserves every moment of anguish over the Anita Hill episode. . . . But while claiming to be 'not adversarial,' he exceeded the call of partisan duty by charging Ms. Hill with perjury" (16A).

Senator Simpson received particularly sharp criticism for his repeated use of innuendo, his cryptic allusions to hidden messages that he might not have had, and his claim to possess incriminating evidence that he might not have actually possessed. Rosenberg concludes that it was Anita Hill rather than Clarence Thomas who was the target of a "high-tech lynching." The executioner was Senator Alan Simpson. Rosenberg writes disparagingly that "on Saturday Simpson gave no details of these allegedly incriminating reports about Hill, and he did not reveal the names of her alleged accusers. But in a TV-tailored move designed to make the point that they were voluminous, he fumbled in the inside of his jacket as if searching for documents" (F1). Such a tactic is disturbingly reminiscent of one Senator Joseph McCarthy used when he waved before a crowd a document that allegedly contained the name of scores of Communists or Communist sympathizers.

The fact that Senator Simpson never revealed either the charges made by "Americans" and "Oklahomans" against Anita Hill or any supportive evidence does not speak well for his ethics or sense of fair play. Rosenberg suggests that Simpson was bluffing, that he would have given the details if he really possessed them, "but if there were no such charges as one suspects, then Simpson himself was lying, and in any case no senator on either side of the aisle challenged him on it" (F3).

Senator Simpson still appears to be committed to the farfetched notion that Hill's charges against Thomas were the result of a major feminist conspiracy. Simpson proved to be a real obstructionist when President Bill Clinton nominated Janet Napolitano—one of a small group of lawyers who advised Hill during the hearing—for the position of U.S. attorney for Arizona. A September 26, 1993, editorial in the *Atlanta Constitution-Journal* strongly condemned Simpson for his actions. The editorial begins with the derisive comment that in "the latest bit of backlash related to the Anita Hill–Clarence Thomas affair, Senator Alan Simpson of Wyoming is once again displaying his true colors. Apparently he has subscribed to the notion that Hill's harassment charges against the Supreme Court nominee were part of a grand feminist conspiracy, as set forth in a recently released book, 'The Real Anita Hill: The Untold Story'" (F6).

A close look at the efforts of the Republican impression management team suggests that in many ways they were deplorable in terms of ethical propriety. Certainly, the key Republican operatives violated many of the standards that frequently have been cited as central to ethical communication (Brembeck and Howell, 1976; Lewis and Saarni, 1993).

Perhaps the most central ethical question that might be raised in this instance is, Where does persuasion end and manipulation begin (Leathers,

1992)? Impression management is particularly susceptible to ethical abuse because nonverbal communication frequently plays such a central role in effective impression management. Nonverbal messages, in turn, often are hidden in that they are perceived at the subconscious level.

Joseph DeVito (1993) maintains that communication is ethical to the extent that it facilitates freedom of choice on the part of the person to whom it is directed. By contrast, communication is unethical to the extent that it relies on hidden messages that mislead and constrain informed and free choice.

In my view, the Republican impression managers in these hearings violated at least five ethical standards: (1) they concealed their true purposes while claiming they were engaged in the objective search for the truth; (2) they repeatedly used the techniques of name-calling and loaded language; (3) they relied heavily on the use of bogus emotional appeal to trigger signal, emotional, and nonreflective responses on the part of the television viewers; (4) they used innuendo and unsubstantiated implications based on inexpert and biased opinion—rather than on facts—to project misleading and negative images of Anita Hill; and (5) they repeatedly used indirect suggestions to try to lead the members of their live and television audiences to reach uncorroborated and unsubstantiated conclusions.

In conclusion, it is perhaps not surprising that Anita Hill's image seems to be more positively perceived as time passes. The Republican impression managers used impression management skillfully to achieve their short-term goals. To do so, however, they employed techniques that are highly questionable from an ethical standpoint. In the long run, the Republicans may be paying the price for their actions. Whereas Anita Hill was left to fend for herself alone during the Senate Judiciary Committee hearings, she no longer finds herself without strong and articulate supporters.

REFERENCES

Boyd, H. (1991, September 21). Thomas proved to be elusive target. *Amsterdam News*, section 3: 3.

Brembeck, W. L., and Howell, W. S. (1976). *Persuasion: A means of social control.* Englewood Cliffs, N.J.: Prentice-Hall.

Brock, D. (1993). *The Real Anita Hill.* New York: Free Press.

Conrad, P. (1991, October 1991). Editorial cartoon. *Los Angeles Times,* 12.

DeVito, J. (1992). *The interpersonal communication book*. 6th ed. New York: Harper Collins.

Duberstein to play role in Thomas Senate hearings (1991, July 3). *Wall Street Journal*, A8.

Eaton, W. J. (1991, August 8). Coaches drill Thomas for his Senate face-off. *Los Angeles Times*, A1.

Ekman, P. (1985). *Telling lies: Clues to deceit in the marketplace, politics, and marriage*. New York: W. W. Norton.

Leathers, D. G. (1988). Impression management training: Conceptualization and application to personal selling. *Journal of Applied Communication Research*, 16: 126–45.

———. (1990). The dynamics of impression management in the sales interview. In D. O'Hair and D. L. Kreps (eds.), *Applied communication theory and research*, 163–83. Hillsdale, N.J.: Erlbaum.

———. (1992). *Successful nonverbal communication*. 2d ed. New York: Macmillan.

Leathers, D. G., and Ross, C. (1992). Theoretical conceptualization of the impression management function of nonverbal communication. Unpublished manuscript.

Leathers, D. G., Vaughn, L., Sanchez, G. X., and Bailey, J. L. (1995). Who was lying in the Hill-Thomas hearings: Nonverbal communication profiles. In P. Siegel (ed.), *Outsiders looking in: A communication perspective on the Hill/Thomas hearings*. New York: Hampton Press.

Lewis, M., and Saarni, C. (eds.). (1993). *Lying and deception in everyday life*. New York: Guilford.

MacNelly, J. (1991, October 9). Editorial cartoon. *Chicago Tribune*, 20.

Morrison, P. (1992, June 14). Review of the book *Capitol Games*. *Los Angeles Times*, BR2, BR9.

Most back Thomas in polls despite harassment claims (1991, October 15). *Boston Globe*, 6.

Mr. Specter's deserved discomfort (1992, September 1). *New York Times*, A16.

Nomination of Judge Clarence Thomas to be associate justice of the Supreme Court of the United States. (1991, October 11, 12, and 13). *Hearings before the Committee on the Judiciary—United States Senate (Part IV)*. 102d Congress, 1st session. Washington, D. C.: U.S. Government Printing Office.

Phelps, T. M., and Winternitz, H. (1992). *Capitol Games: Clarence Thomas, Anita Hill, and the story of a Supreme Court nomination*. New York: Hyperion.

Rosenberg, H. (1991, October 16). Truth only gets paid lip service at hearings. *Los Angeles Times*, F1–F3.

Royko, M. (1991, October 15). Calling Mr. Silver: America needs you. *Chicago Tribune*, 1.

Schlenker, B. R. (1980). *Impression management: The self-concept, social identity, and interpersonal relations.* Monterey, Calif.: Brooks/Cole.

————. (1985). Identity and self-identification. In B. R. Schlenker (ed.), *The self and social life,* 65–99. New York: McGraw-Hill.

————. (1986). Self-identification: Toward an integration of the private and public self. In R. F. Baumeister (ed.), *Public and private self,* 21–62. New York: Springer-Verlag.

Watson, S. (1991, October 13). The devil, smarmy senator says. *Detroit New and Free Press,* F1.

Zuckerman, M., and Driver, R. E. (1989). What sounds beautiful is good: The vocal attractiveness stereotype. *Journal of Nonverbal Behavior,* 13: 67–82.

Part 2

Communication and the Creation of Credibility

6

Looking for Verbal Deception in Clarence Thomas's Testimony

CURTIS D. LEBARON

In September 1991, Anita Hill accused the Supreme Court nominee Clarence Thomas of sexual harassment, which he "categorically denied" (Senate, 1991b, 1). When her allegations became public, the Senate Judiciary Committee vowed to "find the truth" through public hearings, which began on Friday, October 11 (Senate, 1991b, 54). Hill and Thomas testified until Saturday night—for about two days—but the committee failed to resolve contradictions between their testimonies. A few committee members suggested that both testimonies were true; most members admitted that both appeared true; and all members failed to identify signs of verbal deception or patterns of incriminating communication.

Undoubtedly, there are many ways to approach Hill's and Thomas's testimonies in an effort to "find the truth." This essay examines Thomas's testimony the way that FBI agents are trained to examine suspects' statements. When examined this way, it appears that Thomas's testimony had a deceptive bent. This bent can be detected not by looking for overt lies but by discovering subtle indicators of deception. In isolation such indicators might be explained away or dismissed as idiosyncrasies, but in clusters they become meaningful. Throughout Thomas's testimony there are clusters of presuppositions, mannerisms, and omissions that the FBI says are indicative of deception.

The FBI's Approach to Verbal Deception Detection

The FBI Academy in Quantico, Virginia, trains about a thousand law enforcement professionals each year (FBI Academy, 1992). The academy's faculty is described as "uniquely qualified both academically and by virtue of their vast experience in law enforcement" (Field, 1992, 21). The facilities are technologically advanced and well maintained (U.S. Department of Justice, 1972, 1), and the academy continually reviews its courses to "insure that they are current, relevant, and practical" (U.S. Department of Justice, 1979, 4).

One of the academy's courses, Interviewing and Interrogation, teaches students how to interact and communicate with different kinds of people and how to obtain information from witnesses and suspects at different stages of criminal investigations. Part of this course deals with deception and how it can be detected verbally in written statements and oral interviews.

John Hess, who has been an FBI agent for twenty-four years and an instructor at the FBI Academy for nine years, says that while some law enforcement professionals have a knack for detecting deception, the majority have difficulty detecting deception because they look for factual contradictions. "Nothing's a fact—that's the problem," Hess says. Most lies are not overt. Good lies can appear true, and the best lies can be "true," because liars often avoid telling blatant falsehoods and prefer instead to tell a form of the truth (by molding it, deflecting it, and withholding it). Investigators should therefore look not only for factual contradictions but also for "subtle indicators of deception" (Hess, 1991d).

Hess (1991d) claims that the FBI's approach to verbal deception detection is valid—it does help law enforcement professionals detect deception. He considers the FBI's pragmatic approach to be a strength, stating, "There is very little—if any—research to substantiate this. . . . As far as I'm concerned, I don't care, I really don't care whether there's any research. If it gives me an edge and a little insight into things and seems to work, then I'll dance with this one until I find another partner. . . . Coppers don't want to hear about research. They just want to know if it works." The FBI's approach to verbal deception and its detection does emerge from praxis. Although its origin and evolution are nonacademic, FBI praxis seems capable of informing more carefully conceived, disciplined, and focused approaches, such as those found in academia. Praxis can be merged with academic theory. Many sociologists have advocated "the meeting between theory and practice, . . . the meeting of theorists and practitioners . . . the interchange between fieldwork and education institutions" (Ronnby, 1990, 302–3). In other words, method may be a "praxis construction" (Ronnby, 1990, 308). As an example of such combined methodologies, the FBI Academy's approach to verbal deception and its detection is one way of trying to resolve the contradictions between Hill's and Thomas's testimonies.

There are many subtle indicators of deception,[1] but the following three seem especially applicable to Thomas's testimony: deceptive presuppositions (or contradictory assumptions embedded in statements); deceptive mannerisms (which involve how something is said rather than what is said); and deceptive omissions (which involve what is not said).

Thomas's Presuppositions

Presuppositions embody what speakers assume or "know" to be true (Brown and Yule, 1983, 28). For example, Thomas's opening statement on October 11, "I welcome the opportunity to clear my name today" (Senate, 1991b, 1), presupposes that Thomas has a "name," that names can be "cleared," that his name needs to be cleared, and so forth. These are Thomas's assumptions—no one else's—because Thomas composed his statements himself; he had "no handlers, no advisors" (Senate, 1991b, 1).

According to deception experts at the FBI Academy, when assumptions contradict the statements that contain them, the speaker is being inconsistent with self, is denying what he or she assumes or "knows" to be true, and is behaving deceptively (Bennett, 1991c, 10). Deception may be measured against a suspect's mind rather than external conditions. Deception is grounded in personal knowledge rather than absolute truth. Mind and knowledge may be subtly revealed by such things as presuppositions.

Thomas claims that Hill's story was imagined or "concocted to destroy" him (Senate, 1991b, 50), but sometimes his words subtly presuppose otherwise.[2] For example, Thomas says of the hearings, "This is not an opportunity to talk about difficult matters privately or in a closed environment. This is a circus" (Senate, 1991b, 4). Why does Thomas refer to Hill's allegations as "difficult matters"? The word "matters" seems too substantive, too material, for what is supposed to be a figment, a fantasy—literally immaterial. Thomas says "matters" ten times in two days, describing the allegations as "serious matters" (Senate, 1991b, 3) and "sensitive matters" (Senate, 1991b, 57). To whom are these "matters" difficult, serious, and sensitive? Obviously to Thomas; these are his words, his presuppositions.

Other words may also presuppose fact rather than fantasy. Thomas states, "This is a case in which this sleaze, this dirt, was searched for by staffers of members of this committee" (Senate, 1991b, 4). The word "dirt" is akin to "matter"; it suggests substance. Thomas says "this dirt" eight times in two days. By contrast, he refers to Hill's allegations as "lies" only twice and as "stories" only four times—committee members say "lies" and "stories" more than Thomas does. Thus, Hill's allegations seem to be more substantive in Thomas's mind than he claims in his statements.

Some presuppositions involve entire sentences, not just words. Consider three of Thomas's sentences: "If there is anything that I have said that has been misconstrued by Anita Hill or anyone else to be sexual harassment, then I can say that I am so very sorry and I wish I had known. If I did know, I would have stopped immediately and I would not, as I've done over the past two weeks, have to tear away at myself, trying to think of what I could possibly have done. But I have not said or done the things that Anita Hill has alleged" (Senate, 1991b, 2). Perhaps any apology by Thomas is suspect because apologies presuppose at least the possibility of wrongdoing, which Thomas passionately denies. Any apology by Thomas would certainly contradict his claim that Hill's testimony was maliciously concocted. According to deception experts, a compulsion to both deny and rectify is "indicative of guilt" (Hess, 1991e, 25; see also Bennett, 1991b, 14).

This particular apology is especially troubling because it is more than a concession—it is almost a confession. Technically, Thomas does not confess anything because his apology is conditional. His first sentence is an "if-then" statement: if Hill "misconstrued," then he's "sorry." However, there is a sense that Thomas is already sorry. Note his words: "I can say that I am so very sorry and I wish I had known." Why "I am" instead of "I would be"? Why "so very sorry," which seems heartfelt and immediate, as does the second sentence, "If I did know . . . I would not . . . have to tear away at myself"? There is a sense that the conditions for Thomas's sorrow have already been met.

The second sentence in Thomas's apology presupposes the first. As an "if-then" statement, its conditions extend from the conditions of the first sentence. For example, "if I had known" extends from "I wish I had known." At the same time, however, the second sentence contradicts the first. The words "I would have stopped immediately" are inconsistent with the word "misconstrued." Why would Thomas stop, if it is Hill's mistake? What would Thomas stop, if he is not doing anything? The words "I would have stopped" presuppose something other than "misconstrued"—something more like "construed." As the second sentence both extends and undercuts the first sentence, Thomas's concession collapses toward a confession. He quickly recoils into denial; the third sentence tries to mop up the spilt apology.

Sometimes presuppositions are extratextual; the text alludes to them but does not actually contain them. For example, Thomas says he did not watch Hill's testimony before the Senate Judiciary Committee. This information came out as Senator Howell Heflin was making a transition to a new line of questioning:

> Heflin: Now, you, I suppose, have heard Professor Hill's—Ms. Hill—Ms.
>   Anita F. Hill testify today.
> Thomas: No, I haven't.
> Heflin: You didn't listen?
> Thomas: No, I didn't. I've heard enough lies.
> Heflin: You didn't listen to her testimony at all?
> Thomas: No, I didn't.
> Heflin: On television?
> Thomas: No, I didn't. (Senate, 1991b, 5)

Thomas chose not to hear his accuser. He received only secondhand summaries through the FBI (Senate, 1991b, 1) and his wife (Senate, 1991b, 6).

Why did Thomas avoid his accuser? What does this avoidance presuppose? Did he already know what Hill would say? Thomas claims he is "shocked, surprised" at Hill's testimony (Senate, 1991b, 1). Did he feel indifferent? Thomas claims he is "hurt and enormously saddened" (Senate, 1991b, 1). Did he *know* he was blameless? Thomas claims, "I have been racking my brains and eating my insides out trying to think of what I could have said or done to Anita Hill" (Senate, 1991b, 1). Regardless of what Thomas's avoidance presupposes, it seems to contradict his claims. This kind of extratextual presupposition can be particularly indicative of deception. Hess (1991a) explains, "If the person is lying and he's pretty smart, he will have thought through his story pretty well. And he'll have it pretty well covered. . . . But there'll be something that they didn't consider important, but was kind of a transitional type statement, that they'll throw in, that just flies in the face of reason. Listen not just to the details of the story, but to the peripheral stuff" (20). The exchange between Heflin and Thomas is transitional or peripheral. Thomas, it seems, thinks his avoidance is unimportant, while Heflin reacts as though it flies in the face of reason.

In sum, a cross section of Thomas's testimony may show ever-widening rings of deception. Some of his claims may be inconsistent with the subtle presuppositions of his words, sentences, statements, and extratextual messages.

Thomas's Mannerisms

Thomas's manner may also be indicative of deception. Manner is *how* something is said rather than what is said. Instructors at the FBI Academy look at both the posture of a testimony and the mood of a testimony.

Typically, liars have a competitive posture. While truth-tellers expect others to believe them and "don't really feel any need to convince," liars have a compulsion to convince and tend to treat others as an obstacle to their "innocence" (Hess, 1991a, 26). Liars, of course, do not believe themselves. This self-perspective, this self-doubt, seems to leak into their view of things: they seem to presuppose doubt in others. Thus, as the analyst Avinoam Sapir (1991) points out, "a deceptive subject looks upon interrogation as a challenge," as an obstacle (44).

Thomas sees his October confirmation hearings as a challenge, as an obstacle. He states, "Mr. Chairman, in my 43 years on this earth I have been able . . . to defy poverty, avoid prison, overcome segregation, bigotry, racism and obtain one of the finest educations available in this country. But I have not been able to overcome this process. This is worse than any obstacle or anything I have ever faced" (Senate, 1991b, 2). Without question, confirmation hearings would be difficult for anyone, but should they be Thomas's greatest obstacle, given his background?

The hearings were not nearly as challenging to Thomas before Hill's accusations. In September Thomas says he faced "charges of drug abuse, anti-semitism, wife beating, drug use by family members, that [he] was a quota appointment, confirmation conversion, and much, much more" (Senate, 1991b, 2). He successfully refuted all these charges. September, it seems, went better than he had expected. "I expected it to be bad," he says, "I even expected them to attempt to kill me. . . . I even expected, personally, attempts on my life" (Senate, 1991b, 48). Thomas says of the September hearings, "I was treated fairly, senator" (Senate, 1991b, 56). Why, then, did October overwhelm him? Why did one accusation of sexual harassment bring him to say, "I would have preferred an assassin's bullet to this kind of living hell" (Senate, 1991b, 25)? In October, the hearings seem too challenging; his perspective seems self-indicting.

Sometimes a liar's posture is more than competitive—it is aggressive. Deception experts say that aggression is always part of deception to some degree. Sissela Bok (1978) explains that deceit and violence "are the two forms of deliberate assault on human beings," though deceit "controls more subtly" (18). FBI experts have found that deceivers often "try to attack the character of their accuser, or the way the evidence was gained," rather than the evidence itself (Hess, 1991b, 1). Notably, Thomas attacks both his accuser and the way the accusations were gained, though to varying degrees: he slowly undermines Hill's character, and he aggressively attacks the confirmation process.

Thomas undermines Hill's character as the hearings progress. Initially, his criticisms of her are qualified and uncertain. For example, on Friday he states, "As I've had two weeks to think about this and to agonize over this, and as I remember it, I believe that she was considered to be somewhat distant and perhaps aloof" (Senate, 1991b, 10). Notice the words "as I remember it," "I believe," "considered," "somewhat," and "perhaps"—that is a lot of uncertainty for one sentence after two weeks of serious thinking. By the next day, however, his criticisms are more certain, his memory clearer. He states, "She would become entrenched in her own point of view and not understand the other point of view. And she was certainly capable of storming off and going to her office, and that happened on any number of occasions" (Senate, 1991b, 32). These latter statements are not qualified, as are the first.

Similarly, Thomas describes his relationship with Hill in different ways. In his opening statement on Friday morning he insists that their relationship was cordial and that "at no time" did he suspect otherwise (Senate, 1991b, 1). But that night, Thomas introduces something new: "One employee indicated very strongly to me during my tenure at EEOC [Equal Employment Opportunity Commission] that she was, I believe, and I believe this may be a quote, 'my enemy.' And I refused to believe that and argued with him about that and refused to act in accordance with that" (Senate, 1991b, 15). Thomas's statement is somewhat tentative. He questions both his recollection and the legitimacy of his employee's comments.

On Saturday night, however, Thomas subtly bolsters his story, presupposing that Hill was his enemy: "There were some members—at least one member of my staff—who felt that she did not have my best interests at heart, and he would continue to, as I remember it, articulate that point of view. . . . I don't recollect the basis of his conclusions or his statements, but he would say it repeatedly when he saw evidence of it" (Senate, 1991b, 57). Notice that "one employee" has become "some members—at least one member of my staff." The words "I don't recollect the basis" seem to presuppose that there was a basis, though it is forgotten. The words "when he saw evidence of it" presuppose that there was "evidence." Thomas still questions his recollection, but the legitimacy of his employee's comments is presupposed.

Thomas does not attack Hill's character as aggressively as he attacks the confirmation process. Instead, he slowly undermines her character by strengthening the certainty and the extent of his criticisms. Thomas seems to negotiate his attack on Hill with committee members—he says what their questions seem ready to allow. Thus, he plays the role of the reluctant witness. For example, his less tentative statement on Saturday night comes after an invitation by Senator Arlen Specter: "You mentioned . . . [an] associate of yours who classified Hill as your enemy. . . . Can you amplify about what happened in that regard?" (Senate, 1991b, 57). Perhaps such negotiation is natural in this type of communicative interchange. Sometimes, however, deceivers use questions to learn how to lie, to figure out what they can get away with (Hess, 1991d).

Thomas aggressively attacks the confirmation process throughout the October hearings. Consider, for example, his opening statement on Friday evening, immediately after Hill's public appearance. The statement is twenty sentences. In the first sentence, Thomas denies Hill's allegations. In the second sentence, he raises "a second point," which begins a nineteen-sentence attack on the confirmation process. Here are some excerpts: "A second, and I think more important point: I think today is a travesty. I think it is disgusting. I think that this hearing should never occur in America. . . . I think something is dreadfully wrong with this country when any person, any person in this free country would be subjected to this. . . . This is a national disgrace. And from my standpoint as a black American, as far as I'm concerned, it is a high-tech lynching" (Senate, 1991b, 4). Thomas's posture is aggressive, and the pattern of this statement is the pattern of his entire testimony: (1) he attacks the process; (2) he appeals to "America" and to the "country"; (3) he accuses others of racism; and (4) he evades discussions of Hill's allegations.

By attacking the confirmation process, Thomas transforms his hot seat into a judgment seat—he empowers himself and subdues the committee. Thomas refers directly to "the process" thirty-two times in two days and indirectly dozens more times. Committee members, who together say almost twice as much as Thomas, refer to "the process" only twenty-four times, usually in response to one of Thomas's criticisms. By Saturday, Thomas seems to be orchestrating the hearings. Consider his final exchange with Senator Paul Simon:

Simon: I don't know—I don't know how we're going to improve the process.
Thomas: I think this is clearly wrong.
Simon: I think we are in agreement that the process has to be improved.
Thomas: No, it—Senators, in the strongest terms, this process can only go one direction, and that is improvement. This is clearly wrong.
Simon: I have no further questions, Mr. Chairman. (Senate, 1991b, 54)

Deception is a struggle for power, say the experts. Hess (1991d) describes deception as "a battle of the wills." Another expert states, "To the extent that knowledge gives power, to that extent do lies affect the distribution of power" (Bok, 1978, 19). Thomas dominates Senator Simon by attacking the process for which Simon is partly responsible.

Thomas's appeals to "America" and the "country" are also self-empowering. He uses the word "country" twenty-nine times in two days; senators use it seven. He says "America" or "American" fourteen times, twice as often as committee members. Thomas repeatedly projects himself as a surrogate for the nation: "All this hurt has brought my family and I closer—my wife and I, my mother. But that isn't—so there's no pity for me, I think the country has been hurt by this process. I think we are destroying our country, we are destroying our institutions, and I think it's a sad day. . . . You are ruining the country. If it can happen to me, it can happen to anybody. . . . I think that if our country has reached this point, trouble, and you should feel worse for the country than you do for me" (Senate, 1991b, 13–14). Thomas's statements seem to scoot over continually, so that 257 million Americans can sit down beside him. Whether Thomas is on a hot seat or a judgment seat, his appeals to the "country" and "America" intimidate the committee and dissipate his own culpability. Thomas seems to lose himself in a crowd. This, too, may be indicative of deception. Deceivers often "try to enlarge the group they're in," says Hess (1991d). "That's a whole lot more comfort" (Hess, 1991e, 11).

FBI instructors also say that undue claims of prejudicial treatment can be a "signature" of deception (Hess, 1991c, 1). Thomas refers to the hearings as a "high-tech lynching" more than once (Senate, 1991b, 23). He claims, "I've been harmed worse than I've ever been harmed in my life. I wasn't harmed by the Klan. I wasn't harmed by the Knights of Camelia. I wasn't harmed by the Aryan Race. I wasn't harmed by a racist group. I was harmed by this process—this process" (Senate, 1991b, 25). Perhaps this "signature" is not compelling in Thomas's case. He is a person of color before an all-white committee. However, Thomas did not claim to be a victim of prejudice before Hill's appearance, before October.

Thomas's aggressive posture enables him to be evasive. By forcing issues of process, country, and racism to the fore, he displaces talk of Hill, her allegations, and sexual harassment. Examine, for example, the following statement by Thomas: "I don't think I should be here today. I don't think that this inquisition should be going on. I don't think that the FBI file should have been leaked. I don't think that my name should have been destroyed. And I don't think that my family and I should have been put through this ordeal. And I don't think that our country should be brought low by this kind of garbage" (Senate, 1991b, 25). This is a broad, sweeping statement. It touches on the hearing's major themes, yet there is no mention of Hill, her allegations, or sexual harassment. Thomas says he does not think the FBI file should have been leaked. What about the fact that a former friend has "falsely" accused him of sexual harassment? Does that not bother him?

This evasive pattern appears in many of Thomas's unsolicited statements.

Of course, he does talk about Hill, her allegations, and sexual harassment when this is specifically requested or expected. However, his aggressive posture allows him to slide repeatedly away from these issues. He blames Capitol Hill, not Anita Hill. He blames the leak, not the "lies." He talks of country and racism, not sexism. It is not that Thomas tells falsehoods. Perhaps his concerns are "true," but they may serve a deceptive function in his testimony. It seems incredible—literally—that Thomas would repeatedly overlook the very reasons for his October hearings. Hess, of course, teaches that "evasiveness" is an attribute of deception (*Behavioral Symptom Analysis*, 5).

The mood of a testimony, which is the second aspect of manner, can also be revealing. Mood, like posture, discloses self-perspective, and self-perspective is a key to detecting deception because it is molded by what one "knows" to be true. Truth-tellers believe themselves. Liars do not. Truth-tellers are therefore typically optimistic. They expect others to believe them (Hess, 1991a, 26), and they tend to see "only one possible result" when their veracity is questioned: they will be found innocent (Sapir, 1991, 44). Liars, however, are often pessimistic. They see "two possible results" and often expect to be found guilty (Sapir, 1991, 44). Thomas's mood is often more than pessimistic—it is fatalistic. He assumes he is ruined, he believes he is helpless, and he talks of death and hell.

On October 11, Anita Hill testifies, "The last day of my employment . . . I had dinner with Clarence Thomas [and] he said that if I ever told anyone of his behavior that it would ruin his career" (Senate, 1991a, 28). Thomas denies Hill's story, but he also fulfills the prophecy. He believes his career is ruined because of Hill's allegations—he even uses the word "ruined" at one point (Senate, 1991b, 14). On Friday, he exclaims, "This leaked on me and it is drowning my life and my integrity and you can't give it back to me and this committee can't give it back to me and this Senate can't give it back to me. You have robbed me of something that can never be restored" (Senate, 1991b, 6). On Saturday, he is still pessimistic: "I've already lost" (Senate, 1991b, 53). This is not optimism; this is pessimism that seems unwarranted because he is not ruined—Thomas is now sitting on the Supreme Court. This pessimism is self-indicting because he is not expecting others to believe him, even though many Americans and members of Congress do. FBI training techniques would suggest Thomas is behaving deceptively.

A sense of helplessness turns Thomas's pessimism into fatalism. He perceives himself as powerless against Hill's charges, which he says "are impossible to wash off" (Senate, 1991b, 23). "Once you pin that on me I can't get it off," he says (Senate, 1991b, 22). "I have no way of refuting these charges" (Senate, 1991b, 24). His helplessness haunts him: "One thing that has tormented me the last two and a half weeks has been how do I defend myself against [these] charges? How do I defend myself? . . . That's what I've asked myself. How do I defend myself?" (Senate, 1991b, 22). Thomas has already defended himself against "charges of drug abuse, anti-semitism, wife beating, drug use by family members, that [he] was a quota appointment, confirmation conversion, and much, much more" (Senate, 1991b, 2). Why is he suddenly overcome? Why has his mood turned fatalistic? Referring to his son, Thomas confesses, "I don't know what to tell him about this" (Senate, 1991b, 22). If Hill's allegations are false, he should know what to tell him.

Thomas describes himself as "dead." He says that when he was notified by the FBI of Hill's allegations, he "died" (Senate, 1991b, 52). "Let me and my family regain our lives. . . . I want my life and my family's life back," he begs the committee (Senate, 1991b, 3). Death-related words are sprinkled throughout his testimony. He speaks of being "killed" (Senate, 1991b, 50), "assassinated" (Senate, 1991b, 25), "lynched" (Senate, 1991b, 4), "destroyed" (Senate, 1991b, 2), and "drowned" (Senate, 1991b, 6). These cold, stiff words underscore his fatalistic mood.

Thomas has experienced hell ever since he was notified by the FBI—ever since he "died." He says, "I have agonized over this. This has not been an easy matter for me" (Senate, 1991b, 20); "the last two and a half weeks have been a living hell" (Senate, 1991b, 40). His mood, as he describes it, is dark and fatalistic: "Mr. Chairman, something has happened to me in the dark days that have followed since the FBI agents informed me about these allegations. And the days have grown darker [with] enormous pain and great harm. I have never felt such hurt, such pain, such agony. My family and I have been done a grave and irreparable injustice" (Senate, 1991b, 2). This hell, however, seems to be largely self-perceived and self-induced. It comes from within, not without. Although Thomas reminds the committee, "God is my judge, not you" (Senate, 1991b, 41), he is forever torturing himself. He tells of "racking [his] brains and eating [his] insides out" (Senate, 1991b, 1). He admits, "I haven't slept very much in the last two and a half weeks. I've thought unceasingly about this. And my wife simply said, 'Stop torturing yourself'" (Senate, 1991b, 20).

Thomas's self-perception, self-doubt, and self-damnation are self-incriminating. His mood is pessimistic—even fatalistic. When this fatalistic mood is considered along with his aggressive posture, his manner seems deceptive (according to deception techniques taught at the FBI Academy).

Thomas's Omissions

Finally, Thomas's testimony seems riddled with deceptive omissions. Omissions are sometimes difficult to identify because they are literally not there, which is one reason deceivers use them. They involve what *is not* said, or what *should be* said, rather than what *is* said. Nevertheless, omissions can be detected (Bennett, 1991a, 6). Like any cavity, omissions bring attention to themselves when they are too big.

Another reason deceivers use omissions is that they are less painful than overt lies. One FBI expert explains, "It's hard to tell a lie. . . . For a majority of the people we deal with, lying is an effort. It's hard for them to do. And because of that, you'll see that some people tell lies simply by omitting the truth" (Bennett, 1991a, 10).

Thomas is already experiencing pain—he calls it hell—so it is no surprise that there seem to be deceptive omissions in the most sensitive parts of his testimony. For instance, an up-front, direct denial is missing from Thomas's opening statement. Friday morning is Thomas's first chance to formally answer the question in everyone's mind: "Did you sexually harass Hill?" However, he does not answer, at least not initially. First, he talks about how "excruciatingly difficult" the past two weeks have been; then he tells of how "hurt" he was by Hill's charges; then he says that he had always been "proud" that no one had accused him of sexual harassment before—which, of course, is not to say that he had never sexually harassed anyone. Thomas meanders for more than three hundred words before he denies anything, and according to FBI experts, that is suspect. Such a pattern is "not normal" (Hess, 1991d). Truthful answers are typically short, says Hess; "there is no need for a 15 minute diatribe" (Hess, 1991d).

When Thomas does finally deny the allegations, he does not deny them directly. Examine his words: "Contrary to press reports, I categorically denied all of the allegations and denied that I ever attempted to date Anita Hill when first interviewed by the FBI. I strongly reaffirm that denial. Let me describe my relationship with Anita . . ." (Senate, 1991b, 1). This denial seems weak: propped up by the word "strongly," it lies couched in an anecdote about press reports. What makes this denial especially suspicious is that it is indirect. Thomas does not say directly, "I didn't harass"; he says, "I deny that I harassed." This "I deny" pattern is an illusion—it makes a claim only about the present, not the past. It does not make a claim about harassment; it asserts only that "I am saying something," or "I am denying something." In other words, the statement, "I deny that I harassed," is true regardless of whether there was harassment, because the truth of the statement depends on the words "I deny," not "I harassed."

Truth within statements can be tricky. They can create illusions, which is why deceivers may utilize them. For example, some sentences are technically "true," regardless of what they say: "I deny that I did it"; "My answer is no"; "I'm telling you that I am innocent"; and so forth. Some sentences are always "false": "I have no comment"; "I am not saying anything." And some sentences are both true and false at the same time, such as the famous liar's paradox: suppose a man walks into a room and states, "This statement is false." Is his statement true? If it's true, it's false; and if it's false, it's true. No matter how it is grasped, it slips away.

Such technical truth involves subtle distinctions and literal meanings in language. These technicalities are usually unimportant to truth-tellers, who are preoccupied with conventional meanings. To deceivers, however, these technicalities are a haven. Though always attentive to conventional meanings, deceivers manipulate subtle distinctions and literal meanings for deceptive ends. One expert affiliated with the FBI states, "It is not easy to lie. A person will make every effort to run away from the need to say 'no' when this is a lie. . . . Any deviation from the formula 'I didn't do it' constitutes a tactic. . . . Tactics mean: the subject cannot lie frontally, saying, 'I didn't do it'" (Sapir, 1991, 51). Thus, the "I deny that I harassed" pattern in Thomas's opening statement appears to be a tactic: his technically true statement, which is cloaked by his press-reports anecdote, may signal a reluctance to deny directly.

There is a dearth of direct denials in some of the sensitive parts of Thomas's testimony. For example, notice his indirect answers to Senator Patrick Leahy's direct questions:

> Leahy: On the basic substance of what we're talking about here, you're diametrically opposed. Is that correct?
> Thomas: Senator, I just simply said that I deny her allegations, categorically.
> Leahy: If her allegations were correct, if what she has stated under oath was so, that would be sexual harassment, would it not?
> Thomas: Senator, I think it would be.

Leahy: But at the same time you categorically deny that those events ever took place?

Thomas: I categorically deny, Senator, in the strongest terms.

Leahy: It would be sexual harassment if they happened, but you say they did not happen.

Thomas: That's right.

Leahy: Then we have one of two possibilities, obviously. One of you is not telling the truth or . . . could [you both] be seeing the same thing?

Thomas: Senator, my relationship with Anita Hill was cordial and professional, just as it was with the rest of my special assistants, and I maintain that that's all there was. (Senate, 1991b, 42)

Thomas says "I deny" or "I denied" fourteen times in two days. Many other indirect denials come in other forms, such as in his last sentence above: "I maintain," which is just another form of "I deny"—in terms of technical truth, it is always true.

Thomas does make some direct denials, but many of his direct denials follow questions unrelated to Hill's allegations. For instance, when he is asked whether "political influence [was] brought to bear" on a particular administrative decision, Thomas replies, "There was absolutely no political influence" (Senate, 1991b, 5). When he is asked whether he has read the book *The Exorcist*, he says directly, "No, senator" (Senate, 1991b, 25). Although he denies Hill's allegations directly from time to time, direct denials are absent from some of the most sensitive portions of Thomas's testimony.

A second kind of omission is failing to answer questions, which, according to an FBI deception expert, is often an admission of guilt: "If the person doesn't answer the question, then you have your answer" (Bennett, 1991a, 18). For example, if a suspect is accused of breaking a car window and stealing the car, and the suspect only insists, "I didn't break the window," it is likely that the suspect did steal the car. Truth-tellers typically refute allegations fully (Bennett, 1991a, 18).

Thomas does not answer all of the questions that Hill's allegations raise. Consider one of Hill's charges, for example: "He spoke about acts that he had seen in pornographic films involving such matters as women having sex with animals and films showing group sex or rape scenes. He talked about pornographic materials . . ." (Senate, 1991a, 31). Hill alleges two things: first, that Thomas "had seen" such pornographic films and materials; second, that he "spoke about" these with her. Thomas denies only the second allegation—he does not deny viewing such pornography. Thomas might be expected to say something like, "No, I didn't discuss that with her, nor could I have because I've never seen that kind of material." But he does not. If this omission is an admission—if Thomas has viewed such pornography—either Hill's allegations are true or she has made a lucky guess about Thomas's prurient past. When Thomas's denials fall short, he may be being deceptive.

Another kind of omission is lack of commitment. Sometimes Thomas drops commitment from his statements in crucial places. For example, he claims initially that he visited Hill's apartment to have a Coke or a beer on "a number of instances" (Senate, 1991b, 18). "I do remember several times just dropping in," he says (Senate, 1991b, 41). Hill disagrees. She says he visited only once. When Senator Joseph Biden presses Thomas on this point, Thomas retreats:

> Thomas: But it wasn't—I don't remember a large number of times, but it has happened.
> Biden: Can you give us a sense of how often it happened that you would go in and have a Coke or a beer after?
> Thomas: Oh, it couldn't have happened any more than maybe twice, three times. Nothing—it was no—it was nothing major. (Senate, 1991b, 35)

Essentially, Thomas validates Hill's claim—"it couldn't have happened any more than twice" sounds a lot like "once."

Senator Leahy also presses Thomas on this issue. Notice the lack of commitment in Thomas's statements:

> Leahy: She said, other than that time, [you] never drove her home, never came in to visit and talk politics or any other thing. That would not be accurate?
> Thomas: Not to my recollection, senator.
> Leahy: And if [a roommate] said she saw you there only once. . . . that would be inaccurate?
> Thomas: That would not be my recollection, senator.
> Leahy: It would be contrary to what you've just testified to. . . .
> Thomas: My recollection was, as I stated this morning—again, we're talking 10 years ago, senator.
> Leahy: I understand, but I'm talking about what you just stated just a minute ago or two.
> Thomas: That she would have been there, yes, that would have been my recollection. (Senate, 1991b, 41)

What is meant by the words "that would have been my recollection"? Would have been, if what? If Thomas's story were true? The words "would have been" presuppose that it is not.

The words "to the best of my recollection" are also troubling in this context. Thomas's initial claim that he visited Hill's apartment "several times" is unsolicited. It is not prompted by committee members' questions, and it even seems to surprise them (Senate, 1991b, 9). The "memory" springs purely from what Thomas "knows" to be true—or so it seems. However, Thomas's subsequent noncommitment to this memory and his words "to the best of my recollection" are inconsistent with truth-telling (Hess, 1991d). A truth-teller would typically regard Hill's lesser claim of "one visit" as a fragmented or partial recollection. By reducing his unsolicited memory, by retreating, Thomas is momentarily revealing a deceptive stance, which throws his whole testimony into doubt (Bennett, 1991a, 17; see also Hess, 1991a, 22).

Conclusion

Any one indicator of deception, by itself, can probably be explained away as an idiosyncrasy (Hess, 1991d). It is always possible to think of reasons why someone would say something, in a certain way, under certain conditions. That is why FBI experts say that indicators of deception are most meaningful when they appear in clusters (*Behavioral Symptom Analysis,* 3; see also Hess, 1991a, 10; Bennett, 1991c, 4).

The indicators in Thomas's testimony do appear in clusters. For example, peruse the following lengthy, free-flowing statement by Thomas. Nothing in this statement has been quoted or cited previously in this essay, but it demonstrates, in clusters, many of the indicators of deception that have been discussed:

> Senator, as I have said throughout these hearings, the last two-and-a-half weeks have been a living hell. I think I've died a thousand deaths. What it means is living on one hour a night's sleep. It means losing 15 pounds in two weeks. It means being unable to eat, unable to drink, unable to think about anything but this and wondering why, how. It means wanting to give up. It means losing the belief in our system, in this system, in this process, losing a belief in a sense of fairness and honesty and decency. That's what it's meant to me. When I appeared before this committee for my real confirmation hearings, it was hard. I would have preferred it to be better. I would have preferred more members to vote for me. But I had a faith that at least the sys-

tem was working in some fashion, though imperfectly. I don't think this is right. I think it's wrong. I think it's wrong for the country. I think it's hurt me and I think it's hurt the country. I've never been accused of sex harassment. And anybody who knows me, knows I am adamantly opposed to that—adamantly. And yet I sit here accused. And I'll never be able to get my name back. I know it. The day I received the phone call, on Saturday night, last Saturday night about 7:30, and was told that this was going to be in the press, I had—I died. The person you knew, whether you voted for me or against me, died. My view is that that is an injustice. As I indicated injustice to me, but it is a bigger injustice to this country. I don't think any American, whether that person is homeless, whether that person earns minimum wage or is unemployed, whether that person runs a corporation or a small business, black, white, male, female, should have to go through this for any reason. (Senate, 1991b, 49–50)

This statement has a deceptive bent. The words "living hell" and "a thousand deaths" in the first sentences immediately announce Thomas's fatalistic mood. Thomas says "died" three times and "a thousand deaths" once. He talks of not sleeping, eating, or drinking, which makes his death and hell seem self-perceived and self-induced. His "wanting to give up" and his statement "I'll never be able to get my name back. I know it" speak of helplessness and ruin.

Coupled with this fatalism is Thomas's aggressive posture. He repeatedly attacks "the process" and portrays himself as its victim. He speaks of "the system" three times, calling it "wrong," an "injustice." He appeals to "America" and the "country" and offers himself as a surrogate for the nation: "I think it's wrong. I think it's wrong for the country. I think it's hurt me and I think it's hurt the country." The words "black" and "white" allude to his prejudicial claims.

Thomas's fatalistic and aggressive manner enables him to be evasive. This is a broad, sweeping statement that touches on major themes, but there is no mention of Anita Hill, a striking omission—a painful cavity. There is also no direct denial, but only a weak, roundabout attempt at self-exoneration: "I've never been accused of sex harassment. And anybody who knows me, knows I am adamantly opposed to that—adamantly. And yet I sit here accused." It seems incredible that Thomas would extol himself while failing to mention the very reason for the October hearings: Anita Hill. His self-celebrated yet untouchable presence masks Hill's absence. He transforms the hearings into his eulogy, from which he eventually rises to the U.S. Supreme Court.

In conclusion, using the FBI's approach to detecting verbal deception, this analysis suggests that Thomas's testimony has a deceptive bent. Some readers may question the use of FBI techniques to examine Thomas's testimony. In the process of investigating the Hill-Thomas hearings, this essay introduces analytic tools that also deserve scrutiny. This essay thus accomplishes two things: (1) the hearings may be opened and explicated in ways that help resolve contradictions between Hill's and Thomas's testimonies; and (2) readers may be brought to contemplate the way the federal government trains law enforcement professionals to examine suspects' statements.

NOTES

I thank Thomas Huckin for his comments on drafts of this essay.

1. According to FBI instructors, there are hundreds of ways that deception may be manifest in a statement. Agents are taught to analyze statements closely (every sentence and every word) and consider statements as a whole. Special attention is given to word choice, presuppositions, word order, statement structure, time structure, pronouns, verb tense, mood, mannerisms, self-editing, omissions, self-effacement, level of commitment, insignificant inclusions, and changes in language usage generally. Some aspects of their analysis are systematic; other aspects involve a laundry list of things for which to look.

2. Deception experts at the FBI Academy believe that human thoughts and conceptual systems grow out of real-world structures. That is, although words are abstract symbols, they closely correspond to embodied experience (Hess, 1991e, 8). For this reason, FBI agents are taught to pay close attention to individual words and subtle differences between words.

REFERENCES

Behavioral Symptom Analysis. Videocassette. Developed by Headquarters of Inspection and Control, at the Office of Investigations, in cooperation with the Southeast Commissioner of Customs and his staff.

Bennett, M. (1991a, July 30). Statement analysis. Course instruction. FBI Academy at Quantico, Virginia.

———. (1991b, July 31). Scientific content analysis. Handout. FBI Academy at Quantico, Virginia.

————. (1991c, July 31). Statement analysis continued. Course instruction. FBI Academy at Quantico, Virginia.

Bok, S. (1978). *Lying: Moral choice in public and private life.* New York: Vintage.

Brown, G., and Yule, G. (1983). *Discourse analysis.* New York: Cambridge University Press.

FBI Academy. (1992, May 8). Public Relations Office statement.

Field, G. (1992). The FBI Academy. *FBI Law Enforcement Bulletin,* 61: 16–21.

Hess, J. (1991a, July 29). Nonverbal and verbal deception. Course instruction. FBI Academy at Quantico, Virginia.

————. (1991b, July 31). Critical questions. Handout. FBI Academy at Quantico, Virginia.

————. (1991c, July 31). Interviewing techniques. Handout. FBI Academy at Quantico, Virginia.

————. (1991d, July 31). Personal interview on deception and detecting deception. FBI Academy at Quantico, Virginia.

————. (1991e, July 31). Verbal detection of deception. Course instruction. FBI Academy at Quantico, Virginia.

LeBaron, C. D. (1993). The FBI's approach to verbal deception detection. Master's thesis, University of Utah.

Ronnby, A. (1990). Teaching social work. *International Social Work* 33: 299–309.

Sapir, A. (1991). *The L.S.I. course on scientific content analysis.* Phoenix: Laboratory for Scientific Interrogation.

Senate Judiciary Committee hearings on Clarence Thomas. (1991a, October 11). Transcript of Anita Hill's testimony. Computer software. Federal News Service.

————. (1991b, October 11–12). Transcript of Clarence Thomas's testimony. Computer software. Federal News Service.

U.S. Department of Justice. (1972). *Know your FBI.* Washington, D.C.: U.S. Government Printing Office.

————. (1979). *FBI National Academy: A tradition of excellence and accomplishment.* Washington, D.C.: U.S. Government Printing Office.

7

Detection of Deception in the Hill-Thomas Hearings: An Analysis of Nonverbal Behavior

VALERIE CRYER MCKAY

Once a member of the Senate Judiciary Committee leaked Anita Hill's accusations of sexual harassment to the media, the members of the committee, and perhaps the public in general, set about the arduous task of determining whether the allegations, or Clarence Thomas's categorical denials of any incidents of sexual harassment, were the truth or lies. Without question, the confirmation of Clarence Thomas to the U.S. Supreme Court was held in balance while the committee heard and evaluated revealing testimony by Anita Faye Hill. From the moment Hill appeared before the committee on October 11, 1991, the media focused on the determination of the truth of crucial testimony detailing her charges of sexual harassment against the Supreme Court nominee. Even when Hill "passed" a lie detector test on October 13, 1991, the methods and administrator of the test were critically scrutinized.

Despite Thomas's subsequent appointment to the Supreme Court and the return of business as usual, we still do not know who was lying. Will we ever know? The purpose of this essay is to present evidence in response to this question. Utilizing aspects of language pragmatics as the framework for analysis, this essay suggests that (1) nonverbal behaviors characteristic of deceptive messages associated with lying are, to a degree, detectable and (2) documentation of these behaviors can be used as evidence of deceptive behavior (to determine the believability of critical testimony). The essay also discusses the limitations to this line of research.

Language Pragmatics as the Framework for Analysis

During the hearings investigating incidents associated with the Cuban missile crisis, a Soviet delegate who was the target of intense committee questioning engaged in a lengthy pause before answering a critical question. The long hesitation was interpreted as lying; the lie was perceived as a function of the delay between the committee's question and the Soviet delegate's response. The character of the response (as a denial or affirmation of the information in question) could also have been considered a function of the perceived importance of the information requested or the social desirability in responding. In other words, to deny the information could have been a strategy to prevent integral information from being revealed or a way to gain favor and avoid criticism (Baskett and Freedle, 1974). Either way, the hesitation caused the listeners to question the believability of the delegate's testimony.

This example illustrates the perspective of language pragmatics that focuses on the *outcome* of the language process rather than on language structure or semantics. "Language pragmatics is concerned with the relationship between language and the uses to which it is put by speakers and listeners in the language . . . what is done with the information *after* its content has been apprehended" (Baskett and Freedle, 1974, 118). In an experimental study to determine the relationship between information content and believability, Glen Baskett and Roy Freedle (1974) concluded that language pragmatics provides a gestalt framework for analyzing lying and deception; that is, verbal and nonverbal behaviors can affect believability, as in the case of the Soviet delegate. This premise is also the basis for analyzing Anita Hill's and

Clarence Thomas's testimony during the confirmation hearings to determine the truth of that testimony. Is it possible to determine the believability of their testimony by examining the verbal and nonverbal behavior manifested during the hearings?

Extending the pragmatic perspective to the detection of deception in communicator nonverbal behavior only, John Hocking and Dale Leathers (1980) examined observers' ability to detect deceptive behavior and distinctive nonverbal behavior in truthsayers and deceivers. Although the study noted that cultural stereotypes characterizing groups of individuals perceived as deceivers might cause observers to selectively attend to only those behaviors, these researchers determined that motivation might be a crucial factor in the communicator's ability to avoid detection. For example, if deceivers are not motivated (e.g., the consequences of detection are not severe), they will be detected, regardless of whether they engage in stereotypically deceptive behavior. Conversely, motivated liars are more likely to avoid detection through careful control of stereotypical or nonstereotypical behavior. Consistent with the perspective Baskett and Freedle (1974) advanced, consequences resulting from the revelation of important information or the desire to maintain a positive image or character are reasonable motivations for avoiding detection.

In the Hocking and Leathers (1980) study, experimental procedures and content analysis focused on three "classes" of behaviors: body, facial, and vocal. The researchers expected deceivers to exercise conscious control over (1) those behaviors considered stereotypical of deceptive behavior, (2) those behaviors the deceiver could most easily monitor, and (3) those behaviors susceptible to conscious control. Although the results were qualified, motivation was found to be a significant factor in the deceivers' ability to avoid detection. The deceivers not only engaged in more detectable deceptive nonverbal behavior when the consequences were more severe but also were less able to monitor that behavior to avoid detection. These researchers concluded that the level of anxiety, which increases as the consequences of detection become more severe, renders deceivers less able to monitor behavior as they attempt to deceive—further evidence that nonverbal behavior can affect the believability of the speaker's message.

In an examination of the degree to which verbal messages are enhanced and clarified by nonverbal behavior, Dane Archer and Robin Akert (1977) suggested that "nonverbal channels outweigh verbal channels in determining how messages are interpreted" (444). In this study, subjects were asked to determine the truth of either audio or videotaped messages. The results of this study indicated that the deceptive messages available on videotape, which provided both verbal and nonverbal messages, were more easily detectable than in the audiotape alone. These researchers concluded, "In real social settings, verbal and nonverbal cues appear in concert rather than in single-channel isolation. Depending on the situation, specific nonverbal cues appear to modify the significance of words and phrases, emphasizing some and minimizing the importance of others. Nonverbal cues, therefore, appear to provide a qualitative 'script' without which verbal cues cannot be interpreted accurately" (449).

This investigation substantiates the premise that how a communicator encodes messages can be used to interpret the believability and credibility of the words spoken—especially in relation to the nonverbal aspect of messages sent (Archer and Akert, 1977). Consistent with the perspective of language pragmatics, the manner in which a communicator, specifically a deceiver, presents a message can determine whether the speaker is believed. The present essay proposes that certain nonverbal behaviors can be used as indicators of believability; more specifically, certain nonverbal behaviors exhibited by Anita Hill and Clarence Thomas during the confirmation hearings might be used to indicate whose testimony should be believed and whose testimony should be discounted.

Verbal and Nonverbal Indicators of Deception

Research investigating verbal and nonverbal behavior associated with deception appears to fall into two categories: (1) identifying and describing verbal and nonverbal behavior indicative of deception and (2) analyzing observers' ability to detect that behavior. Given that deceivers are attempting to avoid detection, it is not surprising that deceptive behavior is difficult to detect; in fact, "deception can be defined as any intentional verbal or nonverbal act performed in order to direct another away from what the deceiver believes to be the truth" (Riggio and Friedman, 1983, 899). The following review of the literature provides evidence that some verbal and nonverbal behaviors are consistently present in attempts at deception and that trained observers are usually able to detect such deception attempts.

Perhaps the most notable, and certainly among the earliest, research in the area of nonverbal expression of emotion was conducted by Paul Ekman and Wallace Friesen (1975). Focusing on facial expression, these researchers contend that the face is the source of the most trustworthy, though least controllable, nonverbal emotional expression: "It is easier to monitor your words as you speak them than to monitor your facial expressions . . . it is easier to falsify words than facial expressions . . . it is easier to inhibit what you reveal in your words than what you reveal in your face" (136). Consequently, the face, particularly the mouth and lower part of the face, is more likely to reveal attempts at emotional deceit than other parts of the body are.

In contrast, John Hocking, Joyce Bauchner, Edmund Kaminski, and Gerald Miller (1979) contend that whereas the face is more controllable when engaging in factual deception, the body is more revealing where emotions are concerned. Citing previous research as the basis for making the distinction between factual and emotional deception, they conclude that deceivers can control facial/head behavior more effectively than they can the body during situations involving deception; deceivers are more aware of, and thus more capable of controlling, their facial behavior. Results of this study contend that "for factual accuracy, the observers were significantly more accurate at identifying deception when they viewed the respondents' heads than were their body-viewing counterparts" (43). It was easier to detect emotional response by observing body movement only.

Subsequent to this research, Henry D. O'Hair, Michael Cody, and Margaret McLaughlin (1981) investigated cue leakage during attempts to lie about factual information in both prepared and spontaneous situations. They note that being prepared to lie may predispose the deceiver to control more carefully those behaviors indicative of lying, whereas spontaneous situations would not afford the liar time to rehearse. Deceivers might be more skilled in prepared lying because they have rehearsed a text or because they may be mentally prepared to do so. In either case, preparation is a factor in both detection and believability. O'Hair, Cody, and McLaughlin also maintain, "One characteristic of lying behavior that appears to have an impact on the types of cues leaked is the dichotomy between emotional concealment (deceptions in which the subject's underlying affective state is misrepresented) and factual deception (deception in which the subject falsifies information)" (326).

These researchers found that body movement discloses emotional concealment, while the face and head "provide the best source of information about factual deception" (326). Although they note limitations to observers' ability to detect deception, their results also indicate significant differences between prepared lying and spontaneous lying on such upper body indicators as response latency (hesitation), message duration, head nods, body adapters, and frequency/length of laugh/smile. They argue that "in some lying contexts, subjects may anticipate lying and, once the critical question is asked, provide a 'prepared' lie (one that is rehearsed or one that they are mentally prepared to tell) . . . [and that] being prepared to lie may induce liars to control some nonverbal behaviors that they would not be prepared to control during spontaneous lies" (326).

The present essay focuses on factual deception (that is, determining the truth or falsity of testimony during the confirmation hearings) and emotional deception (such as anxiety displays). Because of the format of the hearings, only the head and upper body of Hill and Thomas are available on videotape. According to the conclusions Hocking et al. (1979) reached, factual deception and certainly emotional deception might be difficult to detect by viewing the head only because the face and head are considered to be more controllable. Given the results reported by O'Hair, Cody, and McLaughlin (1981), however, it is possible to detect factual deception by viewing the head and upper body and to distinguish between prepared lies and spontaneous deception. Although it is difficult to determine the degree of preparedness for either Hill or Thomas, it is evident that opening statements were prepared, whereas subsequent testimony was most likely spontaneous.

Extending these implications to the present essay, an incongruency between the factual information being presented (prepared or spontaneous) and nonverbal facial (emotional) expression might indicate a lack of believability; in fact, this distinction has been the focus of previous research. Specifically, performance cues refer to those behaviors indicative of deception and the ability to detect those behaviors even when the content (facts) of the deception is not revealed. In contrast, leakage cues refer to the information or content being revealed, despite attempts to conceal the nonverbal indicators of deception. When the information (content) being revealed is self-serving (which could be the case in the Hill-Thomas testimony), it tends to be less believable. As Robert Kraut (1978) pointed out, observers tend to "believe most in those aspects of a person's performance that the person is least able to deliberately and consciously control" (381). Given this, the incongruity between leakage and performance cues could significantly affect the believability of the Hill and Thomas testimony.

Kraut also incorporated context as an integral factor in detecting performance and leakage cues. He defines context as sparring or "interaction that resembles a context in which the actor tries to present himself in one way and the audience tries to see through this presentation to the actor's real qualities" (380). Defense testimony is a context in which sparring behavior might be observed. This study revealed not only that context was a factor in interpreting the truthfulness associated with either performance or leakage cues but also that these cues differed according to the context in which they were observed.

Two primary dimensions of credibility have consistently emerged in studies of witness testimony: competence and trustworthiness. Antecedents to these have been identified as dynamism, composure, and sociability; if any of these are lacking, then competence and trustworthiness are significantly affected (Miller and Burgoon, 1982). Two classifications of determinants to witness credibility have been delineated: intrinsic and extrinsic. Intrinsic determinants include aspects of verbal and nonverbal behavior; extrinsic determinants are those demographic characteristics or attributes that people bring to the courtroom. Both work in conjunction to influence perceptions of witness credibility.

Illustrating the intrinsic determinants of witness credibility, Gerald Miller and Judee Burgoon (1982) provide six classifications of nonverbal deception cues: (1) underlying anxiety or nervousness (perspiration, shaking, blinking, frequent shifts of the body, self-adapters [drumming fingers on a desk], object adapters [clicking a pen], increased non-fluencies [ah—uh—uh], facial play); (2) underlying reticence or withdrawal (fewer illustrative gestures, less forward body lean, reduced eye contact, longer delay in verbal responses [latency], shorter words/sentences); (3) deviation from personal normative behavior (not possible to detect without baseline behavior pattern); (4) underlying negative affect (reduced immediacy, briefer glances, fewer smiles, displeased mouth movement); (5) underlying vagueness or uncertainty (increase in silence and hesitation before speaking); and (6) contradictory external behavior (nonverbal behavior is incongruent with verbal/vocal rhythm).

The extrinsic determinants included are those characteristics (cultural, demographic, background, personality, and the like) that are attributable to the individual giving testimony. For example, Clarence Thomas was described as "President Bush's conservative Black nominee to the Supreme Court, the self-made man from tiny Pin Point, Georgia, whose key qualification for high office is his supposedly stainless character." Anita Hill, who hailed from a small town in Oklahoma and a farming family, was considered at thirty-five to be "a highly articulate, Black lawyer," who received her law degree from Yale University before working with Thomas at the Department of Education (Smiley, 1991, 16). Not surprisingly, these and other character descriptions laid the groundwork for evaluating the truthfulness of Hill's allegations of sexual harassment and the credibility of both Hill and Thomas as crucial testimony became public during the confirmation hearings.

This review indicates that certain nonverbal behaviors are characteristic of situations involving deception and that these behaviors influence both the believability of the message and the credibility of the communicator. Other factors, such as context, preparedness, and the orientation of the message (factual or emotional), combine to form a complete representation of the complexity characterizing situations involving deception. Yet to be discussed, however, is the role of motivation, which seems to be a significant determinant in the success of deception attempts.

Motivation as a Determinant of Deception Success

Motivation in relation to situations involving deception is conceptualized as a concern with the consequences of having the deception detected. In essence, if deceivers know the consequences will be severe, they are more likely to make a sincere effort to avoid detection; likewise, if the consequences lack severity, deceivers are less concerned with detection (Riggio and Friedman, 1983). Ironically, highly motivated deceivers are both more successful and more detectable as their ability to control nonverbal indicators is reduced. In fact, Bella DePaulo, Keith Lanier, and Tracy Davis (1983) found that "in all channels that included nonverbal cues, the lies of the highly motivated senders were more readily detected than those of the less highly motivated senders" (1101).

Preparedness is also a factor in relation to motivation in deception attempts. According to O'Hair, Cody, and McLaughlin (1981) "Being prepared to lie may induce liars to control some nonverbal behaviors that they would not be prepared to control during spontaneous lies" (326). Perhaps deceivers who are prepared to lie rehearse both verbal and nonverbal aspects of their deception, and detection is therefore a less significant concern. Research examining this claim is inconclusive, however. For example, DePaulo, Lanier, and

Davis (1983) found that even though preparation might enhance verbal performance, nonverbal messages promote leakage of concealed information. Likewise, "a nonverbal cue can amplify the suspiciousness of a statement" and cause the truthfulness of that statement to be discounted (Kraut, 1978, 390). In essence, these results are consistent with the perspective of language pragmatics; that is, verbal and nonverbal behaviors can affect believability. Are motivation and preparedness significant factors in increasing the probability of success at the deception attempt or, on the contrary, enhancing detectability and thus discounting the believability of testimony?

In the case of Anita Hill and Clarence Thomas, motivation and preparedness were integral to the evaluation of prepared and spontaneous testimony. For Thomas, the *consequences* of the hearing included whether he would serve as a Supreme Court justice. For Hill, her position as a law professor at the University of Oklahoma would perhaps be jeopardized by publicizing her allegations of sexual harassment. Without a doubt, the consequences for both Hill and Thomas were severe. With regard to testimony, Thomas's categorical denial of Hill's allegations of sexual harassment was in stark contrast to the detailed testimony Hill provided both prior to and during her appearance at the confirmation hearings. Whose testimony lacked veracity? Inasmuch as both Hill and Thomas did have time to prepare for their opening statements, they might have been more prepared to communicate verbal messages, but are there detectable nonverbal messages that could affect the believability of testimony given? Is there a difference between the prepared testimony given during the opening statements and the spontaneous testimony given in response to questions the members of the judiciary committee posed? Can the believability of testimony be determined?

Method

To determine the incidence of deception during testimony given by Anita Hill and Clarence Thomas, videotapes of both prepared (opening statements) and spontaneous testimony (during the question/answer period) were obtained and content analyzed. Categories of nonverbal behaviors indicative of deception were consistent with those used by Hocking and Leathers (1980) and Dale Leathers, Laura Vaughn, Greg Sanchez, and Jennifer Bailey (1992). The coding scheme for the present study included three classes of nonverbal behaviors: body, facial, and vocal.[1] Specific categories included (1) illustrators, self-adapters, shrugs, postural shifts, and object adapters for body behavior (2) the licking of lips, the shifting of eyes, blinks, rapid eye movement, smiles/ laughs, facial movement, displeased mouth movement, affirmative head nod, and facial adapters as facial indicators; and (3) "ah," stutters, word/phrase repetition, number/length of silent pauses, sentence change, response latency, and speaking rate as vocal indicators.

Coders had over two-and-a-half hours of training prior to individually (and blindly) coding the videotapes of Hill's and Thomas's prepared and spontaneous testimony. The coders were not told that the objective of the coding process was to detect deception; they were only told to determine the presence or absence of targeted nonverbal behaviors. Code sheets were subdivided into six ten-second intervals, totaling one minute each sheet; the one-minute totals were the basis for the final analysis (frequencies, means, and standard-deviations). Reliability was determined by utilizing Ole Holsti's (1968) formula and calculated separately for both Hill's and Thomas's prepared statements (approximately fourteen minutes each) and spontaneous portions (approximately five minutes each). Reliability estimates ranged from .65 to .70, which, although low for scientific research, were considered acceptable for exploratory examination.

Results

Chi-square tests for goodness of fit were performed on the average frequencies (between coders) for all categories of the three classes of behaviors for both Hill and Thomas in the prepared and spontaneous portions of testimony. These tests were performed to determine whether acceptable frequencies of each behavior were present for further analysis. All chi-squares were significant ($p < .05$) except for Thomas's "vocal" categories during prepared testimony.

As a secondary analysis, the Kruskal-Wallis test for independent samples was performed to determine differences in the frequency of body, facial, and vocal behaviors for both Hill's and Thomas's prepared and spontaneous testimony. For Hill, significant differences between the three classes of behaviors were found for both prepared testimony ($H = 2.152$; $df = 2$; $p < .05$) and spontaneous testimony ($H = 7.98$; $df = 2$; $p < .05$). For both prepared and spontaneous situations, facial behavior received the highest rank, indicating the highest frequency. For Thomas, significant differences were also found in prepared testimony ($H = 2.10$; $df = 2$; $p < .05$) and spontaneous testimony ($H = 1.92$; $df = 2$; $p < .01$). For both prepared and spontaneous portions, facial behavior received the highest rank, indicating the highest frequency.

As a final and comparative analysis, Mann-Whitney U tests for equality of means/medians were utilized to determine whether significant differences in the three classes of behaviors existed between Hill's and Thomas's prepared and spontaneous portions of testimony. Results of the Mann-Whitney U for the comparison of prepared testimony indicated that for body ($U = 24$; 7,7; $p > .05$) and facial ($U = 20.5$; 7,7; $p > .05$) categories, no significant differences were found between Hill and Thomas; although Thomas's rankings were higher in both cases, results do not indicate that the frequency of these behaviors was significantly higher for Thomas. For vocal categories during the prepared portions of testimony, no significant differences were found. Hill received the highest ranking and lowest score ($U = 9.5$; 6,6; $p > .05$). This is not surprising, given the initially low frequency for Thomas in vocal cues.

Results of the Mann-Whitney U for body ($U = 17$; 7,7; $p > .05$), face ($U = 20.5$; 7,7; $p > .05$), and vocal ($U = 18$; 6,6; $p > .05$) classes during spontaneous testimony revealed no significant differences between Hill and Thomas. Again, although Thomas's rankings were higher for both body and facial behavior, hypotheses that the frequency of Thomas's behavior would be significantly higher were not supported. Analyses of differences were also performed to compare the frequencies of body, facial, and vocal classes of behavior during prepared and spontaneous testimony for both Thomas and Hill separately. For Thomas, frequencies in body ($U = 13$; 7,7; $p > .05$), facial ($U = 20.5$; 7,7; $p > .05$) and vocal ($U = 8.5$; 6,6; $p > .05$) behavior during prepared testimony did not differ significantly from that observed during his spontaneous testimony. The frequencies during spontaneous testimony were higher in all three classes; however, nondirectional hypotheses were not supported. For Hill, no significant differences were found for frequencies in body ($U = 23$; 7,7; $p > .05$), facial ($U = 28$; 7,7; $p > .05$) or vocal ($U = 13$; 6,6; $p > .05$) behavior during prepared and spontaneous testimony.

Regarding specific nonverbal behaviors in each of the three classifications, no differences were found in comparing prepared and spontaneous testimony for Hill and Thomas. Furthermore, no differences were found in the types of behaviors in which each of the participants engaged. The most commonly observed nonverbal behaviors for both were postural shifts and object adapters for the body; eye shifts, blinks, and rapid eye movement for the face; and ahs and stutters for vocal behavior.

Discussion and Implications

The underlying premise for this research was that either Hill or Thomas was lying during testimony presented before the Senate Judiciary Committee and that (1) nonverbal cues indicative of deception could be detected in videotaped excerpts of the testimony and (2) the higher frequency of nonverbal behavioral cues would reveal who was lying. In essence, although nonverbal cues indicative of deception were observed, no significant differences were detected in any of the areas examined, except in individual classes of behavior during prepared and spontaneous testimony for each participant. There are three possible explanations for these results: (1) the category scheme was limited in its ability to detect the presence of alternative (or more significant) indicators of deception, (2) the perspective that nonverbal cues alone would reveal the presence of deception was reductive, and (3) neither Hill nor Thomas was lying.

The classification of body, facial, and vocal indicators of nonverbal deception and the reliability associated with coding those behaviors were considered satisfactory for the exploratory nature of this study since the coding scheme had been used in previous research. What might be in question, however, is not the reliability of the coding scheme but its validity. Do the classifications and categories cover the full range of behaviors associated with deception or its facsimile? Can the presence or absence of these behaviors predict or explain the perception of believability associated with critical testimony? Does the coding scheme account for culturally specific, nonstereotypical behavior involved in acts of deception? The affirmative answer to these questions is not without reservation and uncertainty. Many of these behaviors are also manifest in various stressful situations—when one is facing confrontation, engaging in an argument, or being questioned by someone of higher status—yet these are not necessarily situations in which deception is omnipresent.

Take, for example, the prepared testimony Hill and Thomas presented. Both focused on Anita Hill's educational background and her association with Clarence Thomas at the Department of Education and the Equal Employment Opportunity Commission in the early 1980s. In fact, much of Thomas's testimony about their past association concurred with Hill's, which perhaps indicated that the testimony during this portion of the proceedings was truthful for both parties. Yet nonverbal indicators of deception were documented; in fact, Chi-square goodness-of-fit tests were significant. Given the significant presence of these indicators, the logical conclusion would be that Thomas and Hill were both lying, despite the factual nature of the testimony and their agreement about it. This conclusion would be both unrealistic and invalid. Yet, without the content of the message, it is logical if one accepts the assumption that these nonverbal behaviors indicate deception.

Which brings us to our second explanation: the reductionist nature of such an assumption. Archer and Akert (1977) maintain that nonverbal messages determine the interpretation of the verbal message; they do not contend that nonverbal messages *take the place of* verbal messages. In fact, to restate an earlier quote from their work, "In real social settings, verbal and nonverbal cues appear in concert rather than in single-channel isolation. Depending on the situation, specific nonverbal cues appear to modify the significance of words and phrases, emphasizing some and minimizing the importance of others. Nonverbal cues, therefore, appear to provide a qualitative 'script' without which verbal cues cannot be interpreted accurately" (449).

The perspective of language pragmatics utilized as the theoretical framework for this essay stipulates that the manner in which the message is presented can determine the truth or falsity of the message. It does not advance that "how" a message is sent dominates "what" the message is conveying; rather, it allows for a more gestalt framework for interpreting the meaning of messages. The issue, then, is not only the validity of the means of interpreting the nature or form of the message but also the content of, and the context in which, the message is presented. At this point, the complexity inherent in the process of interpretation renders the focus on nonverbal behavioral indicators of deception significantly limited in scope.

To argue this point, let's take the issue of believability. Throughout this essay, it has been suggested that perhaps the presence of nonverbal deception is not definitive in determining whether Hill or Thomas was lying; rather, factors both intrinsic and extrinsic to the individuals giving testimony could be determinants of their credibility and the believability of testimony presented. This point can best be explained within the framework of the narrative paradigm. Walter Fisher (1987) contends that "if one's character can be determined and if one's story in regard to a particular issue can be ascertained, it is possible to predict a person's probable actions" (87). If we take this process one step further, an individual's predisposition to endorse another's position on, or interpret another's story about, a particular issue depends on an assessment of values or rational schemes for acceptance. If an issue/statement is within our boundaries of acceptance, it is believed. Those boundaries are defined not only by the issue but also by the manner in which it is presented and by whom.

In the case of Anita Hill and Clarence Thomas, we have two well-educated, determined, and diligent individuals, neither of whom likely had had their credibility and character questioned to this degree at any other point in their professional lives. The positions they had achieved attest to these assessments of character. However, on an almost daily basis in the period during which Hill was testifying, the press presented evidence of exaggeration, lying, motivation, and questionable character on the parts of both Hill and Thomas. On the basis of this information, the public was forced into deciding the veracity of Hill's allegations of Thomas's sexual harassment and ascertaining the reasons behind his categorical denial of all incidents. According to Fisher (1987), the notion of rationality simply provides "a system for determining whether or not one should accept a story, whether or not a story is indeed trustworthy and reliable as a guide to belief and action" (88); it reminds us of the human component of choice in accepting or rejecting the believability of testimony. In essence, the limited information the public was provided does not allow us to judge the truth or falsity of the testimony presented.

Finally, the third explanation simply advances the possibility that neither Hill nor Thomas was lying, that perhaps both believed the testimony they were presenting. If a time machine were available, perhaps everyone could take a trip back to the early 1980s, the period during which the alleged incidents took place. Take a look at the issues, the newspapers, the research, the television programs. How often were the words *sexual harassment* present? What were the relevant issues of the day regarding women's and men's roles in the workplace? How many women were in positions like that held by Anita Hill? Were the operational and legal definitions of sexual harassment in place and understood by employees as well as they are now? Were we as sensitive to the issue of sexual harassment in 1981 as we are now?

My point is not to derogate the issue of sexual harassment. On the contrary, it is to comment on the progress we have made in making it an issue of recognition and action, much of which has occurred as a result of the hearings themselves. What we now define and discipline as sexually harassing behavior was standard operating procedure over a decade ago. Women did not disclose or report (and to a degree still do not) incidents of sexual harassment because they feared losing their jobs (as Anita Hill testified). What was (and still is) considered by many men to be flirting now falls under the legal definition of sexual harassment. Perhaps, even though some or all of the incidents might have occurred, Thomas believed that he was not committing acts of sexual harassment. Given his legal background, one would hope he knew the difference; given the year and human nature, perhaps he did not. What Anita Hill might have felt was the obligation to reveal a significant character flaw in an individual who was about to be appointed as a Supreme Court justice.

NOTE

I wish to acknowledge the assistance and commitment of Glen Heuser, my student assistant in the Speech Communication Department at California State University, Long Beach. I also thank the trained coders, Tamika Kidd and Tim Murphy.

1. This classification is consistent with other research identifying nonverbal cues indicative of deception (see deTurk and Miller, 1985; Harrison et al., 1978; Hocking et al., 1979; Kraut, 1978; Miller, deTurck, and Kalbfleisch, 1983; Riggio and Friedman, 1983; and Taylor, 1986).

REFERENCES

Archer, D., and Akert, R. M. (1977). Words and everything else: Verbal and nonverbal cues in social interpretation. *Journal of Personality and Social Psychology*, 35: 443–49.

Baskett, G. D., and Freedle, R. O. (1974). Aspects of language pragmatics and the social perception of lying. *Journal of Psycholinguistic Research*, 3 (2): 117–31.

DePaulo, B. M., Lanier, K., and Davis, T. (1983). Detecting the deceit of the motivated liar. *Journal of Personality and Social Psychology*, 45: 1096–1103.

deTurk, M. A., and Miller, G. R. (1985). Deception and arousal: Isolating the behavioral correlates of deception. *Human Communication Research*, 12: 181–201.

Ekman, P., and Friesen, W. V. (1975). *Unmasking the face.* Englewood Cliffs, N.J.: Prentice-Hall.

Fisher, W. R. (1987). *Human communication as narration: Toward a philosophy of reason, value, and action.* Columbia: University of South Carolina Press.

Harrison, A. A., Hwalek, M., Raney, D. F., and Fritz, J. G. (1978). Cues to deception in an interview situation. *Social Psychology,* 41 (2): 156–61.

Hocking, J. E., Bauchner, J., Kaminski, E. P., and Miller, G. R. (1979). Detecting deceptive communication from verbal, visual, and paralinguistic cues. *Human Communication Research,* 6: 33–46.

Hocking, J. E., and Leathers, D. G. (1980). Nonverbal indicators of deception: A new theoretical perspective. *Communication Monographs,* 47: 119–31.

Holsti, O. R. (1968). Content analysis. In G. Lindzey and E. Aronson (eds.), *The handbook of social psychology,* 596–692. Reading, Mass.: Addison-Wesley.

Kraut, R. E. (1978). Verbal and nonverbal cues in the perception of lying. *Journal of Personality and Social Psychology,* 36: 380–91.

Leathers, D. G., Vaughn, L., Sanchez, G., and Bailey, J. (1992, November). Who is lying in the Anita Hill–Clarence Thomas hearing? Nonverbal communication profiles. Paper presented at the annual convention of the Speech Communication Association, Chicago.

Miller, G. R., and Burgoon, J. K. (1982). Factors affecting assessments of witness credibility. In N. L. Kerr and R. M. Bray (eds.), *The psychology of the courtroom,* 171–94. New York: Academic Press.

Miller, G. R., deTurck, M. A., and Kalbfleisch, P. J. (1983). Self-monitoring, rehearsal, and deceptive communication. *Human Communication Research,* 10: 97–117.

O'Hair, H. D., Cody, M. J., and McLaughlin, M. L. (1981). Prepared lies, spontaneous lies, machiavellianism, and nonverbal communication. *Human Communication Research,* 7: 325–39.

Riggio, R. E., and Friedman, H. S. (1983). Individual differences and cues to deception. *Journal of Personality and Social Psychology,* 45: 899–915.

Smiley, X. (1991, October 13). Watching for sex lies on videotape: A judge's TV trial. *Sunday Telegraph* (London), 16.

Taylor, J. (1986). Encoding and decoding nonverbal gender display in cross-gender performances. *Women's Studies in Communication,* 9: 76–88.

8

Believability: Narratives and Relational Messages in the Strategies of Anita Hill and Clarence Thomas

JUDITH K. BOWKER

During and immediately following the Senate Judiciary Committee's hearings of testimony by Anita Hill and Clarence Thomas, I was stunned by public reaction. The sweeping disbelief that Clarence Thomas sexually harassed Anita Hill flew in the face of a social reality in which sexual harassment exists as a familiar event. Controversy certainly was to be expected; however, the overwhelming public rejection of both Anita Hill and the human experience she exposed was unexpected.

On October 11, 1991, a CBS news poll indicated that 21 percent of those who responded thought the charges were true; 47 percent believed the charges were not true ("Confirmation," 1991, A18). By October 13, 1991, the *New York Times* reported that 58 percent of those surveyed believed Clarence Thomas and that 24 percent believed Anita Hill (Kolbert, 1991, A1). My own informal discussions with acquaintances, friends, students, and coworkers produced similar responses. Contrary to the majority of responders, I had found the description of the harassment—the narrative provided by Hill and the opposing narrative provided by Thomas—familiar, resounding with my own experiences. Immediately after Thomas's opening statement, I found his account to be believable. However, as the hearings progressed, I was unequivocally convinced that Hill was telling the truth.

For several weeks following the confrontation, I puzzled through transcripts of the hearings, trying to understand why so many men and women believed Thomas. I looked for the rhetorical strategies; in particular, I searched for the central threads of arguments in each story, threads used to create each of the two separate narrative fabrics. I compared and contrasted those threads; that process provided for me some small insight into the question of why people believed Thomas.

But those comparisons did not explain fully the impact of the narratives or the imbalance of power between the two narratives. Why was Thomas believed by so many? What about his narrative or his presentation rang true? Or were people simply disbelieving Hill, siding with Thomas by default? The narrative threads clarified some substantive differences, revealed some of the implied values, and identified issues that each side considered central to the controversy; however, they did not answer questions about persuasive power or the endurance of his story compared with hers. I sought to examine the believability of the narratives within the situational context of the hearings.

Returning to the narratives for information, I looked for the relational messages Hill and Thomas used—messages about relationships between and among Hill and Thomas, the judiciary committee, and the viewing audience. Those relational messages might have been discerned by observers and might have influenced those observers' willingness or desire to identify with one narrative or the other.

I also consulted literature about deception, especially work investigating the context of the deception and how people control deceptive messages (Greene et al., 1985; Kurasawa, 1988; Riggio and Friedman, 1983). During the opening statements and throughout the questioning, Thomas and then Hill were seated behind a large table. Much of the media coverage consisted of close-ups of their faces. Since the literature seems to agree that deceivers can control facial expressions better than other nonverbal cues (Littlepage, Maddox, and Pineault, 1985, 119), focusing on context and control helped identify observable deceptive communication behaviors.

Finally, after concluding these investigations, I conducted a survey after to test my interpretations against those of the viewing audience. The results of the survey added perspective to the conclusions previously drawn.

Method

Before constructing the survey, I sought responses to the hearings from a variety of people in a variety of situations. This informal method of gathering information was used to generate possible perspectives for interpreting the function of the narrative threads, the relational messages, or the nonverbal deceptive behaviors. Perspectives emerged from casual neighborhood discussions, formal and informal essays in the local and national press, written articles, written and oral commentary, audio and visual media, and class discussions. In addition, I conducted a term-long graduate seminar focusing on the proceedings.

Five months after the hearings, a formal survey was conducted to solicit survey participants' explanations of their support of Hill or Thomas. The intervening months, used to establish a context for the survey questions, also served to lower the intensity of the media coverage. The objective of the survey was to gather responses that reflected less of the intensity of the moment and more of the long-term residuals of the competing narratives. Those memories people still held about the Hill-Thomas testimony would represent for each person the salient, ongoing centerpieces of their beliefs and values.

The participants of the survey were 134 male and 113 female college students on a northwestern university campus; they ranged in age from eighteen to fifty-six. Predominantly a Euro-American population (213 of the 247), students responded to several demographic questions (including how they knew about the hearings). Participants were asked to write what they believed about Hill's narrative, what they disbelieved about Hill's narrative, what they believed about Thomas's narrative, and what they disbelieved about Thomas's narrative.

Traditional practice in research of this kind requires the scholar to process results into consumable bits. However, when the information provided is personal and multifaceted—as the information in this survey was—some of the conventional, academic methods of "knowing" appear antithetical to the process of understanding. Integration rather than segregation can provide the means by which to know. For this reason, the following method was used to understand this topic: think carefully, listen to others and incorporate their good thinking, forward an idea, brainstorm with similar and dissimilar thinkers, draw conclusions, and speculate about further investigation.

In the first step, ideas about narrative threads and relational messages emerged from a wide variety of conversations, media presentations, academic investigation, and readings; they resulted from the convergence of the presumptions, beliefs, opinions, and thoughts of many people (though not from survey participants). Participants in the survey provided new information about the narratives and relational messages that could be compared and contrasted with the narrative fabric previously identified.

In this essay, I first present the conspicuous threads of the Thomas narrative and those of the Hill narrative. After describing and analyzing these narrative pieces, I discuss the relational messages embedded in both Hill's and Thomas's presentations. Finally, I compare the responses given by participants in the survey with these threads and relational messages to determine which components participants found compelling.

Narrative Threads

Frankly, the discrepancy I sought to explain appeared to be between my own social reality and that of a majority of the people—male and female—who voiced opinions about this testimony. Although much "scientific" and "academic" pursuit is disguised otherwise, my experience has been that discrepancies between the researcher's perception and those of the world around her or him very often lie at the heart of research. Important to the question of believability, then, was the determination of the threads most conspicuous and most central to the narratives used during the hearings.

Narrative threads emerged in a number of ways. Some were detected by participants in the term-long seminar on Hill and Thomas. Some resulted from everyday discussions and conversations that I pursued with any willing participant. Some arose in media presentations—news shows, talk shows, commentary, or editorials. Some were suggested by Anita Hill in subsequent public speeches (for example, her speech at the Georgetown University Law Center on October 16, 1992). Transcriptions and video tapes of the proceedings provided the texts in which the threads of the narratives were traced for frequency or dominance.

Gender, race, and politically correct ideologies complicated the emergence of narrative threads. Also, the sex, race, and ethnicity of both the researcher—a white Danish-American woman—and the survey participants—males and females, mostly white, and mostly Euro-American—both expand and limit the study in different ways. As a consequence, conclusions are applied not generally but situationally. I have addressed the more general problems intrinsic to sexual harassment, particularly power issues, in another article (Bowker, 1993).

The Thomas Narrative

Multiple threads, woven in intricate complexity, twine through the narratives of Anita Hill and Clarence Thomas. Threads evident in the Thomas narrative were created by Thomas, by members of the Senate Judiciary Committee (particularly Orrin Hatch, Arlen Specter, and Alan Simpson), by witnesses for Thomas, and by the press. One headline in the *New York Times* attests to this: "Judge's Backers Take Up His Defense, Posing Motive and Method for Accuser" (Lewis, 1991, I28).

Two important threads involved fantasy and time. The thread that centered on fantasy, drawn particularly clearly by Specter, depicted Anita Hill as a woman given to fantasy about men's interest in her ("The Thomas Nomination," 1991, L13; "Thomas Rebuts," 1991, I14). This theme avowed that Hill's fantasies about men led her to interpret Thomas's actions in ways that were not in keeping with reality; the message contends that Hill embellished not only the actions at the time they occurred but also her story as she revealed the episodes to the committee.

Unraveling from this thread were strings of images of a "scorned woman," one desperately seeking the attention of men and not getting it (Phelps and Winternitz, 1992, 269, 319–21, 323–24, 358, 361–62, 371–77, 398, 407). This line of thinking was supported by Hatch's suggestion that Hill had taken details from *The Exorcist* to invent the infamous Coke can episode ("Accuser Put under Attack," 1991, I29; Phelps and Winternitz, 1992, 343–44). Witnesses for

Thomas were closely questioned about Hill's fantasies, thus threading the idea through witness testimony as well as the testimony of Thomas himself, as can be seen in the following question: "You do know Dean Kothe and he does know Judge Thomas. And this is his concluding statement. Quote, I find the references to the alleged sexual harassment not only unbelievable but preposterous. I'm convinced that such are the product of fantasy, closed quote. Would you care to comment on that?" (quoted in "The Thomas Nomination," 1991, L13).

A second popularly cited narrative thread questioned the amount of time Hill allowed to pass before she told her story to the public. Deriving from this part of the narrative were arguments that Hill could not have experienced significant discomfort since she was able to keep silent so long. Also evolving from those arguments were inquiries about why Hill transferred from the Department of Education to the Equal Employment Opportunity Commission (EEOC) with Thomas and why she stayed in contact with him, such as the following:

> Senator Specter [questioning Ellen M. Wells, witness for Anita Hill]: . . . we have a situation where Professor Hill went from the Department of Education to the E.E.O.C., and she was a classification attorney where she could have kept her job. And then she went with him voluntarily on a trip to Oral Roberts [University]. . . . knowing Professor Hill as you do, and in light of your statement, so outraged, have to do something, what would that something have been? Would it have been to follow him from one job to another, to call him up, drive him to the airport? Or would it [at] least have been not to maintain that kind of an association? (quoted in "Questions to Those," 1991, A13–14)

Further inquiries were made about Hill's contact with Thomas:

> Senator Simpson: . . . Does it seem odd to any of you here that these universally crude and obscene things, which we have all heard. . . . So here it is, this foul, foul stack of stench, justifiably offensive in any category, that she was offended justifiably, embarrassed, justifiably, and that she was repelled, justifiably. And I ask you, why then after she left his power, after she left his presence, after she left his influence and his domination or whatever it was that gave her fear, and call it fear or revulsion, or repulsion, why did she twice after that visit personally with him in Tulsa, Oklahoma, had dinner with him in the presence of others, had breakfast with him in the presence of others, rode to the airport alone with him in the presence of one. (quoted in "Questions to Those," 1991, A13)

The issue of the passage of time was raised throughout the testimony—especially by the senators—and seemed to be pursued ardently by the media and general observers.

A third narrative thread, contributed largely by the press and the public, questioned Hill's motives. In Thomas's opening statement, he made clear his inability to remember anything he could have said or done to elicit Hill's accusations ("Thomas, Hill Make Statements," 1991, 2980). People voiced concern that Hill made the charges hoping to gain publicity and a high public profile, leading her to lucrative contracts and writing assignments. Outlying arguments included allegations about her work record as a lawyer, her teaching record in Oklahoma, and her possible coercion by "slick lawyers" (Lewis, 1991, I28).

The fourth narrative thread recast the interaction between Hill and Thomas. This part of the narrative developed for and by Thomas acknowledges that some form of interaction did indeed occur between them; however, according to this narrative, that interaction was commonplace conversation between a man and a woman, not sexual harassment. Unlike the implications of the "scorned woman," this thread replaces Hill's translations of events with translations that affirm Thomas's behaviors but recast them as commonplace.

Phyllis Berry, a woman who worked in Thomas's office, suggested that Hill might have had a crush on Thomas ("With Each Round of Testimony," 1991, A11). J. C. Alvarez, a staffer at the EEOC, maintained that Hill "had a crush on the chairman" and "wished she could have had a greater relationship with the chairman than just professional" (quoted in "With Each Round of Testimony," 1991, A11). Some did acknowledge, in some measure, that Thomas engaged in at least some of the behaviors alleged by Hill. As one white female observer said, Anita Hill was "making mountains out of molehills. I suppose he did harass her a little bit. I personally believe he probably did all of those things. But they are making too big a deal out of it. It's not like he's been raping women and beating children" (quoted in Johnson, 1991, A16). The culpable component of this event was identified as Hill's overly sensitive reactions to Thomas's mundane actions.

The Hill Narrative

Unlike the Thomas narrative, which was constructed as a reaction to another story, the Hill narrative determined the arena of controversy. Details in her narrative—for example, the dates, the professional connection between Thomas and her, the pornographic bounds of the incident, the extent to which she chose to express the pornography, and the nature of the harassment she alleged—combined to establish the setting for both her own narrative and Thomas's. Unlike Thomas's narrative, in which significant segments were constructed during the hearings through questions composed by members of the Senate Judiciary Committee, Hill's narrative was constructed largely by her. Her narrative, like Thomas's, was reiterated by witnesses, judiciary members, the media, and the public. Four threads that emerged in her narrative included reticence about reporting, unequivocal examples of sexual harassment, descriptions of powerlessness, and acknowledgement of inexperience.

Of the many threads in Hill's narrative, one she presented early and repeated often concerned her "agonizing consideration" about forwarding these allegations (quoted in "Thomas, Hill Make Statements," 1991, 2981). This part of the narrative characterized Hill as a private person, not given to public display of her personal life. Unwinding from this thread are the claims that she would not gain either economically or professionally from these disclosures. Hill's narrative casts ethical and moral obligations as catalysts that compelled her testimony.

Another important thread of the Hill narrative declared unequivocally that sexual harassment had occurred and that it had occurred without provocation. Hill's story presented images of discrete actions, actions not easily misinterpreted. Graphic, pornographic details established Thomas's alleged behavior as outside the social norms for office demeanor; although the narrative did not include legal parameters for 1981, the parameters for social appropriateness clearly were breached. Related to this part of the narrative were exchanges about Hill's preference not to date people with whom she worked, her behavior in Thomas's presence as observed by others, and her verbal rejections of Thomas's invitations.

A third narrative thread followed Hill's perceptions that she had no recourse about Thomas's actions because he was the chair of the Equal Employment Opportunity Commission and because she believed her job opportunities would be destroyed by reporting the harassment. This portion of Hill's narrative elicited reaction from those constructing the Thomas narrative, and the stories compete conspicuously on this point. From the intersection of these two stories evolved issues about whether Hill knew other high-level officials to whom she could report and how marketable she was at the time.

A fourth narrative thread, again put forward for the most part only by Hill herself, cited her youth and inexperience as foundations for the choices she made. In her opening statement, Hill indicated her young age was part of the reason she chose not to disclose the harassment at the time it occurred ("Thomas, Hill Make Statements," 1991, 2982). The age issue is referred to by Hill's witnesses but is not in Thomas's narrative.

This part of the Hill story provides a metaphor for this process, especially senatorial support of Hill's narrative. Little evidence emerges of the extension or amplification of any component of the Hill narrative. Unlike the Thomas narrative—which is extended, amplified, and even created by other participants in the hearings—Hill's narrative is woven nearly entirely by Hill herself.

Relational Messages

To help explain believability, I investigated the relational messages Hill and Thomas used because relational messages can arbitrate meaning. The relational messages contributed to the situational context, adding critical meaning to the persuasive narrative. In this case, I am using relational messages to mean messages exchanged—usually nonverbally—that established between the people communicating issues of power, status, personal value, and prerogative. I examined the messages for underlying presumptions about those issues, presumptions that may resound in familiar ways to observers of the hearings. If the relational messages conflicted with other narrative messages, observers would have to choose between them. Discovering the other information exchanged during the hearings might provide another perspective for understanding how people chose the story they believed.

Hill's Relational Messages

Anita Hill established many relational messages during the hearings; in particular, four of those messages established how she perceived herself in relation to the specific audience at the hearings, especially the judiciary committee and Thomas. In those four messages, she made clear her position as a woman, a professional, and a victim of sexual harassment. Although the following messages appeared, their existence did not ensure their validation by anyone not hearing the testimony.

That she chose to make public her narrative established the message that a woman has the province to identify male behaviors of these kinds and to label those behaviors as sexual harassment. Further, Hill established that assessments of sexual harassment may be made by a single woman—meaning an unmarried woman—and that they may be made public in a national forum. This message affected Hill's public relationship with Thomas; however, its most significant impact concerned the all-male Senate committee and the viewing audience.

Second, Hill established that allegations of sexual harassment may be made by a single woman—meaning only one woman. Without other women to corroborate the story, Hill presented the information for public scrutiny. Her decision to expose her narrative was not predicated on corroborating testimony. This message had the greatest effect on the relationship she had with the senators, although it also concerned her relationship with the viewing audience. Insofar as it presumed her status to be on a par with Thomas (i.e., not needing similar, corroborating experiences of another victim), this message affected her private and personal relationship with Thomas.

Third, one of Hill's relational messages validated a perspective that a woman's career and her choices about career and marriage are as viable as a man's. Hill's appearance as a lawyer among lawyers provided a public, nonfiction model of a female professionally interacting in a characteristically male arena. The juxtaposition of Hill as a single person and Thomas as a married one reversed the more common expectation for men and women in this culture. More than the others, this relational message provoked virulent responses, perhaps marking it as having challenged a deep-seated cultural value.

A fourth relational message emerged more subtly than the others. This featured Hill as a single woman playing a part in an all-male production. While Hill's appearance asserted one relational message—that a single woman may present this topic—another theme counteracted this one, censuring Hill's choice to speak and indicting her for choosing an inappropriate social role. J. C. Alvarez, a witness for Thomas, described Hill as "a very hard, tough woman" (quoted in "With Each Round," 1991, A11). The countering message appeared particularly salient in the African American community. Alvin F. Poussaint, a Harvard psychiatrist, notes, "There's a high level of anger among black men, be they low-income or professional, that black women will betray them; that black women are given preference over them; that white men like to put black women in between them to use them. Black men feel that white men are using this black woman [referring to Anita Hill] to get another black man" (quoted in "Many Blacks Say," 1991, A16). Euro-Americans held Hill suspect for this reason as well, asserting that Hill was hoping to derail Thomas's nomination to the Supreme Court.

Discussions of Hill's marital status, her dating behaviors, her relationships with males, and her status as a professional (both past and present) all derived from this fourth theme. The message was borne out in subtle, often nonverbal ways: the manner in which questions were asked, the number of questions asked, the unwillingness of senators to serve as patrons for Hill (as Arlen Specter and Orrin Hatch had for Thomas), the questions to witnesses concerning Hill's dating behaviors but not Thomas's, the committee's willingness to confine areas of questioning in regard to Thomas, and so forth.

Last, Hill authenticated a life experience that might not have been shared by others—particularly men—in her specific audience. In so doing, she challenged their realities; she created an interchange in which that group was asked to accept intellectually a reality that they could not experientially create. Since men cannot experience sexual harassment in precisely the same way that women can, Hill's narrative exacted from them intellectual exertion. This last theme most directly affected Hill's relationship with committee members.

To reiterate, these messages were about Hill's relationship with Thomas, the committee, or the viewing audience. Whether the audience decoded these messages, understood them, accepted them, or rejected them partly explains why people believed one narrative or the other. Comparing and contrasting these four messages with those disclosed by participants in the survey may help distinguish the messages most important to observers who were choosing whom to believe.

Thomas's Relational Messages

Thomas's assertion of power in his relationship with the committee affected not only the style of interchange between the committee and him but also the kind of information that would be revealed. He also used relational messages to establish his status regarding Hill's testimony. Female witnesses on Thomas's behalf presented their accounts of the relationship that he had in general with women who worked under his supervision.

One clear, repeated relational message that Thomas created was that he had the authority to mandate what questions to him were allowable in this hearing. Unlike the narrative threads, many of which were co-created by Thomas and others, this relational message was delivered both verbally and nonverbally by Thomas directly to the Senate Judiciary Committee in such statements as this: "I will not allow myself to be further humiliated in order to be confirmed. I am here specifically to respond to allegations of sex harassment in the workplace. . . . I will not allow this committee or anyone else to probe into my private life" (quoted in "Thomas, Hill Make Statements," 1991, 2980–81). He accomplished this message both by instruction and by his refusal to answer questions dealing with certain topics.

A second relational message, also created solely by Thomas, established Thomas's relation to Hill's charges. By not listening to Hill's testimony ("Thomas, Hill Field Questions," 1991, 3070), Thomas confirmed his position; he could ignore Hill's messages if he so desired. His choice of disconfirmation rather than rejection indicates his assertion of status and power relative to Hill's. By not presenting a different version of the time line—Thomas repeatedly stated that he could think of "nothing" that could have prompted Hill's allegations ("Thomas, Hill Make Statements," 1991, 2981)—he further displayed that he could exercise his prerogative to dismiss Hill's narrative without needing to provide any action in its place.

A third relational message was translated by witnesses for Thomas. The Thomas defense included female witnesses, some of whom testified in the televised hearings. All these witnesses either currently worked for or had worked for Thomas; all testified that Thomas had never harassed them. The relational message, then, was that Thomas did not abuse power or status in the relationships he had with women in general. He established his authority to deny a single woman's individual reality. The power differential was marked by Thomas's relational affiliation with his office staff.

Finally, Thomas presented a posture in relation to the senators. Using race as the vehicle, he established a relationship of power wherein he had authorization to indict his prosecutors. Thomas called the hearings a "high-tech lynching" and indicated that the committee had played "into the most bigoted, racist stereotypes that any black man will face" (quoted in Berke, 1991, 11). With his message that this Euro-American panel was abusing him, an African American man, he expressed not only that he was in a position of one who could indict but also that the Euro-American abuse of African Americans applied only to him. Although Hill also was African American, Thomas did not include her in his relational posturing. His two-fold message asserted his position as a player equal to or superior to the committee and his position as separate and distinct from Hill.

Assessing the Narratives and the Relational Messages

The initial overwhelming support for Thomas becomes more understandable after examining both the narratives and the relational messages. While the narrative thread of fantasy appears less central than the others, the practical issues of the passage of time and possible monetary gain clearly would appeal to a middle-class viewing audience. When combined with relational issues that Thomas used to present himself as an assertive, powerful individual who was being indicted by a racially bigoted panel, Thomas's appeal can be explained.

In addition, the culpability issue directly relates to Ronald Riggio and Howard Friedman's (1983) conclusions that personality and social skills play important roles in deception detection. At the time of the hearings, women charging sexual harassment generally were regarded with suspicion (unlike the store owner, for example, who can charge embezzlement and cast suspicion on the person accused). That suspicion could account for how large numbers of the viewing audience selected and interpreted deception cues differently.

Hill's narrative existed completely within the frame of the sexual harassment allegation. As such, her presentation also was subject to the same selection and interpretation screen as was Thomas's culpability argument. Other than a few descriptors at the beginning of her opening statement, Hill presented little about herself that was not within the realm of the harassment situation; senators who questioned her did not move her out of that context except when she introduced her family before her testimony began.

Thomas, however, established his relationship with the committee as one in which he determined the boundaries of the presentation before the committee. He presented himself as a son (indicting the senators for causing his mother great physical pain), as an African American, and as a Supreme Court nominee. Differences in the relationship constructed between Thomas and the panel and between Hill and the panel affected significantly the ways in which the audience might assess each.

Survey Results

The survey was used to collect others' responses to the hearings and to compare and contrast participants' reasons for believing Hill or Thomas with the conclusions of the analysis of narratives and relational messages. The survey revealed two gross but significant findings. The first, and most surprising, was that nearly half the respondents marked that they were inclined in some degree to believe that Thomas harassed Hill. Less than one-fourth (22 percent) of the participants marked that they were inclined in some degree to believe that he did not. This reversal of opinion from those opinions expressed during and immediately following the hearings added complexity to the consideration of the question about why so many more people believed Thomas than Hill during the hearings.

The second finding echoed the message heard during and immediately following the hearings: differences in who believed what did not split along sex lines. On nearly all questions, both those answered by the scales and those answered by essays, the proportion of answers by males and females was equal or nearly equal. In other words, both males and females believed in approximately equal numbers that Hill told the truth; likewise, both believed that Thomas told the truth. An equal number identified this particular sexual harassment case as interesting and important.

Upon discovering that twice as many participants in this survey believed Hill's narrative than believed Thomas's, I became particularly interested in those narrative threads or relational messages that had endured over the six months. Any threads or messages not in evidence from these respondents might have been effectual short-term strategies but not enduring ones. I also considered what intervening actions might have continued to work as persuasive means by which beliefs were changed.

Participants' Reported Beliefs

People who believed Hill had been harassed tended to believe Hill's examples about the harassing behaviors. The most common way people expressed their belief was saying that they believed Thomas had engaged in "sexually inappropriate" behavior, that he had harassed Hill and others, and that he made sexual advances in the office.

This category of responses echoes the narrative thread established by Hill:

identifiable sexual harassment had occurred. Participants' comments recalling examples and specific behaviors Hill described suggest that the people who wrote these answers might have experienced sexual harassment in the past or known someone who had. Interestingly, however, only 40 percent of the people who marked themselves as most extreme ("absolutely sure" or "very sure" that Thomas harassed Hill) reported that they had been sexually harassed.

To understand more fully why Hill's examples and assertions were believed, other categories of answers on the survey were considered. Although the largest number of responses expressed the belief that sexual harassment occurred, five other smaller groups of responses emerged. The amalgamation of those groups provides clarification.

That Hill "simply told the truth" is supported by belief in her sincerity. "She was convincing," wrote several respondents, "because she had no reason to lie." Others believed that Hill did not expect this hearing and that as a young professional she would have been afraid at the time to pursue a complaint. These remarks reiterated Hill's narrative thread that she gained nothing by this disclosure.

Participants noted Hill's demeanor and emotional appeal as credible. Several participants wrote that Hill's description of Thomas's "lewd remarks," sexual vocabulary, and Thomas's style of talk was believable. In the last small group of comments, respondents wrote they believed that Hill believed she had been sexually harassed. When asked what they believed about Anita Hill's testimony, only one respondent wrote, "All of it." Approximately one-fourth reported that they either had no answer or did not know or remember enough to respond.

In the group who believed Hill was harassed, then, the most enduring factors seemed to be the threads of her narrative theme rather than her relational messages. In particular, the group believed that Hill had been harassed based on Hill's examples of behavior and depictions of language. They recalled and believed her narrative about having no reason to lie; they extended her narrative by responding to the criticism developed in Thomas's narrative that Hill had waited too long to confront him.

A synthesis of responses from people who believed Thomas had not harassed Hill had a strong central theme: "I believe everything Thomas said." Nearly one-fourth of the respondents who marked that they were "absolutely sure" or "very sure" Thomas had not harassed Hill also answered that they believed everything or almost everything in the Thomas narrative. Another fourth reported they had no answer to the question, "What do you believe about what Clarence Thomas said in his testimony?"

The other half of the participants in the survey did not offer a variety of responses. Unlike the people who believed harassment occurred, these participants had more answers that were similar. Participants cited the testimony of Thomas's female coworkers and the fact that no other complaints had been lodged against him as reasons they believed Thomas. These answers support Thomas's relational message in which he aligned himself with the women who worked in his department. They also deny Hill's relational assertion that she—one woman alone—could put forward this account.

Several people noted that interaction did occur between Hill and Thomas but that the interaction was not sexual harassment. For example, one wrote that Thomas's "off-hand things were not meant as they were taken." Another suggested that Thomas had probably asked Hill out but that their relationship was professional. That Thomas "did nothing to harm her" followed in this category. People who responded in this way relied on Thomas's narrative thread that assigned culpability to Hill for misinterpreting mundane behaviors.

Other comments pointed to Thomas's respect for Hill; he would not "use his position" to harass her. No one mentioned the parts of the Thomas narrative that developed the fantasy thread or the passage time. No mention of language or lying appeared. Surprisingly, no one brought up Thomas's accusations of racial slander as a reason why they believed his story.

Conclusion

Why did people so overwhelmingly believe Thomas? And why did participants in the survey done five months after the event indicate that support had shifted? Although I still am not fully satisfied with answers to these questions, I have discovered information through this study.

First, the fantasy thread of Thomas's narrative evaporated. At the time of the hearings, the fantasy thread constituted a large part of the Thomas narrative. It was cited as the reason for believing Thomas. Yet, after five months reflection, that part of the argument had faded. Perhaps this shift can be accounted for by sexual harassment stories made public in the intervening months between the hearings and the survey. Those stories might have modified reality by familiarizing people with patterns of behavior identified as sexual harassment. Survey respondents who believed the sexual harassment charge recognized language, behavior patterns, and styles of talk.

Interestingly, the very relational messages Thomas made about Hill (his disconfirmation of her by not listening to her testimony) and the narrative thread that she fantasized the sexual harassment are the themes I recognized from my own experiences with sexual harassment. The absence of sexual harassment stories as part of our social lore kept the stories invalidated—fantasies. Hill's relational messages created the channel through which those stories could be made public; even though her messages were not accepted immediately by some of the committee members or by most of the public, they were received by some people in the viewing audience who later reassessed the stories in the light of the emerging stories of sexual harassment.

The same reassessment did not occur with regard to reassigning culpability. Survey participants continued to disbelieve Hill because they reasoned that Thomas might have approached Hill but that his actions did not constitute sexual harassment. Participants cited Thomas's position—not specifically as head of the Equal Employment Opportunity Commission but generally as the chief supervisor in a business environment—as a reason he would not indulge in sexually harassing behaviors. Research on how assumptions about one's position affect the reporting, assessment, and outcomes of sexual harassment cases could be useful.

Another insight this study provided concerns the very question of believability. Perhaps the question of sexual harassment is not just about believing or disbelieving the narrative. Those people who changed their views in response to new narratives may be able to process in a different way new information presented rhetorically; those people who resorted to generalization ("I believe everything") may be operating not from process to conclusion but from conclusion to process.

Deception literature identifies trained and untrained receivers. Perhaps an investigation of the relationship between skill in deception detection and flexibility in attitude change might reveal important information. Considering the two groups together—trained and untrained or skilled and unskilled— may lead to inaccurate conclusions about how the group as a whole processes believability.

Finally, how well a rhetorical framework fits with the idea it carries may affect the audience's immediate response. In this case, one of the rhetorical frameworks included examples and testimony intended to convince listeners that Hill's story was fantasy. This framework—which at the time accomplished the intended response—was not coherent enough to endure long-term scrutiny. The framework dissipated, leaving only generalizations.

The framework Hill used seems to have fit the ideas within it; that framework seems to have endured and persisted. Thomas's framework is much less intact; respondents could not cite their reasons for believing the Thomas narrative with the specificity and detail used by those believing the Hill narrative. Perhaps that lack of fit was an essential ingredient in the dissonance that prompted this research.

Research might focus on identifying which threads or narratives in such controversial situations function to service attitudes already formed and which operate as constructs for new reasons to believe a story. In other words, the fantasy thread seemed to operate as a placebo for people who were predisposed not to believe Hill. It provided a reason. When that reason dissolved upon the revelation of multiple similar stories, participants resorted to believing "everything" Thomas said. Closer study of those participants on both sides of the issue who relied on "everything" as a way to explain their belief might reveal interesting relationships between their pre-testimony and post-testimony positions.

REFERENCES

Accuser put under attack as senators question judge. (1991, October 13). *New York Times*, I29.
Berke, R. L. (1991, October 13). Thomas backers attack Hill; judge, vowing he won't quit, says he is victim of race stigma. *New York Times*, I1.
Bowker, J. K. (1993). Reporting sexual harassment: Reconciling power, knowledge, and perspective. In Gary Kreps (ed.), *Sexual harassment: Communication implications*, 195–205. Cresskill, N.J.: Hampton Press.
Confirmation of Clarence Thomas: The public's view. (1991, October 11). *New York Times*, A1, A18.
Greene, J. O., O'Hair, H. D., Cody, M. J., and Yen, C. (1985). Planning and control of behavior during deception. *Human Communication Research*, 11: 335–64.
Hill, A. F. (1992, October 16). Marriage and patronage: The empowerment and disempowerment of African-American women. Speech delivered at the Georgetown University Law Center in Washington, D.C.

Johnson, D. (1991, October 14). Puzzled and disgusted but fixated on hearings. *New York Times*, A16.

Kolbert, E. (1991, October 15). Most in national survey say judge is the more believable. *New York Times*, A1.

Kurasawa, T. (1988). Effects of contextual expectancies on deception-detection. *Japanese Psychological Research*, 30: 114–21.

Lewis, N. A. (1991, October 13). Judge's backers take up his defense, posing motive and method for accuser. *New York Times*, I28.

Littlepage, G. E., Maddox, J., and Pineault, M. A. (1985). Recognition of discrepant nonverbal messages and detection of deception. *Perceptual and Motor Skills*, 60: 119–24.

Many blacks say Thomas case hurts them all. (1991, October 14). *New York Times*, A16.

Phelps, T. M., and Winternitz, H. (1992). *Capitol Games: Clarence Thomas, Anita Hill, and the story of a Supreme Court nomination*. New York: Hyperion.

Questions to those who corroborated Hill account. (1991, October 14). *New York Times*, A13–14.

Riggio, R. E., and Friedman, H. S. (1983). Individual differences and cues to deception. *Journal of Personality and Social Psychology*, 45: 899–915.

Thomas, Hill field questions before Judiciary Committee. (1991, October 13). *Congressional Quarterly Weekly Report*, 49: 3068–74.

Thomas, Hill make statements as panel begins hearings. (1991, October 12). *Congressional Quarterly Weekly Report*, 49: 2979–82.

The Thomas nomination: Republicans and Democrats alternate in questioning. (1991, October 12). *New York Times*, L13.

Thomas rebuts accuser: I deny each and every allegation. (1991, October 12). *New York Times*, I14.

With each round of testimony, the mood at the Thomas hearings sways. (1991, October 14). *New York Times*, A1.

Tracking Reactions: Audience Evaluations of the Hill–Thomas Hearings

LYNDA LEE KAID, JOHN TEDESCO,
AND CLIFFORD A. JONES

The events of October 11–14, 1991, will surely go down in history as some of the most controversial proceedings in American politics. A black conservative male nominated for a position on the U.S. Supreme Court was accused of sexually harassing a black female lawyer who formerly served as his assistant. The hearings turned into a trial that television brought into the living rooms of Americans. The accused labeled the hearings a "high-tech lynching," and the intimate testimony of Clarence Thomas and Anita Hill was competing for ratings against such programs as *Days of Our Lives* and *General Hospital.* As the drama unfolded, Americans were positioned to take sides in this mediated trial. From the initial public acknowledgement of Hill's affidavit in the October 6 *Newsday* to the end of the hearings on October 14, evaluations of Hill and Thomas and the treatment of them by the Senate Judiciary Committee shifted rapidly. Since the hearings there has continued to be a great deal of media attention to them, and they have become the focus of many interpersonal debates. There are still many unanswered questions communication scholars could ask related to people's reactions to the hearings. As the hearings proceeded, at what points did public opinion shift? Are there differences in the evaluations of Hill and Thomas along lines of gender and political affiliation? What are the elements of Hill's and Thomas's testimony that make them believable or unbelievable? How was the questioning of Hill and Thomas by the Senate Judiciary Committee members evaluated?

The purpose and method of research reported in this essay is similar to that undertaken by Lynda Lee Kaid, Valerie Downs, and Sandra Ragan (1990) in their analysis of the infamous 1988 George Bush–Dan Rather encounter on the CBS Evening News. The purpose is to provide an in-depth look at the proceedings of the Hill-Thomas hearings. A pretest/posttest design was used to measure the effects of the various segments of the hearings and to measure change in audience evaluations.

Confirmation Hearings

The confirmation hearings proceeded much like a trial. The defendant and plaintiff, Thomas and Hill, were allowed to give opening statements and then were put on the witness stand, so to speak, for scrutiny by the Senate Judiciary Committee. Over the course of the three-day event, Thomas gave an opening defense, followed by Hill's opening charges, questioning of Hill, and Thomas's questioning and defense.

In many ways, the hearings resembled an attack–rebuttal sequence. Kaid, Downs, and Ragan's research (1990) sets a good precedent for the applicability of this setting and its relation to negative political advertising research and argumentation research. Researchers have found that there is a relationship between an attack and the image of the attacker and the target (Kaid, Downs, and Ragan, 1990; Kaid and Boydston, 1987). Findings indicate that backlash from an attack can occur and that the image of the attacker can be damaged (Merritt, 1984). It has also been found that an unrefuted attack can hurt the attacked (Bailey, 1988). Additional research in the area of negative political advertising has found that the evaluation of the attacker can become more negative as a result of rebutting the attack (Garramone, 1985). By evaluating Thomas's opening statement, Hill's opening statement, Hill's questioning, and Thomas's rebuttal, the researchers hoped to uncover whether the attack-rebuttal sequence produced any marked difference in the evaluations of Hill and Thomas and whether Thomas's failure to address the specifics of Hill's attack had any effect on the evaluations. The first research question was, What were the differences in audience evaluations of Hill and Thomas as the hearings proceeded?

Gender and Political Affiliation

Two clear variables that affected the evaluations of Hill and Thomas were gender and political affiliation. From the beginning to the end of the hearings, opinion polls attempted to measure Hill's and Thomas's support. A poll by ABC News and the *Washington Post* showed interesting shifts of support for Hill and Thomas from October 6, the day the story about Hill's affidavit was published in *Newsday*, until October 15, the day of the Senate vote. Prior to the *Newsday* story, support for Thomas's confirmation among men and women differed by four points; 65 percent of men and 61 percent of women favored it. Shortly after Hill's charges were made public, the gap between men and women doubled; 51 percent of men supported Thomas to 43 percent of women. These figures indicate a 14 percent drop in male support for Thomas and an 18 point drop in female support for Thomas. Hill's testimony did much in the way of adding to differences in the support Thomas received. Following her testimony, there was a 16 percent gap between males and females; 59 percent of males and 43 percent of females thought Thomas should be confirmed. This indicates that Hill's testimony apparently did not decrease the percentage of women who would support Thomas but did increase the percentage of men who thought Thomas should be confirmed. This appears to support the notion of backlash from an attack that is found in the negative political advertising research (Merritt, 1984). However, by the time the hearings were complete, gender support for Thomas was back to a 4 percent difference, with 61 percent of men and 57 percent of women supporting Thomas (Alston, 1991). It is unclear, though, whether the gap in time between the hearings and this research had allowed opinions on Hill and Thomas to solidify or whether reactions to the testimony segments would still create a difference in evaluations of Hill and Thomas.

Since the hearings, there has been much debate about partisan politics and the battle lines that were drawn during the hearings. For example, in *Capitol Games*, Timothy Phelps and Helen Winternitz (1992) argue that the Bush administration supported Clarence Thomas's nomination as part of its attempt to limit women's freedoms. They assert that the Bush administration sought to control women's reproductive, economic, political, and social power by nominating a conservative. Democrats were criticized for failing to hold Thomas responsible for his poor civil rights record. "Likewise," Margaret Burnham (1992) argues, "women were not mobilized because of Thomas' anti-women's-rights record so far as civil rights is concerned; rather, abortion became the central issue of women's rights organizations, and the senators followed suit" (316). Democrats made an issue of Thomas's clear opposition to the Democratic platform (a platform supported by most blacks), but they failed in their attempt to mobilize their opposition to Thomas's confirmation (Burnham, 1992).

The failure of the Democrats is also clear in their questioning of Thomas. Many observers have suggested that Thomas was not put through nearly as tough a segment of questioning as Hill was. Members of the Senate Judiciary Committee did not probe Thomas's categorical denial of all allegations, and they did not ask Thomas to recount and support his defense.

Gender and political affiliation thus seemed important in the Thomas confirmation. These variables lead the researchers to ask the following questions: Were differences in evaluations based on gender or political affiliation and how did the audience judge the questioning of Hill and Thomas? Another interesting question about the Hill-Thomas hearings is, Did prior media exposure to the hearings affect audience reactions to Hill and Thomas?

Methodology

A total of 121 undergraduate students from three major research universities located in different parts of the country were shown videotaped recordings of the Hill-Thomas hearings. Approximately an hour and a half of edited coverage of the confirmation hearings was compiled for the purposes of this study. The taped coverage was divided into four segments to measure changes in posttest evaluations of the hearings. A pretest was administered to all subjects to measure their perceptions of Clarence Thomas and Anita Hill. Subjects were then shown portions of the hearings and asked to complete a questionnaire following each segment. The pretest/posttest design was chosen because it helped to control for prior perceptions of Clarence Thomas and Anita Hill. The pretest/posttest design offered a measure to determine whether exposure to taped coverage of the hearings elicited change, even though subjects might have had a decided pretest preference.

Subjects at one research location were randomly assigned to one of two study groups. Both groups at this location received the same treatment that the groups at the other universities did; however, responses for one group were recorded throughout the hearings by utilizing a computerized audience response system.

Hearings Materials Selected

Researchers determined how the hearings could be edited to create a tape that reflected the entire hearings process. The resulting hour and a half of coverage was broken down into four sections. Segment one, which was about fifteen-and-a-half minutes long, contained Thomas's opening statement, in which he was sworn in and proceeded to deny the allegations of sexual harassment and detail the relationship he had with Hill. Segment two, which was also about fifteen minutes long, contained most of Hill's opening statement, in which she detailed the charges of sexual harassment against Thomas. Section three, about twenty-six minutes long, contained extensive questioning of Hill by the committee. Section four, about thirty-four minutes long, contained Thomas's response statement, in which he "categorically" denied all allegations of sexual harassment, and excerpts from his questioning.

Test Instruments

The test instruments were developed to measure the research questions of this study. First, subjects answered pretest questionnaires. The pretest questionnaires contained three major question areas: (1) demographic information about the subjects, (2) feelings toward Hill and Thomas, and (3) previous exposure to the hearings. Subjects also recorded their reactions to Hill and Thomas on seven-point semantic differential scales containing twelve bipolar adjectives (e.g., believable/unbelievable).[1] These scales were developed from similar scales that have been successfully used to measure image since 1968 (Kaid and Boydston, 1985; Sanders and Pace, 1977). As with the previous studies, the scales produced high reliability. For this study, Cronbach's alpha equaled .76 for the Thomas pretest, .80 for the Hill pretest, .84 for the Thomas posttest, and .80 for the Hill posttest. Feelings about Hill and Thomas also were recorded on a feeling thermometer, which allowed a range of 0 to 100. The University of Michigan Center for Political Studies has used this thermometer in their traditional voter election studies (Miller and Levitin, 1976). Subjects also were asked to indicate, using a seven-point disagree-agree scale, agreement with statements about who was telling the truth. Posttest questionnaires were administered following each segment of the hearings described above.

Posttest questionnaires contained the semantic differential scales; the feeling thermometer; the questions concerning who was telling the truth; and questions about whether the hearing process was appropriate, fair, biased, or difficult for the participants. Open-ended questions also asked subjects to record what stood out in their minds about the hearings and how they felt about the participants. Additionally, for one of the groups, a continuous computerized measurement system was used to measure subject responses to Thomas and Hill throughout the portions of the hearings. The continuous measurement system is a hand-held electronic device with a seven-point dial. The respondents were asked to move the dial from one to seven to indicate how positively or negatively they felt about the participant speaking at the moment (one for very negative to seven for very positive). If they had no feelings or were not sure about the speaker, they were instructed to indicate that by a neutral response, which was a four on the dial. Each of the hand-held dials was linked to a computer, which recorded the continuous responses to the individual speaking. The computer overlaid this information on a video copy of the hearings as they progressed. This measurement was important to indicate statements and periods in which Hill and Thomas received their highest and lowest ratings from respondents.

Test Groups

The test group for this study contained 121 undergraduate communication students.[2] The study was conducted at the following three large research universities in an attempt to control for locational bias: the University of Oklahoma, where the group consisted of 25 females and 15 males (N = 40); Ohio University in Athens, where there were 32 female and 16 male subjects (N = 48); and the University of North Carolina at Chapel Hill, where there were 28 females and 5 males in the study (N = 33).

Results

One of the first concerns in analyzing the results of this study was whether the three separate locations would affect the evaluations. Analysis of pretest evaluations of Hill and Thomas in all three locations based on t-tests of differences on the semantic differential scales and on the initial feeling thermometer measure indicated that there was little difference among the three locales. Basically, the participants in all three locales had the same initial impressions of Hill and Thomas. The only exception was that the participants in North Carolina had a somewhat lower evaluation of Thomas than did those in Ohio. Because of these overall similarities, the data from all three locales were combined for the analysis reported here.

Differences in Audience Evaluations during the Hearings

Before viewing the hearings, participants had essentially the same overall evaluations of Hill and Thomas (see table 1). Even though two years had passed, the participants rated both figures exactly the same on the pretest semantic differential scales measuring overall images (each was given a score of 4.63 as the summed average of all twelve scales). The same equivalence of evaluation also was apparent in the ratings of both on the feeling thermometer, on which Hill received a warmth rating of 51.60 and Thomas a rating of 51.34. Before viewing, participants also judged the truth-telling likelihood of each to be about the same (4.16 for Hill and 4.11 for Thomas).

At the conclusion of the viewing in this study, however, there had been a decided shift in favor of Clarence Thomas (see table 1). Not only did Thomas's overall image evaluation show a significant positive shift (while Hill's stayed the same), but his warmth rating increased a full ten points, to 61.06 The judgment of his truth-telling also rose substantially. By contrast, Hill's warmth rating declined to 42.68, and judgment of her truth-telling also declined nearly a full point, to 3.23.

TABLE 1. Differences in Evaluations of Hill and Thomas[a]

	Hill	Thomas
Overall image evaluations		
Before viewing	4.63	4.63
After viewing	4.65	5.19[b]
Feeling thermometer		
Before viewing	51.60	51.34
After Thomas opening	47.71	59.80[c]
After Hill opening	51.98	53.12
After Hill questioning	45.80	58.03[c]
After Thomas questioning	42.68	61.06[c]
Believe telling the truth		
Before viewing	4.16	4.11
After Thomas opening	3.45	4.96[c]
After Hill opening	4.31	4.26
After Hill questioning	3.60	4.61[c]
After Thomas questioning	3.23	5.00[c]

a. N = 121.

b. T-test indicates that difference between before and after viewing is significant at
p ≤ .001.

c. T-test indicates that difference between evaluation of Hill and Thomas is significant at p ≤ .05.

Perhaps even more interesting is what table 1 reveals about the process of the decline in Hill's evaluations and the rise in Thomas's. Although they started out with the same ratings on the feeling thermometer and in terms of truth-telling, Thomas's opening statement gave him a clear lift. When it was over, his warmth rating and truth-telling evaluation had risen substantially, and Hill's had fallen to the point that Thomas then had a statistically significant edge over her on both items.

Hill's own opening statement obviously repaired some of that damage, raising her warmth and truth-telling ratings and producing a decline in Thomas's ratings. After her opening, there was again a leveling of the scores for Hill and Thomas to the point that after her opening there was again no significant difference between their standing on either rating item.

The turning point for both Thomas and Hill was the questioning of Hill by the senators on the Judiciary Committee. After they questioned her, her ratings fell substantially on both the warmth thermometer and the truth-telling index. Thomas's ratings climbed back up so that he was once again rated as significantly higher than Hill. These results were further magnified when

Thomas returned for his response and questioning. By the time his question-ing period concluded, his warmth and truth-telling ratings not only were substantially higher than his before-viewing ratings but also were significantly higher than Hill's.

Differences Based on Gender

The data in this study indicate that there were substantial differences between how males and females evaluated the two protagonists at every stage in the hearing process. As table 2 shows, before the viewing in this study began, fe-males had significantly higher overall evaluations of Hill (4.81) than of Thom-as (4.56), while males evaluated Thomas (4.78) more favorably than Hill (4.22). A similar pattern is apparent in the initial feeling thermometer (warmth) rat-ings and the truth-telling index.

At the conclusion of the viewing, however, both males and females evalu-ated Thomas more favorably than Hill. Again, as in the overall data, it is easy

TABLE 2. Differences in Hill-Thomas Ratings Based on Gender[a]

	Female (n = 85)		Male (n = 36)	
	Hill	Thomas	Hill	Thomas
Overall image evaluation				
Before viewing	4.81	4.56[b]	4.22	4.78[b]
After viewing	4.84	5.14[b]	4.21	5.29[b]
Feeling thermometer				
Before viewing	56.28	47.27	40.53	60.94
After Thomas opening	51.52	56.78	38.72	66.92
After Hill opening	57.12	49.47	39.83	61.75
After Hill questioning	51.38	54.94	32.61	65.33
After Thomas questioning	48.29	57.07	29.42	70.47
Believe telling truth				
Before viewing	4.51	3.73	3.33	4.67
After Thomas opening	3.71	4.72	2.86	5.53
After Hill opening	4.69	3.98	3.42	4.92
After Hill questioning	3.99	4.36	2.67	5.19
After Thomas questioning	3.56	4.72	2.44	5.67

a. T-tests indicate that there is a significant difference between male and female evaluations of Hill and Thomas on all items, except for the After-Viewing Image Evaluation of Thomas.

b. T-test indicates that difference in how each gender evaluated Hill versus Thomas is significant at p ≤ .05.

to see how the evaluations progressed throughout the stages of the hearings to give an edge to Thomas on all of the measures at the conclusion of the hearings. As before, for both men and women, the ratings swung back and forth between Hill and Thomas, until after the senators' questioning of Anita Hill, at which point Hill's evaluations declined across all measures as Thomas's ratings rose.

It is important to note, though, that even as the pattern repeated itself across the stages of the hearings, females always rated Hill significantly higher and Thomas significantly lower than did males. Thus, although the direction of the changes for Hill and Thomas was the same, gender was an important determinant of the comparative rating level for each.

Differences in Evaluations Based on Partisanship

The expected differences by party affiliation also were present in this study, as can be seen in table 3. Like gender, partisanship was a significant indicator

TABLE 3. Differences in Hill-Thomas Evaluations Based on Party Affiliation

	Democrat (n = 32)		Republican (n = 51)	
	Hill	Thomas	Hill	Thomas
Overall image evaluation				
Before viewing	4.97	4.43[a]	4.61	4.65[a]
After viewing	4.93	4.98[a]	4.89	5.31[a]
Feeling thermometer				
Before viewing	59.79	41.93	48.10	57.55
After Thomas opening	54.79	50.44	44.96	65.80
After Hill opening	63.42	43.42	47.86	58.35
After Hill questioning	55.35	48.98	42.08	63.20
After Thomas questioning	51.37	52.30	38.98	65.86
Believe telling truth				
Before viewing	5.00	3.19	3.71	4.49
After Thomas opening	4.12	4.26	3.04	5.33
After Hill opening	5.16	3.42	3.86	4.65
After Hill questioning	4.40	4.00	3.20	4.82
After Thomas questioning	3.93	4.35	2.90	5.31

a. T-test indicates that difference within party for evaluation of Hill versus Thomas is significant at p ≤ .05.
   In every case on the feeling thermometer and the truth-telling index, t-tests indicated that the difference between Republicans and Democrats for both Hill and Thomas is significant at p ≤ .05.

of responses. Democrats viewed Hill significantly more positively than Republicans did at the outset. As the encounter progressed, however, these differences leveled off for Democrats, who came to view Thomas with more "warmth" (on the feeling thermometer) and to believe that he was telling the truth. Republicans not only increased their regard for Thomas but also found themselves even more critical of Hill on all measures by the end of the viewing period.

Evaluating the Questioning of Hill and Thomas

The findings indicating that the critical turning point in the evaluations of the protagonists was the senators' questioning of Anita Hill makes an understanding of the questioning process even more important. Respondents were asked to indicate their level of agreement or disagreement with a series of statements evaluating the questioning process for Hill and Thomas. When the responses are grouped into summary agree/disagree ratings for each question, it is easy to see that the majority of respondents believed that Anita Hill was asked more stringent and trying questions than Thomas was. For instance, whereas 53.6 percent of the respondents believed that the questioning of Thomas had been "fair," only 40.0 percent believed that Hill had been treated fairly. Over 65.0 percent of the respondents believed that Hill "had been asked difficult questions," but only 38.0 percent felt the same about Thomas's questions.

There also was a strong difference in beliefs about the bias of the questions. Nearly half of the respondents (47 percent) thought that the questioning of Anita Hill had been "biased." Only 35 percent saw bias in the questioning of Clarence Thomas.

Effect of Prior Exposure to Hearings on Evaluations

One obvious concern in a study of this type was whether prior exposure to the hearings or to media reports about them might have affected respondents' evaluations of Hill and Thomas. To test this, questions were asked about whether the respondents had seen the hearings when they were held live and how much they had heard about the hearings in the media.

Surprisingly few respondents had seen the hearings before the experimental session. In fact, 70 percent of the respondents said they had not seen the hearings at all. Only eight people (6.6 percent) of the sample said they had seen all or most of the hearings. Most people had, however, heard something about the hearings: 25 percent had heard "a great deal," and 48 percent had heard "some" information. Despite the notoriety of the event, 24 percent of the sample said they had seen very little about it, and 3 percent had seen nothing at all in the media about it.

Perhaps more important than the amount of actual exposure is whether the exposure shaped the respondents' views of Hill and Thomas. To test this, the amount of exposure to the hearings in the media was correlated with the pre-exposure image evaluations (semantic differential scales) of Hill and Thomas. The amount of media exposure did correlate significantly with Hill's evaluation ($r = .19$; $p \le .05$), indicating that the more exposure a respondent had to media reports about the hearings, the more positively Hill was evaluated. No such significant correlation existed between media exposure and Thomas's evaluation.

Discussion

These results comparing evaluations of Hill and Thomas over the course of the hearings do a great deal to confirm prior speculation about the effect of the hearing process. The respondents in this study were relatively uncontaminated in that most had not seen the hearings before and they started out with the same evaluations of Hill and Thomas. It is not unfair, then, to suggest that the effects of this abbreviated exposure to the hearings were a very realistic test of how viewers might have responded at the time of the actual hearings. If that is the case, then these results indicate that the outcome in Clarence Thomas's favor is a direct result of the tough questioning of Anita Hill by the Senate Judiciary Committee members.

This result, documented in the segment-by-segment data analysis above, is also mirrored in the findings from the computer automated response system utilized by one group of the respondents. The continuous response system helps us understand why the trial nature of the hearings worked to help Thomas and hurt Hill. The confirmation hearings were characterized by some, including members of the Senate Judiciary Committee, as a trial, at least in some respects. In reality, it was not a trial, and few of the traditional safeguards of fairness were observed. Consciously or unconsciously, the committee endowed the proceedings with some of the trappings of judicial procedure, creating the impression that fairness was a consideration. The reality was that many aspects of the hearing procedures and conduct contravened rules traditionally applied to ensure fair trials. Some of these deviations from convention directly contributed to perceptions measured during the viewing of the stimulus materials in this study.

One curious aspect of the procedure was that Thomas began the hearings on Anita Hill's allegations by presenting his defense before Hill had presented her charges. Thomas thus claimed the advantage of primacy and had the opportunity to establish his position and his credibility before the charges were aired. The continuous measurement system indicates that he was successful in this; his mean ratings began at the neutral position (four) and ended on a positive note, ranging throughout from four to five. This procedure is contrary to traditional concepts of fairness in judicial proceedings.

One traditional notion of fairness in American jurisprudence is that the burden of proof is on the accuser—the accused is innocent until proven guilty. In recognition of this burden, the accuser has the privilege of going first and last—a sort of judicial primacy-recency theory. The Thomas confirmation hearings violated this premise in that Thomas was permitted to go first to establish his defense before Hill presented her testimony in support of her allegations. At the same time, the committee frequently reminded everyone that Thomas was innocent until proven guilty, thereby not only giving Thomas the tactical persuasive advantage of opening the proceedings but also cloaking him with a presumption of innocence, appropriate to a criminal trial but somewhat out of place in a confirmation hearing.

The continuous computer measurement system ratings strongly suggested another advantage that accrued to Thomas through methods prohibited in real trials. During one portion of Thomas's statement, he rhetorically questioned how the average person or the members of the Judiciary Committee would like these things said about them, referring to "false" and "sleaze." He repeated these rhetorical questions three times, during which his ratings quickly rose from 4.36 to 5.02 within seconds, indicating that he had struck a sympathetic and responsive chord with the experimental subjects. In trial practice, this sort of argument is called a Golden Rule argument—do unto others as you would have others do unto you—and is flatly forbidden as a form of improper and prejudicial argument that appeals to sympathy as a basis for decision rather than to fact or evidence. Yet Thomas employed it with graphically demonstrable success.

One accusation/question by Senator Arlen Specter that produced a strong negative reaction to Hill on the continuous measurement graph was his professed opinion that Hill had committed perjury. This statement, injected as a "question" to Thomas, is another example of how traditional trial procedures designed to ensure fairness were not observed. First, it was not a question at all but was an accusation that Hill had committed a crime. Second, it was repeated at least three times, which would not normally be allowed. Third, it represented Specter's injection of his own belief or opinion, a tactic that not only would cause it to be stricken if in a trial but also would subject Specter to professional discipline as a violation of the American Bar Association Rules of Professional Conduct, Rule 3.4(e).

Another incident producing a strong negative reaction to Hill on the continuous measurement graph was an affidavit by John Doggett accusing Hill of imagining that he had a romantic interest in her. Whether Doggett ever had an interest in Hill, whether Hill ever had an interest in Doggett, or whether either of them had an overactive imagination about that incident was not at issue in the Thomas hearings. In a real trial, neither the Doggett affidavit nor Doggett testimony regarding such an incident would have been permitted.

The continuous measurement graph also signaled a strong positive response for Thomas when both Thomas and members of the committee argued that only Hill had accused Thomas of sexual harassment and that no other women had come forward to accuse Thomas of harassing them. During Thomas's testimony on this point, his mean rating rose from 4.57 to 4.82. Thomas presented witnesses, referred to in his testimony, who testified that Thomas never harassed them and that they did not see him harass Hill. Such testimony by witnesses or senators would not be admitted in a real trial. Proof that Thomas did not harass a dozen other people no more disproves that Thomas harassed Hill than proof that Lee Harvey Oswald never shot Dwight Eisenhower disproves that Oswald did shoot John Kennedy. A murderer is not excused for killing one person on the grounds that he did not kill anyone else. The implication, of course, was that if Hill alone had claimed harassment, she must be lying. This argument is not only irrelevant but also prejudicial in that it presumes that harassers necessarily deal in bulk or wholesale quantities, or not at all. However, this argument permeated the hearings.

Traditional trial procedures were utterly disregarded in the questioning of Hill and Thomas, although the violations were to Hill's disadvantage in almost every case. Senators routinely, almost exclusively, propounded "questions" that would not be permitted in a courtroom. Most "questions" were speeches or unsworn testimony by the senators, not questions to the witnesses. Many "questions" included material that was not in evidence or was not intended to be offered as evidence. Many were editorials or pontifications that might be appropriate in a speech but could not be considered questions. Repetitions ran rampant. Over the course of the hearings, senators constantly repeated the same statement/questions to the same witness for the sake of emphasis and repetition, conduct that would not have been allowed in a trial. The putative questioning of Thomas was used by the committee not to press Thomas for details or substantiation but to repeat the senators' own opinions and statements. During much of Thomas's second appearance, he often did not even respond to the "questions" of the senators, because they were not questions. The continuous response system demonstrated that Thomas benefited greatly from these tactics.

The findings from the continuous computer responses also provide support for the differences between male and female evaluations and differences based on political partisanship. The overall mean score differences for Thomas and Hill on the computerized dials were about the same during Hill's and Thomas's opening statements, but the mean scores for Thomas's opening statement ranged from 4.17 to 5.50 for males and 4.07 to 5.00 for females. For both males and females, Thomas received his lowest rating during the first thirty seconds of his statement, indicating that Thomas's statement was rated very positively as it progressed. The highest mean score evaluation for both males and females occurred during Thomas's discussion of how he treated Hill as he did every other member of his staff—with support and respect.

Hill's opening statement received much lower mean scores than did Thomas's. Hill's high and low mean scores ranged from 4.08 to 2.17 for males and 4.07 to 3.13 for females (see table 4). Hill scored her highest evaluations from both males and females when she discussed the positive working relationship that she and Thomas had at the Department of Education and her decision to accept a job with Thomas. Although the low mean scores for males and females differed by almost a point, the low scores for both came when Hill introduced graphic depictions of the harassment. The low score of 2.17 for males was recorded during Hill's discussion of the "Coke can incident," and the low score of 3.13 for females was recorded during her description of the

TABLE 4. High and Low Mean Scores from Computer Response[a]

Group	During Opening		During Questioning	
	Thomas	Hill	Hill	Thomas
Males (n = 12)				
High	5.50	4.08	3.67	5.83
Low	4.17	2.17	2.00	4.58
Females (n = 15)				
High	5.00	4.07	4.33	4.67
Low	4.07	3.13	2.80	3.67
Republicans (n = 12)				
High	5.83	4.00	3.75	5.67
Low	4.25	1.92	1.58	4.17
Democrats (n = 8)				
High	5.13	4.75	4.50	4.10
Low	3.50	3.50	3.50	3.38
Independents (n = 7)				
High	4.43	3.86	4.14	5.43
Low	3.86	2.86	2.57	3.86
Mean (n = 27)				
High	5.14	4.07	4.04	5.00
Low	4.36	2.93	2.54	4.25

a. N = 27.

type of pornographic films that Thomas discussed with her. Although males evaluated the graphic details more harshly, it is clear that the graphic description did not work in Hill's favor.

Even more dramatic differences in male and female evaluations of Hill and Thomas came during the questioning segments (see table 4). The mean scores for Hill's questioning ranged from a low of 2.00 to a high of 3.67 for males and a low of 2.80 to a high of 4.33 for females, indicating that females were less harsh on Hill during this difficult questioning phase. The findings are very puzzling though when analyzed by what is said during the high scores for Hill. During this segment both males and females rated Hill the highest when she was recounting again the incident with the Coke can. A possible justification for this could be that the audience was no longer shocked by this description and had become supportive over the course of the hearing process. The increased support for this graphic incident also may indicate increased support for Hill's accusations.

Hill received her lowest mean score from males when the letter from Doggett, which accused Hill of scorning him for leading her on, was introduced. This letter was obviously introduced to discredit Hill's ability to differentiate a friendly conversation from a flirtatious conversation. It worked well to reduce male support for Hill. Females were more critical of Hill when it was suggested that she had accused Thomas as a means to "quietly and behind the scenes" force him to withdraw his nomination. In both cases, her lowest scores occurred when accusations against her by persons outside the hearing process were recounted. Although the credibility of the men who were making accusations about Hill's character is not known, it appears from the scores during Hill's questioning that the introduction of this outside material did much to discredit her character.

The final segment, Thomas's questioning, also reveals some interesting differences between male and female evaluations. Once again, this segment produced a large disparity in mean score evaluations. Mean scores for Thomas ranged from 4.58 to 5.83 for males and from 3.67 to 4.67 for females (see table 4). Males did not view any aspect of Thomas's questioning negatively. This segment resembled closing remarks by Thomas more than a questioning phase, and his sweeping statements received high scores from both males and females. The high scores for males came during Thomas's discussion of stereotypes that the black male has to face in this country. His description of the struggles of the black man did much to add to his credibility among males. Females were more supportive of his scorn for the hearing process and of his statement that the hearing process was more like a circus and a "high-tech lynching."

It is clear from the evaluations and the topics that were discussed at high and low points throughout the evaluations that males and females differed in their responses to Hill and Thomas. It is also clear that the greater disparity in the questioning segments of the hearings caused greater factionalism to develop and males and females to see the hearings along gender lines.

Similar results are found when Republicans, Democrats, and Independents are analyzed. There appears to be greater disparity in evaluations of Hill and Thomas when political affiliation is introduced as a variable (see table 4). In general, Republicans were much more supportive of Thomas than were Democrats or Independents, and Independents were much more supportive of Thomas than they were of Hill. As the hearings progressed, Independents became much more supportive of Thomas; his high mean score evaluations from the first segment to the final segments increased by a full point, from 4.43 to 5.43. Independents' support for Thomas is very similar to that of the Republicans when what is being said during points of high and low evaluations is analyzed. Even more interesting is that Republican and Democrat support appears to mirror the support by males and females. Male and Republican support for Thomas was very similar, and female and Democrat support was very similar. High evaluation scores for Thomas during his opening statement reached a zenith for Republicans and Independents when Thomas discussed his treatment of Hill at the Department of Education. This mirrors the support that males gave Thomas at this same point. Independents were more critical of Thomas when he stated that he categorically denied the allegations Hill made, suggesting that Independents wanted more discussion or proof for Thomas's denial.

Support for Thomas developed along similar lines during his questioning segment. Support for Thomas was high when he took control of the questioning and recounted the stereotypical sexual attitudes in this country and their link to the black man. Thomas's high scores among Democrats were parallel to the support Thomas received from women. During his opening statement, Democrats were supportive of Thomas when he reported his cordial working relationship with Hill. During Thomas's closing remarks, Democrats were most supportive of Thomas when he described his disgust with the hearings process. In his opening statement, Thomas received his lowest score when he discussed the anguish and fear he had felt since Hill's accusations. Democrats were least supportive of Thomas during the few moments that committee members actually asked questions. During the questioning segment, Thomas's low mean score of 3.38 was recorded during his denial of Hill's accusations. His standard "No senator" responses did not appear to hold much weight with Democrats.

What is interesting is that these denials produced the lowest evaluations of Thomas by Independents and Democrats at different points of the hearings. Independents gave Thomas his lowest evaluations when he denied harassment during his opening statement, and Democrats gave Thomas his lowest evaluation during his denial in the closing statements. One might infer from these findings that Democrats' support for Hill would increase throughout the hearings and Independents' support would decrease; however, that was not the case. Independents became more supportive of Hill as the hearings progressed, while Democrat support for Hill remained virtually constant.

It is also interesting that during Hill's questioning, she received highest evaluations among all groups when she discussed the "Coke can incident." Her lowest evaluations occurred when outside attacks on her character were made. It appears from these findings that support for Hill's statements was increasing until the point at which Senator Specter (a Republican from Pennsylvania) introduced damaging attacks on Hill's character. Thomas escaped the hearing process without senators' introducing such damaging attacks to discredit him.

Another aspect of the findings that might shed light on the reasons for the responses in this study comes from the open-ended answers respondents gave after viewing each segment. After each viewing segment, respondents were asked to write in their own words what they "remembered most" about Hill's or Thomas's performance in that segment, what "stood out" in their minds, what their "feelings" were after watching. After Clarence Thomas's opening statement, the most frequently mentioned responses on this part of the questionnaire were that he "was telling the truth," that he seemed "honest" and "sincere," and that he seemed to treat the situation "professionally." Many mentioned that they were impressed with how "emphatically he denied the charges" and with his statement that he was always "speaking against sexual harassment." Many respondents specifically remembered his statements about how harmful these accusations had been to his family, how his elderly mother, "unable to stop crying," was confined to bed. Not every comment was positive; some thought Thomas was simply "a very good liar" and that his "well-rehearsed speech" was designed to "cover up" his actions. Overall, however, the respondents were favorable to Thomas after his opening remarks, and he was very successful in creating sympathy for himself with his references to how the situation was harming his family.

Reactions to Anita Hill's opening statement were more mixed. Some respondents also thought she was "telling the truth," while others specifically commented that she was not being truthful. Several respondents thought she was using her childhood and biographical data as a ploy to "convey innocence." Hill was perceived as a much less polished speaker than Thomas. Some respondents said so explicitly; others commented that she seemed "extremely nervous," upset, and agitated and that her delivery was "choppy." Several specifically felt that her nervousness reduced her credibility and that her halting, sometimes hesitant delivery made her seem unconvincing. Substantively, respondents were most hesitant about believing her because she had waited so long to make the charges and had not said anything about his behavior at the time.

Since the analysis indicated that the senators' questioning of Hill was the crucial point in turning the tide against her, it is particularly interesting to look at the open-ended responses following the viewing of that segment. Again, respondents focused more on the style of her presentation than on its substance. They commented that she seemed "nervous," was "uncomfortable," gave a poor "representation of herself," seemed "meek," and was "hesitant" and "unsure." Beyond these comments about her style, the most frequently mentioned observations after the questioning period were (1) Hill seemed "unable to recall details" and seemed "vague" and unprepared, and (2) she appeared to be contradicting herself. Many respondents came away from this segment believing that Hill had had to "piece her story together." Very few respondents recalled anything positive about Hill from this segment, although a few saw her as sincere, honest, and believable. There is no question, however, from both the tone and respondents' substantive comments after this segment that the senators had been very successful in making her testimony appear "contradictory," "lacking in detail," "inconsistent," and "vague." This points up a strong difference in the way ordinary persons might have responded to Hill's presentation. Where professional observers (some elsewhere in this volume) felt that Hill's problem might have been that she was too calm, too forthcoming, and too at odds with social expectations of women and victims, many observers allowed their impressions of her testimony to be framed by opposing senators and cast the blame onto her.

In the final segment viewed by the respondents in this study, Thomas came back to the committee and made a short statement and was questioned briefly by the senators. Respondents indicated that the most impressive thing about this segment was the absolute fervor with which Thomas denied all the charges. Again, respondents found him to be an excellent, well-prepared, and controlled speaker who was consistent in his story, and they were impressed with the emotional forcefulness and anger he showed at being subjected to the "outrage" of the hearings. Many specifically remembered his reiteration that "enough is enough." These findings seem to indicate that Thomas's anger worked for him instead of signaling that he might be "protesting too much."

His aggressive denial did not suggest to ordinary viewers, as it would to FBI experts (according to Curtis D. LeBaron's essay in this volume), that he might be lying.

Nonetheless the comments after this final segment do show that not all respondents were convinced, despite the overall ratings in Thomas's favor. Some said he "looked guilty," that he was "hot-tempered" and "uncooperative," that he played to male committee members' feelings, and that he capitalized on the racial angle, although it was not relevant to this case.

Finally, it is important to note that these results confirm findings from negative advertising on the importance of rebuttals. Audiences were apparently impressed with Thomas's vehement denials. They cared less for explanations or elaborations; a "categorical" denial was more definitive and believable, letting the viewer off the hook and requiring less soul-searching and none of the difficult critical evaluation process needed to sift through conflicting stories and evidence. Anita Hill's failure might have been at least partly because of her tentativeness, the tendency to qualify and equivocate ingrained in most scholars, and her decision to give up the chance to "have the last word" to rebut the charges leveled against her character.

NOTES

1. The adjectives in the bipolar semantic differential scales were unqualified/qualified; unsophisticated/sophisticated; dishonest/honest; believable/unbelievable; unsuccessful/successful; attractive/unattractive; unfriendly/friendly; insincere/sincere; calm/excitable; aggressive/unaggressive; strong/weak; inactive/active.

2. The authors thank Professor Anne Johnston (School of Journalism and Mass Communication at the University of North Carolina–Chapel Hill) and Professor Christina Beck (Department of Interpersonal Communication at Ohio University) for their assistance in gathering data for this study.

REFERENCES

Alston, C. (1991, October 19). Political fallout from Thomas' quote could cut any number of ways. *Congressional Quarterly Weekly Report, 49*: 3028–29.

Bailey, D. (1988, January). Famous for 15 minutes. *Campaigns and Elections, 9* (1): 47–52.

Burnham, M. A. (1992). The Supreme Court appointment process and the politics of race and sex. In T. Morrison (ed.), *Race-ing justice, en-gender-ing power: Essays on Anita Hill, Clarence Thomas, and the construction of social reality*, 290–322. New York: Pantheon.

Garramone, G. M. (1985). Effects of negative political advertising: The role of sponsor and rebuttal. *Journal of Broadcasting and Electronic Media*, 29: 147–59.

Kaid, L. L., and Boydston, J. (1987). An experimental study of the effectiveness of negative political advertising. *Communication Quarterly*, 35: 193–201.

Kaid, L. L., Downs, V. C., and Ragan, S. (1990). Political argumentation and violations of audience expectations: An analysis of the Bush-Rather encounter. *Journal of Broadcasting and Electronic Media*, 34: 1–15.

Merritt, S. (1984). Negative political advertising: Some empirical findings. *Journal of Advertising*, 13: 27–38.

Miller, W. E., and Levitin, T. E. (1976). *Leadership and change*. Cambridge, Mass.: Winthrop.

Phelps, T., and Winternitz, H. (1992). *Capitol games: Clarence Thomas, Anita Hill, and the story of a Supreme Court nomination*. New York: Hyperion.

Sanders, K. R., and Pace, T. J. (1977). The influence of speech communication on the image of a political candidate: "Limited effects" revisited. In B. D. Ruben (ed.), *Communication yearbook I*, 456–72. New Brunswick, N.J.: Transaction.

The specter of this kind of male judgment, along with misnaming and thwarting of her needs by a culture controlled by males, has created problems for the woman writer: problems of contact with herself, problems of language and style, problems of energy and survival.

ADRIENNE RICH, *On Lies, Secrets, and Silence*

10

Telling the Truth: The Rhetoric of Consistency and Credibility in the Hill–Thomas Hearings

THOMAS J. DARWIN

Few events in our recent past have stormed across the cultural landscape as the Hill-Thomas hearings did. As Nellie McKay (1992) describes it, "It was over in a few days, coming like a hurricane that whipped across the landscape of our lives, leaving a trail of wreckage and a less apparent rainbow in its wake" (269).

This essay analyzes how the "male judgment" of several Republican senators discredited Anita Hill by portraying her as either someone whose behavior was inconsistent with culturally defined roles (and therefore was not credible) or someone who was lying. In this way, the senators were able to silence those explanations of Hill's actions that would make sense if one perceived her as a victim of sexual harassment. The rhetorical strategies the Republican senators employed in the hearings made Hill recognizable to the public only as a lying woman seeking revenge, which thoroughly discredited her and silenced her suffering.

The hearings were as confusing as they were compelling. They raised questions about partisan politics. Why had the Senate agreed to hear this "eleventh hour" testimony? Perhaps Democrats saw a chance to discredit a nominee they strongly opposed. Perhaps the members of the Senate Judiciary Committee believed that they had to give this woman a chance to speak, a chance to tell her story. After all, as many of them said, they were concerned about women's issues.[1] Perhaps they sensed that ignoring the story of a woman making such a serious allegation was bad politics (indeed, the hearings became a significant political issue in congressional races in both Illinois and Pennsylvania).

They also raised questions about relationships between men and women, what was "just the way people are," and what was sexual harassment. No one who watched the hearings could stay neutral. The hearings entangled far more people than just those in the Senate chambers. They also confronted millions of Americans with the issues of power, gender, and race that swirled around and through the hearings. The hearings confronted many different publics with tough issues, forcing them to construct a version of the events in question that made sense. There was, as Nancy Fraser (1992) put it, "the official public sphere within [the hearings]; the extra-governmental public constituted by the mass media; the various counter-publics associated with social movements like feminism [and] . . . the ephemeral but intense constitution of informal public spheres at various sites in everyday life—at workplaces, restaurants, campuses, street corners, shopping centers, private homes, wherever people gathered to discuss the events . . ." (597). Perhaps the stakes were highest for the "ephemeral but intense" public of everyday life. It is in everyday life that the issues of race, class, and gender that motivated the hearings move from abstract philosophical arguments to struggles over jobs, self-image, and quality of life. This public was undecided, not because they were uncommitted but precisely because they carried the commitments born of struggle on a daily basis. They watched the hearings with special interest, caught up in the "hurricane" of fascination and outrage, trying to find answers wherever they could. As Toni Morrison (1992) states:

Everyone interested in the outcome of this nomination, regardless of race, class, gender, religion, or profession, turns to as many forms of media as are available. They read local papers to see if the reactions among their neighbors is similar to their own, or they try to figure out on what information their own response should be based. They have listened to newscasters and anchor people for the bits and bites that pointed to, or deflected attention from, the machinery of campaigns to reject or accept the nominee. They have watched television screens that seem to watch back, that dismiss viewers or call upon them for flavor, reinforcement, or routine dissent. Polls assure and shock, gratify and discredit those who took them into serious account. (viii)

Constructions of the events became the stuff of intense personal debate. The stakes of taking a stand on who was telling the truth were highest in personal circles, where the values and beliefs implied by believing Hill or Thomas had a direct impact on our relationships, as Morrison (1992) notes:

> But most of all, people talked to one another. There are passionate, some-times acrimonious discussions between mothers and daughters, fathers and sons, husbands and wives, siblings, friends, acquaintances, colleagues with whom, now, there is reason to embrace or to expel from their close circle. Sophisticated legal debates merge with locker-room guffaws; poised exchanges about the ethics and moral responsibilities of governance are debased by cold indifference to individual claims and private vulnerabilities. (viii–ix)

The problem confronting the public as it tried to make sense of these hearings was how to make sense of Anita Hill's actions. How people make sense of each other's actions has been treated extensively by philosophers (Kant, 1953; Nagel, 1974) and anthropologists (Shweder and Levine, 1984; Vendler, 1984). Because individuals and the circumstances in which they find themselves are unique, there are no universal rules for understanding another's actions. However, we can project ourselves into their situation and ask ourselves what it must be like to be in that situation. What would we feel? How would we react? The understanding of an agent, in other words, requires empathy, "that is, the reproduction, by means of imaginary transference, of the agent's consciousness in one's own mind so that his conduct may appear as a result of free, but rational choice. Because of course, 'mad' acts cannot be understood. Freedom does not exclude but requires rationality . . ." (Vendler, 1984, 208–9).

Notice the function of expectations in this account of empathy. We are able to understand or recognize someone else's actions because they behave in ways that we recognize as rational. If they do not act rationally, we either can make no sense of their actions or assume they are "mad."

Expanding on this model of empathy for understanding human action, certain philosophers (Johnson, 1993; MacIntyre, 1981) have argued that moral judgments (i.e., whether what someone is doing is right or wrong) are based on our constructions of actions into sequences or narratives. In other words, we are able not only to understand others but also to judge them by virtue of how well their actions fit a narrative we have constructed based on past experiences. Or, as Alasdair MacIntyre (1981) put it, "I can only answer the question 'What am I to do?' if I can answer the prior question 'Of what story or stories do I find myself a part?' We enter human society, that is, with one or more imputed characters—roles into which we have been drafted and we have to learn what they are in order to be able to understand how others respond to us and how our responses to them are apt to be construed" (216).

Flipping the logic, we can only answer the question "What is someone else to do?" by fitting their actions into a role within a narrative that we or society have fashioned. We understand what someone has done and what they should do by matching their actions up against the expectations of roles they play in narratives of which we take them to be a part. Moreover, the narratives we construct for ourselves and each other prize consistency and rationality above all else. To be made sense of, we must fit people's action into an account or assume they are mad.

As I show in this essay, Republican attacks relied on this model of moral judgment to construct Hill as someone who was either unsound morally or lying. My analysis casts Republican strategies as the construction of a narrative for Hill in which she was not trustworthy because she contradicted the expectations of certain roles. Hill's attackers relied on this logic to force her into a double bind of being recognizable only as someone dangerous to the community because she operated according to different moral constraints or as a liar. What is most interesting to me is not only that the Republican attacks relied on this logic of human action but also how this logic of human action enabled them to completely silence the suffering of Anita Hill and by extension countless other victims. What happened to Anita Hill speaks to the power of an account of human behavior that relies on consistency for understanding and credibility.

This reading of the hearings therefore articulates what was available for people to recognize as they tried to understand Hill's actions. Only by understanding Hill's actions could the "everyday" public find her believable. To those undecided in this confrontation, accounts of Hill constructed through the questions and answers of the hearings become rhetorical resources from which they formed their own accounts. Although different people would reach different conclusions, their respective conclusions were constrained by the accounts constructed during the hearings.

More important, this reading reveals the power dynamics of the hearings—how cultural assumptions about what counts as "normal" behavior were used to limit the range of recognition, silencing other accounts that would make sense of Hill's actions as those of a victim of sexual harassment. Since the Republican account dominated the others, tracing its logic also serves as a starting point to account for the disparities between those who believed her and those who did not.[2]

The following discussion traces the rhetorical strategies Republicans used to discredit Hill and make her recognizable only as a lying, vengeful woman who was anything but a victim of sexual harassment. First, this analysis shows how those who attacked Hill based their attacks on the assumption that normal, and therefore credible, people act in ways consistent with certain culturally defined roles. This allowed them to conclude that because Hill did not act as one would expect a lawyer or a victim to act, she was lying. Second, this analysis shows how attributing motives for lying allowed her attackers to identify her with derogatory stereotypes, further discrediting her. Subsequently, it is argued that Senator Orrin Hatch's conjecture about the sources of her allegations further denied she was a victim of sexual harassment by implying that she could not even be sure which of her experiences were really hers. Finally, this analysis reflects on how the Republican strategy to silence an "Anita Hill" that is recognizable and sympathetic as a victim was consistent with the use of pain as a political weapon against oppressed groups.

The Trial of Anita Hill: Constructing (In)credibility

Those who attacked Hill had the immediate advantage of not having to confront physical evidence or witnesses. If there were no evidence, no witnesses, and no "physical" harm done by the harassment,[3] then how could anyone know what happened or that anything at all happened? Hill had made no written record of the harassment and had not told any of her friends about it directly. (Joel Paul, for example, testified that Hill had hinted at it, though never mentioned Thomas directly).

Truth therefore became a question of credibility—which meant interrogating Hill's character and motives. This focus was consistent with the fact that from the beginning the hearings took the form of a trial. As a commentator on the hearings argued about charges with no witnesses, "Normal courtroom defense to such charges is to try to even the score by eliciting details that damage the accuser's credibility and by testing various theories of her motivation" (Garment, 1992, 34).

Isolating Hill

Proceeding as if the hearings were a trial, Republican attackers and Democrat defenders focused entirely on Hill's character and motives. Hill was isolated from the outset, because Thomas was not forced to account for his actions or motives. Thomas very deftly proscribed discussion of his own credibility in his opening statement by ruling out questions about his private life: "I'm not here to be further humiliated by this committee or anyone else, or to put my private life on display for prurient interests or other reasons. I will not allow this committee or anyone else to probe into my private life" (Hearings, 1991, 6).

Since most of the theorizing that took place in the hearings about credibility amounted to folk-theorizing about psychology, by ruling out talk about his private life, Thomas shielded himself against questions about his own credibility or motives. Determining motives requires that we "go in someone's head." Invoking the right to privacy, Thomas recast any attempts by the committee to get inside his head as illegal search and seizure. Any direct questioning therefore became a violation of Thomas's basic rights.

Thomas also blunted potential probes into his private life and motives by playing the racism card. By calling the hearings a "high-tech lynching for uppity blacks" (Hearings, 1991, 157), Thomas took advantage of the clear racial overtones of the hearings. He placed the committee in a pernicious bind. Members had to appear impartial in these proceedings. By casting the hearings as a lynching, Thomas made impartiality impossible except for one scenario: a scenario in which they did not push him on his private life.

Thomas did not have to account for himself even though there was good reason for him to say more. As many commentators have pointed out (e.g., Applebone, 1991), senators knew details about Thomas's habits that could (or should) have led to more direct questioning of Thomas. They knew, for example, about what the *New York Times* called his "well documented taste for watching and discussing pornographic movies while he was at Yale Law School" (Dowd, 1991; Wines, 1991). Also, they chose not to hear testimony from Angela Wright, a second black woman who claimed to have been harassed by Thomas and had told somebody at the time.[4]

Inconsistency and Lying

Having established the hearings as a trial and having isolated Hill, Republicans relied on a traditional model of action and motivation in which how people should act is measured by how well they follow culturally established roles. Through his questions, Senator Arlen Specter's strategy was to show how Hill contradicted expectations dictated by certain roles she played. It worked to the extent that an undecided audience identified these roles and their prescribed actions and therefore doubted Hill because she contradicted them.

Specter's logic was that if, in fact, she had been sexually harassed, she would not have contradicted the following roles. As a law professor, she would not have concluded that he would be fitting for the court in any respect, if she had all this personal information about him (Hearings, 1991, 50). As an experienced attorney and as someone experienced in sexual harassment cases, she certainly would have made her "evidentiary position" stronger by taking notes (Hearings, 1991, 51). Given that the typical statute of limitations for filing charges in most civil rights cases is six years, surely she should have thought it unfair to make charges nine years after the fact (Hearings, 1991, 54).

These charges focused the narrative constructed for Hill on her status as a legal expert. Specter questioned Hill throughout with a tone of incredulity, which is reflected in the use of such words as "certainly" and "surely." According to Specter's account, Hill, in her role as a professional, had an obligation to protect the law and the institutions that administer it. If Thomas was unfit, she had an obligation to do something about Thomas's nomination immediately, not to wait until the eleventh hour to come forward. So, either she was shirking her responsibility, or she was lying. As a professional, she knew what kind of evidence would have been necessary to prove such allegations. Either she was incompetent, or she was lying. As a professional, she had an ethical obligation to play fair and observe the statute of limitations. Either she was unethical professionally, or she was lying. By arguing that she acted inconsistently, Specter forced Hill and everyone trying to account for her behavior to conclude that she was irresponsible, incompetent, and unethical or that she was lying.

Specter faced the fact that Hill's action might be reasonable for a victim of sexual harassment, so he compared Hill's actions with his version of what a victim of sexual harassment should do. Following this line of questioning, the hearings devoted much time considering two questions: Why did Hill follow Thomas from one job to another, given that she would not have any difficulty getting another job (something they say she should have known) (Hearings, 1991, 56), and why did she keep contact with him by telephone (Hearings, 1991, 80)? (The latter led to the long, drawn out discussion about telephone logs.)

Throughout this line of questioning, Republicans hammered Hill with their logic of how a victim of any transgression should respond. Surely, they argued, those who had undergone such a terrible ordeal would not have stayed in the situation. Or, if they had stayed, they certainly would not have remained on good terms with their abusers. By not reacting in these ways, Hill violated the assumption that a reasonable person who is harmed should seek redress. In a society founded on the idea of equality and balance (not to mention one as litigious as ours), not to seek damages for harm done is quite out of character. One is supposed to fight back against a transgression, especially someone who is as well-educated and financially secure as Anita Hill. So again, Hill's attackers implied that either there was something "wrong" with her, or she was lying.

The contrast that Hill's attackers painted as they showed her contradicting this clear set of expectations was most bluntly illustrated in J. C. Alvarez's testimony on Hill. Alvarez's assessment of Hill could not have fit the Republican strategy better if they had scripted it for her: "I, too, have experienced sexual harassment in the past. . . . it is an issue I have experienced, I understand, and I take it very seriously. But having lived through it myself, I find Anita Hill's behavior inconsistent with these charges. I can assure you that when I come into town, the last thing I want to do is call either of these two men up and say hello, or see if they want to get together. . . . Women who have really been harassed would agree" (Hearings, 1991, 267). Alvarez then moved to the same conclusion the Republicans were pushing, that is, Hill was lying: "Her behavior just isn't consistent with the behavior of a woman who has been harassed, and it just doesn't make sense. . . . It has to make us all suspicious of her motives" (267).

In her opening statement, Alvarez crafted her persona as perhaps the quintessential upstanding citizen, recounting how she broke up a mugging and underlining how down to earth she was by telling stories about her family and her troubles getting to the hearings. She was thus able to embody the standard against which Republicans were holding Hill as she explained her reasons for coming forward to defend Thomas: "You know, I talked with my mom before I came here, and she reminded me that I was always raised to stand up for what I believe. I have seen an innocent man being mugged in broad daylight, and I have not looked the other way. This John Q. Public came here and got involved" (Hearings, 1991, 267).

Talking to her mother, standing up for what she believed, coming to Washington to get involved, Alvarez positioned herself in stark contrast to the "Anita Hills" constructed in the hearings. Alvarez portrayed herself as one guided by the highest principles, both professionally and personally. Hill, by contrast, was portrayed as having no principles.

Moreover, Alvarez stated the implicit Republican argument against Hill in both lines of questioning—she was inconsistent and therefore must have been lying. In each case, they limited the possibilities of Hill's behavior to their version of what should have been done. In the case of how she should have behaved as a victim of sexual harassment, they did not consult any experts on the matter. They did not give her the opportunity to make sense of her actions by fully explaining what motivates someone who has suffered sexual harassment. Rather, Specter created the standard of sensible behavior, held Hill up to it through his questions, and, when she did not fit the reasoning, implied that she must have been lying.

The logic underpinning Specter's attack was that credibility derives from actions consistent with certain culturally defined roles. These roles are so clearly defined that there can be no mistaking the constraints they place on behavior. Deviation from these roles and their constraints is therefore a clear indication there is something wrong with this person. The public is compelled to follow the following logic: "I, member of the public, know that a lawyer or a victim of some crime should keep records, should get angry, should seek redress, should at the very least say something to someone about this situation. Anita Hill says nothing, in fact stays on good terms with someone who supposedly harmed her. This makes absolutely no sense; therefore, she must be lying or delusional."

In other words, Specter's logic fits the cultural logic of making sense of another's actions that was explained earlier—to be intelligible, a person's actions must rationally follow the constraints of cultural roles. If a person's actions are inconsistent, it can only be for bad reasons. In Hill's case, the Republican explanation for her deviations was that she was lying. But if she was not lying, then she violated the ethical and professional standards of a lawyer and the standards of what any normal person should do if harmed. The implication is that if Hill was a victim, she was not an honorable person.

Motives and Stereotypes

Confident that they "showed" Hill to be lying because she contradicted certain expectations, Republican senators continued to construct Anita Hill by accounting for her motives. They had to account for motives to be consistent with their own logic. To lie, Hill must have known the truth and willfully distorted it. Republicans needed to show a motive for lying to say that Hill was lying.

Attributing motives to Hill, however, did more than keep their logic consistent. It enabled them to discredit Hill further. By articulating motives for Hill, they offered still more versions of Anita Hill, all of which not only discredited her but also made her dangerous. Fraser (1992) describes some of the many Anita Hills: "During the course of the struggle, it was variously suggested that Hill was a lesbian, a heterosexual erotomaniac, a delusional schizophrenic, a fantasist, a vengeful spurned woman, a perjurer, and a malleable tool of liberal interest groups . . ." (600–601). The thesis that Hill was an erotomaniac emerged in the testimony of John Doggett, who filed several affidavits and testified that Hill had fantasized about him (Hearings, 1991, 72). Moreover, coworkers testifying for Thomas further "tarred" her with numerous classic sexist stereotypes: stridently aggressive, arrogant, ambitious, aloof, tough, opinionated. Again, J. C. Alvarez put it most bluntly: "She was a very hard, tough woman. She was opinionated. She was arrogant. She was a relentless debater. . . . She was aloof, and she always acted as if she was a little bit superior to everyone, a little holier-than-thou" (Hearings, 1991, 264).

Perhaps the most insidious and pernicious (or clever, depending on one's perspective) way Republican questioners attacked Hill was by allowing Thomas himself to speak for her. Thomas described Hill as distant and aloof from the other staffers. Hill, as constructed by Thomas, caused problems, problems that he attributed to her "being *young*—but usually involved her taking a firm position . . .—and being *unyielding to the other members of the staff*, and then storming off or *throwing a temper tantrum* of some sort, that *either myself or the chief of staff would have to iron out*" (Hearings, 1991, 101, emphasis added). Hill, the troublemaker, was no surprise to Thomas. After all, he concluded, Hill was the stereotypical "strong" woman: "Anita would not be considered a meek woman. She was an aggressive debater. She stood her ground. When she got her dander up she would storm off. I would say that she was a bright person, a capable person. . . . [asked if she is a vindictive woman] I think senator that she argued forcefully for her position, and I took it as a sign of immaturity, perhaps, that when she didn't get her way that she would tend to get—reinforce her position and get a bit angry" (Hearings, 1991, 109).

The picture of Hill that emerged in these passages was almost a cliché but was no less damaging. Hill was the stereotypical "strong woman," but her strength was not the strength of conviction and character. It was the stubbornness of being immature and opinionated. Instead of standing her ground for what she believed in and refusing to engage at times as a protest to inequity, she threw a tantrum and refused to be reasonable. The language in these passages is telling: Hill is compared to a storm, unpredictable and dangerous because she took no responsibility for her actions (Thomas, not Hill, had to "iron out" the problems she caused).

Perhaps the most damage was done, ironically enough, by Democratic attempts to blunt Republican attacks on Hill. In the clearest example, Senator Howell Heflin attempted to invalidate Specter's insinuation that Hill was motivated by revenge for rebuffed advances. Heflin asked her if she was a "scorned woman" or a "zealot civil rights believer," if she had a "martyr complex," if she desired to be a "civil rights hero," if she was "given to fantasies," and finally if she wanted to write a book about these experiences (i.e., was self-serving). Heflin's point was to show that these different motives were ridiculous and that the whole line of questioning was therefore ridiculous. Hill, of course, answered no to each question, maintaining that she had to come forward because her story had been made public (the infamous leak) and now wanted to speak for herself.

As the testimony of Thomas's supporters showed, Heflin's satire held the problem of all satire—some people took it seriously. Calling attention to stereotypes to invalidate them nonetheless perpetuated them. Despite the fact that Heflin intended to make light of these motives, for someone trying to make sense of Hill's actions, these became possible interpretations of Hill: yes, Heflin was being sarcastic, but he could have been on to something.

Again, the picture was quite damaging. Such words as "zealot," "martyr," and "hero," compounded by her being "scorned" and "given to fantasies," made Hill more than a strong woman—they made her dangerous. If Heflin was right, Hill was driven by hate, with a touch of delusion, to do anything for the cause of civil rights and women's rights. Martyrs and zealots are dangerous because they will go to any length, even death, to achieve their warped goals. These are terms usually reserved for terrorists. In his attempt to discredit the attacks on Hill's motives, Heflin painted her as a civil rights terrorist, made more dangerous by being mentally unbalanced. He inadvertently touched on a conservative (both political and cultural) paranoia about systematic liberal attempts to subvert American values.

Her Story Is Not Her Story

Republican efforts to completely (re)construct Hill went so far as to deny her experience. For example, Senator Hatch even found a "source" for the "disgusting, dreadful things" that Thomas "supposedly" said to her (Hearings, 1991, 203–4, 206). In one sense, Hatch was compelled to do this because—even if Hill did not document what happened—her account seemed potentially credible. After all, stories, however unbelievable, do not just come out of nowhere. If the story could not be explained away, there was the possibility that Hill might be believable.

Hatch's need to completely remake and discredit Hill resulted in one of the more bizarre moments of the hearings. In explaining how Hill got the details she described—which constituted her experience of sexual harassment—Hatch implied that parts of her account could be attributed to sources other than Thomas. For example, Hatch suggested that the idea that Thomas discussed his sexual prowess and endowment came from sexual/racial stereotypes about black men (Hearings, 1991, 125–26). The remark about "Long Dong Silver," Hatch said, came from a sexual harassment case that was heard in the Tenth Circuit, of which Oklahoma was a part. One of the allegations in that case was that the man harassed the women with pictures of "Long Dong Silver." Hatch insinuated that Hill could have gotten this accusation from this case, "This is a public opinion that is available in any law library. I have to tell you, I'm sure it's available there at the law school in Oklahoma, and it's a sexual harassment case." Finally, in Hatch's greatest stretch, he attributed the pubic hair comment that Thomas allegedly made to a passage from *The Exorcist*, which he quoted for the audience (127–29).

As her attackers did in attributing motives to Hill, Hatch literally tried to tell Hill's story for her. By tracing "her story" to racial stereotypes and *The Exorcist*, Hatch further exploited the disparaging stereotypes already cast on Hill. Not only was her story not her story, Hatch implied, her "sources" showed her to be racist and bizarre (delusional).

As noted at the outset, Hatch did more than account for Hill's story; he further erased her by denying her experience. Hatch's accusations implied that Hill's life was completely fabricated. If Hill was capable of making up something so terrible and life-changing from scraps of law cases and *The Exorcist*, what substance could there be to the rest of her life? What kind of self did Anita Hill have after all? What kind of self did she have that was even capable of suffering as she claimed that she did? Not only that, by casting her as someone who made up her life from novels, Hatch strengthened the construction of Hill as delusional, dangerous, and untrustworthy. By denying Hill's experience, Hatch projected his own bizarre reading of the situation onto Hill.

In the end, then, Republicans "showed" how Hill contradicted certain clearly defined and accepted cultural roles—lawyer, victim. Appealing to a logic that says people never deviate for a "good" reason, the Republican construction led to the conclusion that Hill was either lying or dishonorable. By attributing motives to Hill, they cast her in still more roles. She was the strong woman, strident and immature, stormy and hard to control. She was the woman who, from the conservative standpoint, threatened American values by her unwillingness to stay in her place, whether in the family, at work, or in society. It was her brand of anger and impetuosity that threatened to destabilize society and culture. Or, she was a cultural terrorist driven by scorn and vengeance to bring down society. She was all the more dangerous because, in addition to everything else, she was delusional. Moreover, she was devoid of any identity, taking her experiences and thus her identity from disparate scraps of other people's experience. This logic was meant to lead to the conclusion that Hill's allegations were prompted by these nefarious motives. Not only was Hill not credible, but also she came to represent everything that threatens society. Her plot against a justice on the Supreme Court was but one small part in a much larger effort to rend the very fabric of America.

Denying the Voice of Suffering

In the midst of these efforts to discredit Hill, any attempt to tell the story of sexual harassment was completely covered up. It was covered up despite the efforts of Judge Susan Hoerchner and Ellen Wells to explain the actions of a victim of sexual harassment. Ellen Wells's testimony described all the characteristics of sexual harassment that have been detailed by experts on the matter. For others who were willing (and able) to listen, Hill's story was told. No one could argue, then, that Hill's story, and the story of any victim of sexual harassment, failed for lack of trying. It failed to come across because it was constantly deflected and ultimately silenced by the attacks on Anita Hill.

First, Wells described how a victim is inclined to silence because sexual matters are personal and embarrassing in a public setting: "I should note that I did not ask for details for two reasons: Neither Professor Hill nor I would have been comfortable discussing such matters. Women typically don't talk in sexually explicit terms" (Hearings, 1991, 205). Those who work with victims of sexual harassment argue that embarrassment is a strong silencing force. According to them, "Upbringing or experience may make the subject of harassment seem too painful or laden with other taboos for some women to come forward" (Petrocelli and Repa, 1992, chap. 3:5).

Cultural taboos notwithstanding, silence is compelled by the inherent power imbalance between men and women in the workplace. Sexual harassment, fundamentally, is not about sex, as William Petrocelli and Barbara Repa (1992) point out: "Sexual harassment is not about sexual attractiveness or a testosterone-induced urge to get close. It's not about sex at all. Sexual harassment on the job is almost always an abuse of power designed to discourage women from continuing in the work force or getting more desirable, better paying jobs" (chap. 3:5). Victims of sexual harassment face incurring "job-connected injuries"; losing their jobs; losing wages and benefits; being reassigned to jobs of less quality; or quitting their jobs altogether because the situation is intolerable (Petrocelli and Repa, 1992, chap. 1:11–13). Catharine MacKinnon (1987) succinctly defines sexual harassment as "sexual pressure imposed on someone who is not in an economic power to refuse it" (103). Wells also expressed the economic nature of sexual harassment by describing the fear of losing one's job: "When you're confronted with something like that, you feel powerless and vulnerable, and unless you have a private income, you have no recourse. And since this is generally done in privacy, there are no witnesses, and so it's your word, an underling, against that of a superior, someone who is obviously well thought of . . . if you hope to go forward and . . . move out from their power and control, you sometimes have to put up with things that no one should be expected to put up with" (Hearings, 1991, 225). Because the guilty person usually has a public reputation and power over the victim, coming forward puts a victim immediately in a position of being suspect and subject to public humiliation.

Finally, as Petrocelli and Repa (1992) indicate, a victim of sexual harassment takes responsibility for the crime: "Women have long been socialized to be the sexual gatekeepers, responsible for setting the bounds of closeness in their relationships with men. The foremost thought on the minds of many women who have been harassed is: What have I done wrong?" (chap. 3:5). Similarly, Wells expressed the victim's willingness to take responsibility for what happened: "One of the first things you would ask yourself is, 'What did I do?' You blame yourself. . . . and so you try to change your behavior because it must be me, I must be the wrong party here. And then I think you perhaps start to get angry and frustrated. But there's always that sense of being powerless. And you're also ashamed. . . . And so you keep it in; you don't say anything" (Hearings, 1991, 238).

It is important to note that Hill's story was recognizable to those who already knew her story and to those who have been sexually harassed. As McKay (1992) observed:

> Anita Hill was a woman confronted with the difficult choice of telling or not telling the dirty details of what millions of women in this country suffer daily and are too afraid to dare tell. And in her telling, millions of women identified with her, and understood perfectly well (even if some senators pretended they never did) the power relations that kept her from pressing charges against her harasser-employer at the time, and caused her to promote an amicable relationship with him long after she left his staff. During and after her testimony millions of American women of all races dredged up long-buried memories of similar harassments in their pasts. . . . (277)

But, for the undecided public, Hill never was able to articulate the grounds and logic that would make her story recognizable.[5] The pattern of oppression described by Wells and those who confront sexual harassment,[6] like Hill's testimony, never received a complete hearing because the defense was always dictated by the nature of the attack. Hill's witnesses tried to construct a favorable narrative for her, but they were unable to because they had to respond to questions designed to discredit Hill and make her recognizable only as a liar. Although Hill and her witnesses constructed a narrative for Hill, the narrative was ultimately controlled by Republican senators. It is one thing to explain what victims of sexual harassment go through and why their behavior may seem inconsistent to an audience that is open to the account and shares some common ground on which to receive the account. The hearings did not provide this opportunity, however. Attempts to explain Hill's behavior were elicited as proof that Hill was telling the truth, which in the absence of evidence, is unprovable. Hill's defenders who tried to tell the story of sexual harassment were given an impossible task.

Furthermore, if the Republicans succeeded in showing that Hill was lying about having been harassed (by destroying her credibility), then Wells's account was not germane. Even if Wells spoke the truth about sexual harassment, since Hill was lying about being harassed, Wells's account did not apply to her. At that point, Hill's defense became irrelevant, especially to those who reduced her to a legal expert who acted out of character or to Specter's version of a victim of harassment.

The Republicans not only attempted to make Wells's testimony irrelevant by arguing that Hill was lying but also questioned her motives, as they had Hill's. Specter attempted to portray Wells as not helping Hill. He also tried to get Wells to contradict Hill, and thus her own testimony, by repeatedly asking her if she would have taken the same action that Hill did. He asked Wells if she should not have taken some action on Hill's behalf. He finally pushed her to silence:

> Specter: So in essence you're saying that even though you said if so outraged you have to do something, that ultimately you would have done nothing?
> Wells: I think that is the case.
> Specter: And would she have maintained that kind of friendly relationship . . . ?
> Wells: I don't know all those—all the circumstances, but given the kind of work—I'm sorry. (Hearings, 1991, 312)

Specter forced Wells into avoiding a contradiction—either she would have acted a certain way, or she would not have. He pitted Wells against Hill, that is, Wells's need to be consistent with her own outrage against her defense of Hill's lack of action. Specter moved Wells from an eloquent expression of what it is like to experience sexual harassment to an apology for not fitting into his category system. In the process, he defused the power of her testimony.

Some may argue that putting Hill and those who spoke for her on the defensive was perfectly justified. After all, the hearings were constructed as a trial, with Hill cast as the accuser who had the burden of proof. However, the proceedings were supposed to be hearings, not a trial. The Senate did not have explicit rules of evidence to control arguments in hearings. As Suzanne Garment (1992) pointed out, it was not set up like a courtroom, "in which professionals from each side would have questioned both Thomas and Hill before an impartial judge" (35). Neither did the Senate have "the benefit of anything like a grand jury, which sifts through raw data and decides which information is good enough to serve for further government action" (35). Finally, and perhaps most important, "in public hearings on issues of individual guilt and innocence, the absence of rules means that the contest is drenched in free floating poison. The odds are even slimmer than usual of ever finding a semblance of the truth" (35). Garment did not elaborate on the nature of the "free floating poison," but a substantial part of it was the systematic denial of any opportunity for those who have suffered sexual harassment to account for it in their own terms, according to their own logic.

Concluding Remarks: Silence and Oppression

The Republican strategy against Hill was ultimately based on her lack of tangible evidence to address their skepticism. In an article on sexual harassment, MacKinnon (1987) notes that in 1982 the Equal Employment Opportunity Commission (EEOC), ironically enough, "held that if a victim was sexually harassed without a corroborating witness, proof was inadequate as a matter of law" (113). Although the EEOC in 1983 allowed that corroboration is impossible in some cases, it never changed its original position (MacKinnon, 1987). Because she had no witnesses, Anita Hill could not meet the standard of evidence. During the hearings and until the present, it remained her word against his word. And, because her word was discredited, she had no proof— she was silenced.

Also silenced, of course, were Hill's pain and, by extension, the pain of countless other victims of sexual harassment who are not given the opportunity to voice their pain. They are not given the opportunity to voice their pain precisely because they are held to a standard of evidence that dictates something must be shown in order to be real. Pain runs afoul of this injunction because it is at once unmistakable and unsharable in normal discourse. As Elaine Scarry (1985) observes, "So, for the person in pain, so incontestably and unnegotiably is it present that 'having pain' may come to be thought of as the most vibrant example of what it is to 'have certainty,' while for the other person it is so elusive that 'hearing about pain' may exist as the primary model of what it is to 'have doubt.' Thus pain comes unsharably into our midst as at once that which cannot be denied and that which cannot be confirmed" (4).

Scarry argues that pain is the quintessential political weapon precisely because it cannot be proven or shown in language that predicates existence on being able to be seen. It is difficult to make pain a political issue because it is impossible to agree on how to make it public. Since pain cannot be made a political issue, it cannot be redressed in the mainstream—it forces the suffering to find other expressions. According to Scarry, the most common outlet of pain is art. In other words, pain requires a creative response, a response that will always seem outlandish compared with those experiences that can be "shown" in simpler, everyday terms.

The outlandishness of pain's response is exemplified in women's attempts to express their experience to the mainstream. "The entire history of women's struggle for self-determination," Rich (1979) argues, "has been muffled in silence over and over. One serious cultural obstacle encountered by any feminist writer is that each feminist work has tended to be received as if it emerged from nowhere . . . [thus] women's work and thinking has been made to seem sporadic, errant, orphaned of any tradition of its own" (11).

One could add to Rich's list the many stereotypes attached to Hill, expressed in such words as "calloused," "hard," "irrational," "fantastic," and "immature." The lack of recognition about which Rich writes and the response to a perceived outlandishness about which Scarry writes are exemplified in the exercise of power that silences Anita Hill. In the same way that pain is an effective political weapon because it cannot be seen, the oppressive power of Republican attacks on Hill and her witnesses derived from the absence of tangible evidence—because there were no witnesses, it simply did not happen. The charge of oppression can always be denied by those who oppress with the simple but deadly demand, "Prove it." Of course, the Republicans went much further than challenging Hill to prove her allegations; they used the fact that she could not prove her allegations as the foundation for their efforts to construct her as a liar and a threat.

The outlandishness that made Anita Hill a threat is clearest in the way she was stereotyped as a threat to mainstream culture. The stereotypes used to construct the various Anita Hills are not surprising, nor is the fact that they were invoked necessarily news. What is instructive, as traced in this essay, is how these stereotypes were mobilized in the context of deeper cultural logics of identity and credibility. The oppressive power operated in the hearings in more than just the attribution of damaging stereotypes. Power was exercised more fundamentally by prescribing what one must do to be credible and using such prescriptions against Hill. The hearings worked according to a logic that suggests one must be consistent with roles that are clear and acceptable, or idealized versions of such roles, to be credible. Using this logic to attack Hill's character and credibility created the opportunity for the stereotypes to take hold in the first place.

Had the Republicans simply accused Hill of being a delusional liar, they might have appeared more blatantly mean-spirited and brought more protest on themselves. But, put in the context of cultural assumptions about consistency and identity, stereotypes provided necessary, if disquieting, answers. After all, the logic of consistency and identity requires us to account for all behavior by making it consistent with some recognizable role. Attempts were made to account for Hill's behavior from the standpoint of what is consistent for a victim of sexual harassment. However, because of the way these attempts were fit into the overall scheme of the hearings, they were suppressed and silenced, except to those who already understood them. For the undecided public struggling to identify with some position in the debates, none of the dominant versions of Anita Hill made her believable. Even worse, they pointed to her as a threat to the values and stability of those who would identify with her.

Of course, the ostensible purpose of the hearings was to determine if Hill had, in fact, been sexually harassed by Thomas. Even if the events did not happen as she described them, even if the events never happened, there was more at stake than determining the truth. The people who constituted "the public" cared about the truth because it might help them be clearer about how they felt about the issues raised by the hearings. The different rhetorics developed to account for the alleged events, to impugn and defend, traveled far beyond the Senate chambers. They were integrated into or, in some cases, became the substance of positions taken in family discussions, discussions at work, discussions in classrooms, and discussions on the street. They were used to defend actions, and they were no doubt used to silence uncomfortable truths in the same way Republicans sought to silence Anita Hill's truth.

By "truth," I do not mean to imply any judgment on whether Anita Hill was telling the truth. Whether she was telling the truth, or whether the truth was somewhere in the midst of the various accounts, the truth of sexual harassment is indisputable. This is why the hearings implicated the public so intensely. The various accounts that were so hotly contested only mirror the vast struggle over gender and power that runs through our own culture. It is no wonder we watched with anger, puzzlement, disgust, and fascination.

NOTES

1. Senators Patrick Leahy, Orrin Hatch, and Alan Simpson all made a point of saying that women in their lives have suffered sexual harassment or sexual discrimination. In addition, as my colleague Joanne Gilbert pointed out to me, during debates the day after the hearings ended and before Thomas's confirmation vote, many members professed their concern for women's issues.

2. The many public opinion polls taken at the time showed that most people believed Thomas. On October 21, 1991, *Newsweek* reported on a poll done during the hearings, indicating that men believed Thomas by a margin of two to one, women by a margin of three to two. On October 15, 1991, the *New York Times* showed that in a poll after the hearings the margin increased to well over two to one for both men and women.

3. Interestingly, no one asked Hill about any physical harm she might have suffered as a result of being harassed. Those who work with victims of sexual harassment report that it is usually accompanied by physical manifestations of the psychological damage (Petrocelli and Repa, 1992, chap. 1:10).

4. For Angela Wright's story of her relationship with Clarence Thomas, see Applebone, 1991.

5. Imagine, as many critics of the hearings have pointed out, if the Senate Judiciary Committee had been composed entirely of women or had had more people of color.

6. A number of books have been written on sexual harassment. One of the best known is MacKinnon (1979). In the months that followed the hearings, several new books on sexual harassment also were published, including Petrocelli and

Repa (1992), written by two sexual harassment lawyers, and Sumrall and Taylor (1992), who collected numerous stories from victims of sexual harassment and framed them with a powerful introduction by Andrea Dworkin.

REFERENCES

Applebone, P. (1991, October 12). Common threads between the two accusing Thomas of sexual improprieties. *New York Times*, A11.

Dowd, M. (1991, October 16). Image more than reality became issue, losers say. *New York Times*, A14.

Fraser, N. (1992). Sex, lies, and the public sphere: Some reflections on the confirmation of Clarence Thomas. *Critical Inquiry*, 18: 595–612.

Garment, S. (1992, January). Why Anita Hill lost. *Commentary*, 26–35.

Hearings before the Committee on the Judiciary on the nomination of Judge Clarence Thomas to serve as an associate justice of the Supreme Court of the United States. (1991, October 11, 12, and 13). U.S. Senate, 102d Congress, 1st session. Washington, D.C.: U.S. Government Printing Office.

Johnson, M. (1993). *Moral imagination: Implications of cognitive science for ethics.* Chicago: University of Chicago Press.

Kant, I. (1953). Critique of pure reason. Trans. Norman Kemp Smith. London: Macmillan.

MacIntyre, A. (1981). *After virtue: A study in moral theory.* Notre Dame, Ind.: University of Notre Dame Press.

MacKinnon, C. A. (1979). *Sexual harassment of working women: A case of sexual discrimination.* New Haven, Conn.: Yale University Press.

———. (1987). *Feminism unmodified: Discourses on life and law.* Cambridge, Mass.: Harvard University Press.

McKay, N. (1992). Remembering Anita Hill and Clarence Thomas: What really happened when one black woman spoke out. In Morrison (ed.), *Race-ing justice, en-gendering power,* 269–89.

Morrison, T. (ed.). (1992). *Race-ing justice, en-gendering power: Essays on Anita Hill, Clarence Thomas, and the construction of social reality.* New York: Pantheon.

Nagel, T. (1974). What is it like to be a bat? *Philosophical Review*, 83: 435–50.

Petrocelli, W., and Repa, B. K. (1992). *Sexual harassment on the job.* Berkeley, Calif.: Nolo Press.

Rich, A. (1979). *On lies, secrets, and silence: Selected prose 1966–1978.* New York: W. W. Norton.

Scarry, E. (1985). *The body in pain: The making and unmaking of the world.* New York: Oxford University Press.

Shweder, R., and LeVine, R. (eds.). (1984). *Culture theory: Essays on mind, self, and emotion.* Cambridge: Cambridge University Press.

Sumrall, A. C., and Taylor, D. (eds.). (1992). *Sexual harassment: Women speak out.* Freedom, Calif.: Crossing Press.

Vendler, Z. (1984). Understanding people. In Shweder and LeVine (eds.), *Culture theory,* 200–213.

Wines, M. (1991, October 10). Stark conflict marks accounts given by Thomas. *New York Times,* A18.

Part 3

*Implications of Hearings for Politics
and the Workplace*

The Pragmatics of Sexual Harassment: Two Devices for Creating a "Hostile Environment"

DARRIN HICKS AND PHILLIP J. GLENN

Anita Hill's charges during the Clarence Thomas confirmation hearings proved a lightning rod for nationwide discussion in the workplace. Many people thought of such actions as a "problem" for the first time as a result of the Senate hearings. Some expressed frustration at the ambiguity of the law, especially on what actions contribute to a "hostile environment." A review of recent court cases shows various legal bodies struggling with this very issue, with inconsistent outcomes. One basis for ambiguity lies in an attempt to define harassing behaviors in isolation from their sequential context. In contrast to this position, we argue that to understand better how harassment occurs, we need to look at what actions and utterances do in interaction. Instead of asking, "What counts as sexual harassment?" we pose the question,

"How does one do sexual harassment?" Since a "hostile environment" is a jointly created context, we also ask, "How does a victim come to participate in harassing interactions?"

In the wake of the Hill-Thomas hearings, communication scholars are beginning to view sexual harassment as a communicative phenomenon. In a recent issue of the *Journal of Applied Communication Research*, several narratives recounting sexual harassment were collected and analyzed from differing viewpoints (Strine, 1992; Taylor and Conrad, 1992; Wood, 1992).

Julia Wood (1992) provides a powerful reminder of the political significance of naming. Sexual harassment, because it is experienced by those in subordinate positions, has only recently been recognized as a discriminatory action that perpetuates inequality. Wood argues that for those not harmed by sexual harassment "it was not worth naming; it did not exist" (352). It was not until individuals and institutions were assigned financial liability for sexually harassing actions that sexual harassment became known and studied. Wood points out that the struggle over recognizing the harmful effects of sexual harassment is far from over. The meaning and significance of sexual harassment depend on relating it to various culturally embedded practices and social contexts. In this essay we trace how the rulings on sexual harassment have been grounded in a "reasonable woman" legal standard to illustrate the political significance of naming. Furthermore, we demonstrate how the contestation over various interpretations of "context" by the courts distorts the experience of sexual harassment.

Mary Strine (1992) gives a poststructuralist reading of narratives recounting episodes of sexual harassment, claiming that the poststructuralist insight that a person "is now more accurately thought of as an evolving composite of differing, even contradictory, social subject-positions that an individual body occupies over the course of a lifetime" offers a way of understanding sexual harassment (393). Strine argues that "culturally variable, deeply embedded constraints on identity formation" work to create contradictions in the various identities occupied by a particular body as well as ruptures in cultural expectations (393). For example, the identities of woman and professionals have historically been articulated as contradictory. Sexual harassment, according to Strine, can be read as the resistance of males, whose own subjectivity is constituted by this contradiction, by "signalling and containing" the entrance of women into professional occupations as a "social transgression" (394). While we agree with Strine, in this essay we take a step back and detail the ways that identities established in patriarchal relations of dominance are created, maintained, and transformed in and through sexually harassing talk.

Brian Taylor and Charles Conrad's (1992) analysis of the narratives recounting sexual harassment in academic settings found sexual harassment described as a communicative practice. Sexual harassment, as with all types of "political" communication, works to establish and sustain relations of power through the regulation of social space. Like Taylor and Conrad, we view sexual harassment as an organized, describable phenomenon constituted by a "variety of practices and experiences which contribute to the suppression of rationally conducted, open, and accountable dialogue" (468). In this project, we elaborate on Taylor and Conrad's work by describing some of the interactional methods used to create and maintain contexts that suppress dialogue.

As much light as previous research sheds on the nature of sexual harassment, without detailed accounts of how sexual harassment is accomplished in and through communicative action, as Wood (1992) points out, "we are limited in our grasp of how sexual harassment actually transpires, why participants engage in it, what professional, psychological, and cognitive consequences (both 'payoffs' and problems) it entails, and what conditions in individuals, relationships, organizations, and culture allow, perpetuate, and sometime promote it" (355). We contend that through detailed description of the methods used to create and preserve hostile sexual environments, we may come to find the methods necessary to transform them.

There are obvious difficulties inherent in attempting to collect instances of naturally occurring sexual harassment for empirical examination. Researchers have collected personal narratives, conducted interviews, and even examined fictional sources. Consonant with Wood's (1993) call for studies of "individuals' descriptions of sexual harassment" (17), we analyze Professor Anita Hill's statements about her interactions with Justice Clarence Thomas in which harassment allegedly occurred. Whatever their basis in fact, Hill's public statements provide clear descriptions of harassing episodes. From analyzing these instances, we can identify two distinct ways of "doing sexual harassment." One involves repeatedly, even relentlessly pursuing consent to social invitations, including dismissing and ignoring covert and overt rejections. The second involves dominating and controlling the topic of conversation by always initiating the topic and refusing to go along with the other party's attempts to shift it. These devices, *pursuit of consent* and *control of topic,* place the other party in the increasingly difficult situation of either having to leave the scene or become extremely rude (e.g., slapping or yelling). Under the constraints of work relationships and the need for employment, the "victim" may not feel that even these options are available or may feel that resorting to these options carries heavy consequences (and indeed, it often does; people have been fired, shunned, and scapegoated for exercising them). The repeated use of pursuit of consent and topic control in the workplace contributes to the creation of a hostile working environment, thus creating sexual harassment.

In this essay we argue that recent court rulings on the hostile environment as the basis for sexual harassment cases reveal fundamental problems and inconsistencies for which the pragmatic analysis of harassment we offer here provides some remedy. We then examine Anita Hill's testimony in the light of previous research on the sequential organization of talk to explicate these two devices for doing sexual harassment (pursuit of consent and topic control). Finally, we raise some implications for legal rulings and workplace training.

Current Treatment of Sexual Harassment Claims

Sexual harassment is a legal cause of action under Title VII of the Civil Rights Act of 1964. Title VII makes it illegal for employers "to fail or refuse to hire or to discharge any individual, or otherwise to discriminate against any individual with respect to his compensation, terms, conditions, or privileges of employment, because of such individual's race, color, religion, sex, or national origin" (2000e–2002a). The word *conditions* is operative in conceptualizing sexual harassment. When employees are subject to sexual harassment, they are subject to a condition of employment that is invidiously discriminatory. The Equal Employment Opportunity Commission (EEOC) guidelines outline the current definitions of sexual harassment the courts use:

> Harassment on the basis of sex is a violation of Title VII. Unwelcome sexual advances, requests for sexual favors, and other verbal and physical conduct of a sexual nature constitute sexual harassment when (1) submission to such conduct is made explicitly or implicitly a term or condition of an individual's employment, (2) submission to or rejection of such conduct by an individual is used as the basis of employment decisions affecting such individual or (3) such conduct has the purpose or effect of unreasonably

interfering with an individual's work performance or creating an intimidating, hostile, or offensive working environment. (1988, sec. 1604.11)

The EEOC guidelines set out two types of sexual harassment claims: quid pro quo and hostile environment. The first and second conditions set out in the guidelines constitute the quid pro quo claim, or, as Catharine A. MacKinnon (1979) would put it, "the more or less explicit exchange: the woman must comply sexually or forfeit an employment benefit" (32). Quid pro quo is the most easily recognized form of sexual harassment since, as Wendy Pollack (1990) observes, "it fits the traditional model of a subordinate within the workplace hierarchy who suffers or is threatened with a tangible loss" (48). The hostile environment claim is much harder to define. Hostile environment harassment does not necessarily result in an economic loss to the victim. The hostile environment claim addresses more intangible, nondiscrete harms that often occur over several years. The third condition of the EEOC guidelines defines any verbal or physical action of a sexual nature that has the effect of creating a hostile working environment as sexual harassment. When unwanted sexual comments or touching, pornography, and other actions perceived as sexually demeaning result in a hostile working environment, the employee has been subject to sex discrimination and is therefore entitled to legal remedy.

The Supreme Court, in the case of *Meritor Savings Bank v. Vinson* (1986), legitimized the use of the hostile environment standard. Mechele Vinson alleged that her supervisor forced her to engage in sexual relations and made open, unwelcome sexual advances on the job. Even though Vinson was not fired or directly threatened with job loss or other economic losses if she failed to comply with her supervisor's requests for sexual favors, the court held that the conditions of her employment were indeed intimidating and that a hostile environment therefore existed. The Court dismissed as irrelevant arguments that Vinson voluntarily participated in sexual conduct with her supervisor since she was never directly threatened with job loss and continued to work at the bank, knowing her supervisor would continue making sexual advances. The Court argued that the "gravamen of any sexual harassment claim is that the alleged sexual advances were unwelcome" (68). Thus, as long as the harassment is unwelcome and sufficiently severe and pervasive enough to inflict psychological damages, a hostile environment claim may be sustained (Pollack, 1990, 55). The Court had yet to test a sexual harassment claim of the type envisioned in the EEOC guidelines: the creation of a hostile environment through verbal conduct of a sexual nature.

In *Rabidue v. Osceola Refining Company* (1986) the Court ruled that pornography and other types of sexually demeaning discourse have a minimal effect on the "reasonable person" and that the workplace was therefore not hostile. The Court interpreted the term *unreasonably* in the 1988 EEOC guidelines to mean that the truth and authenticity of a sexual harassment allegation should be determined according to a test of whether the harassment was reasonable in the wider "social context":

> In the Court's viewpoint the word "unreasonably" opens the door to an important conceptual development of the sex harassment theory. This word entitles the judiciary to consider the nature of the employment environment in which the given plaintiff suffered the alleged harassment. This in turn authorizes courts to consider factors such as the educational background of the plaintiff co-workers and supervisors, the physical makeup of the plaintiff work area, and the reasonable expectation of the plaintiff with the kind of conduct that constitutes sex harassment. (430)

This line of reasoning led the Court to conclude that, given the generally "uncivilized" behavior exhibited among men of little education who work in traditionally blue-collar occupations, any person could "reasonably" expect that the workplace would be full of sexual comments and pornography: "Thus, under the approach sketched above, the standard for determining sex harassment would be different depending on the work environment. Indeed it cannot seriously be disputed that in some work environments, humor and language are rough hewn and vulgar. Sexual jokes, sexual conversations and girlie magazines may abound" (430).

The Court argued that the overwhelming presence of pornography in the "social context" of daily life desensitizes the "reasonable person" so that its presence does not affect work performance and psychological well-being in any significant way: "For better or worse, modern America features open displays of written and pictorial erotica. Shopping centers, candy stores and prime time television regularly display pictures of naked bodies and erotic real or simulated sex acts. Living in this milieu, the average American should not be legally offended by sexually explicit posters" (433).

The Court, finding that pornography and sexually explicit comments in the workplace had a minimal effect on Vivienne Rabidue, dismissed the charges of harassment. By situating Vivienne Rabidue's claims in the larger "social context," the Court argued that her experiences were not unusual and that she therefore could "reasonably" expect these things and had no grounds for a charge of sexual harassment. This treatment of context provided the Court with an analytical weapon for dismissing women's lived experience of sexual harassment, since potentially, anyone who claims that the working environment is hostile may be labeled as "unreasonable."

The Court's use of "context" to disregard claims of sexual harassment in the *Rabidue* case came under sharp attack in *Robinson v. Jacksonville Shipyards, Inc.* (1991). Lori Robinson, a welder at Jacksonville Shipyards Incorporated, alleged that the display of pornography in her work areas and in the offices of her supervisors, along with a constant barrage of sexual comments and lewd jokes, created a hostile working environment. The defendants, citing the precedent set in *Rabidue*, argued that in the larger "social context" and in particular in the "context" of a shipyard, pornography and sexual comments and jokes are commonplace and therefore "reasonable." The Court found that the "social context" arguments of the defense had no value in determining the issues of the case. To combat the legal precedent set forth in *Rabidue*, the Court offered three arguments against the prior use of "context" as a standard for determining hostile environment sexual harassment.

First, the Court argued that the prevalence of pornography and other demeaning sexual discourse in society is irrelevant for determining if these create a hostile workplace. Rather, "the whole point of the sexual harassment claim is that behavior that may be permissible in some settings can be abusive in the workplace" (1525).

Second, the Court maintained that the "social context" argument offered in *Rabidue* undermines Title VII's promise to open the workplace to women. If the Court used the preexisting state of the workplace as a standard to assess the amount of hostility and discrimination that is "reasonable" given a particular "context," only those women who could and would accept the level of abuse inherent to a given workplace would apply to and continue to work there.

The third argument the Court made against using "social context" to assess hostile environment claims in the *Robinson* case focused on the Court's use in the *Rabidue* case of the widest possible view of context ("society" and the "reasonable person") to limit hostile environment sexual harassment from its analysis. Once the scope of analysis was enlarged, it became clear that the interpretive constraints operating in the "contexts" of the "workplace" and in "society" differed. The same was true of the interpretive constraints at work in the "contexts" of a reasonable person" and a "reasonable woman." Hence, a different standard for assessing what conduct constitutes an "unreasonable" amount of hostility should operate when considering the claims of women in a workplace setting. This move from a "reasonable person" to a "reasonable woman" standard introduced in *Robinson* was extended in *Ellison v. Brady* (1991).

In a unanimous decision the Supreme Court held that neither the standard set out in *Robinson* and *Ellison* nor the standard set forth in *Meritor* and *Rabidue* should be used to assess whether conduct is sufficient to create a hostile working environment. Rather, in *Harris v. Forklift Systems, Inc.* (1993), the Court took "a middle path between making actionable any conduct that is merely offensive and requiring the conduct to cause a tangible psychological injury" (370). On the one hand, it argued that the utterance of an epithet that "merely" offends is not sufficient to create an "objectively" abusive or hostile working environment. On the other hand, it argued:

> Title VII comes into play before the harassing conduct leads to a nervous breakdown. A discriminatorily abusive work environment, even one that does not seriously affect the employee's psychological well-being, can and often will distract from employees' job performance, discourage employees from remaining on the job, or keep them from advancing in their careers. Moreover, even without regard to these tangible effects, the very fact that the discriminatory conduct was so severe or pervasive that it created a work environment abusive to employees because of their race, gender, religion, or national origin offends Title VII's broad rule of workplace equality. (370–71)

The Court did not propose an alternative to the standards of either "offensive conduct" established in *Robinson* and *Ellison* or "psychological injury" established in *Meritor* and *Rabidue*. Instead, the Court argued that no "mathematically precise test" could ever be established for determining if a given workplace was hostile and abusive, and it refused to privilege any single factor as sufficient to measure the hostility of a particular workplace. It added:

> But we can say that whether an environment is "hostile" and "abusive" can be determined only by looking at all the circumstances. These may include

the frequency of the discriminatory conduct; its severity; whether it is physically threatening or humiliating, or a mere offensive utterance; and whether it unreasonably interferes with an employee's work performance. The effect on the employee's psychological well-being is, of course, relevant to determining whether the plaintiff actually found the environment abusive. But while psychological harm, like any other relevant factor, may be taken into account, no single factor is required. (372)

One objection to the Court's decision in *Harris* is that it failed to articulate any clear standard for assessing whether some particular conduct is sufficient to create a hostile working environment. As loose as the "offensive" conduct standard set up in *Ellison* and as severe as the "psychological injury" standard set forth in *Meritor* and *Rabidue* (1986) were, they both provided a mechanism for determining if some particular conduct creates an abusive and hostile environment.

In his concurring opinion, Justice Antonin Scalia argued that the Court's decision failed to set "a very clear standard" (372). Furthermore, he argued that the clarity of the standard (or lack of one) was not at all increased by adding the adjective "objectively" or by appealing to the "reasonable person's" notion of what constitutes an abusive or hostile environment. By not setting any kind of clear standard, the *Harris* decision did not give any guidance to the lower courts that will be deciding how hostile environments are created and maintained in future sexual harassment cases. Indeed, for the time being, it seems as if the questions of what a hostile environment is and how it comes into being remain unanswered.

Critique of the Court's Rulings

Two doctrinal issues, both at the core of the hostile environment theory as currently articulated by the courts, seriously hinder any chance of discovering how a hostile environment gets constructed and, therefore, how a workplace might be transformed. First, grounding the authenticity of an allegation of sexual harassment in the ability of the plaintiff to show damages focuses solely on the victim rather than on the interactive conduct constituting a hostile environment. Second, defining a hostile environment as the presence of discourse that either a "reasonable person" or a "reasonable woman" finds "humiliating," "abusive," or "offensive" focuses on the semantic content rather than on the pragmatic uses of the discourse in question. If the courts are to move toward a full account of how a hostile environment is made or revised, both doctrines must be respecified.

The standard set out in *Harris* for determining an abusive and hostile workplace creates a nearly impossible burden of proof and forces the plaintiff into a double bind. Plaintiffs can show that the conduct was physically threatening and humiliating (as opposed to merely offensive) or that it unreasonably interfered with their job performance. The physical threat standard provides little help to plaintiffs, however, for most cases of hostile environment harassment do not involve physical threats. In fact, if plaintiffs could prove that they were physically threatened if they did not comply with requests for sexual favors, they would have grounds for a quid pro quo claim. Since *Harris* suggested no mechanism for determining whether some conduct was "humiliating" or "merely offensive," it is unlikely that many courts will employ this test. *Harris* did, however, make numerous references to job performance, suggesting that this would be the preferred standard for adjudicating hostile environment claims in the future. Yet grounding a claim of sexual harassment on diminished job performance is as dangerous for plaintiffs as having to prove psychological injury. If plaintiffs can prove that their job performance has diminished since the advent of the alleged harassing conduct, the defense may argue that plaintiffs are using harassing conduct as an excuse for poor work performance and will set out to show that plaintiffs were poor employees. The defense has numerous resources (such as performance evaluations and the testimony of other workers) to cast plaintiffs as poor employees. If, however, plaintiffs claim that they were able to perform their job competently even while being harassed, the defense may argue that the plaintiffs failed to meet the minimal definition of a "victim" and that the charge of sexual harassment should therefore be disregarded. Both the psychological injury standard set out in *Meritor* and extended in *Rabidue* and the job performance standard suggested in *Harris* place an almost impossible burden of proof on the plaintiffs. The claim of damage is far too difficult for most (if not all) plaintiffs to meet, for there is no way to prove a direct causal relation between a set of statements and actions and the onset of psychological injury or diminished job performance.

The courts currently judge allegations of sexual harassment according to a test of plaintiffs' endurance. If they could endure no more of the harassment without incurring psychological damage or a diminished ability to do their job, their allegation of hostile environment has a chance of being sustained. As Pollack (1990) points out, "The court looks to the victim, not for her perspective on what behavior she affirmatively and freely accepts and what she does not, not for what is harmful to her and to what extent she has been harmed, but for her ability to cope with the harassment" (60). Shifting the focus from the actions constituting a hostile environment to the victim's endurance legitimatizes sexual harassment by making legal any behavior that degrades and demeans yet cannot be proven directly to cause psychological injury or diminished job performance.

One result of moving away from the offender's conduct to the plaintiff's tolerance has been the court's search for an objective standard to assess whether some particular conduct should be legally offensive, intimidating, and hostile. The courts, fearing that some women may be oversensitive to sexual comments and hence would chill "normal" sexual talk at work, claim that any sexual conduct that humiliates, offends, or intimidates a "reasonable woman" constitutes sexual harassment. Who is this reasonable woman? By labeling some women as "reasonable," the Court implies that some women bring charges that are "unreasonable," "hyper-sensitive," and "crazy." The reasonable woman standard is anything but objective. The Court decides what actions befit a "reasonable woman." The reasonable woman standard ignores differences among women—or, more accurately excludes those who exhibit difference—and posits "woman" as a homogeneous, static category, implying an oversimplified and incorrect view of gender.

Gender is not an inherent property of the biological species male or female. Rather, as Candace West and Don Zimmermann (1985) point out, gender is a "routine, methodical, and reoccurring accomplishment" performed through "the activity of managing situated conduct in light of normative conceptions of attitudes and activities appropriate for one's sex category" (126–27). That is, the identity "woman" is an effect of communicative practices. No one person can be identified solely as a "woman." Rather, any one person consists of multiple identities, with "woman" being one of many possibilities. Thus, a "woman" cannot be defined as "reasonable" or "unreasonable" without taking into account the discourse that constituted her as such.

Sexually demeaning discourse at work may create a hostile environment, not because "reasonable" women find it humiliating or offensive but because it equates "woman" with "object of sexual aggression." This may in turn control how "women" are allowed to participate in talk at the workplace, because "women" may be seen as not having the capacity, desire, and the right to participate fully, except in ways deemed appropriate by those controlling the design and implementation of forums for talk and decision making. Of course, exclusion from full participation may apply to other categories of people. Racial and ethnic minorities, homosexuals, people with mental disabilities, children, and the like historically have been denied rights to speak.

The courts currently ignore the fact that the reason some women find sexually demeaning discourse disturbing enough to constitute a hostile environment has nothing to do with some women being more "reasonable" than others. Any discourse locking people into a workplace identity (e.g., "woman," "nigger," or both) that entails disrespect, inequality, and a constant need to monitor behavior creates a hostile environment.

The *Harris* decision, which moved away from the reasonable woman standard set out in *Robinson* and *Ellison* and back to the reasonable person standard used in *Rabidue,* did not alleviate the problem because it also excluded difference and is likely to be used as a tool for disregarding the experiences of plaintiffs because they are cast as "unreasonable." In fact, a reasonable woman standard would be preferable to a reasonable person standard because at least it uses the perspective of the oppressed group to judge the truth and authenticity of the plaintiff's account. However, it is the reasonableness part of the standard that is the problem with both the reasonable person and reasonable woman standards. Both standards ignore how the identities of both "person" and "woman" are accomplished in and through communicative practices. As a result, any unequal social conditions that would be used to construct a "person" and a "woman" are treated as "reasonable" and will be used to dismiss the very real experiences of hostility, abuse, and intimidation that may exist in the workplace.

By limiting the scope of their analysis to defining conduct that "reasonable" persons or women find objectionable, the courts failed to articulate any account of how or why that conduct is perceived as intimidating, hostile, and abusive. Without such an account, the courts cannot identify the methods by which people create conditions promoting inequality and discrimination in the workplace. Hence, no possibilities for transforming workplace norms, short of a massive cultural revolution, appear available.

If, however, we begin by describing the methods used to make a workplace into a hostile environment, we find that sexual harassment is an organized, describable accomplishment of situated actors. By identifying procedures used to achieve a hostile environment, we may also begin to identify those procedures for respecifying the workplace into a democratically organized, equitable, and nonhostile setting. Such analysis begins by examining actual accounts of hostile environment harassment to reconstruct those discursive moves that create and maintain a hostile working environment.

Respecifying Sexual Harassment as Communicative Accomplishment

> I envision a two-way process of interaction between the relevant legal concepts and women's experience. The strictures of the concept of sex discrimination will ultimately constrain those aspects of women's oppression that will be legally recognized as discriminatory. At the same time, women's experiences, expressed in their own way, can push to expand that concept. Such an approach not only enriches the law. It begins to shape it so that what really happens to women, not some male version of what happens to women, is at the core of the legal prohibition. Women's lived-through experience, in as whole and truthful a fashion as can be approximated at this point, should begin to provide the starting point and context out of which is constructed the narrower forms of abuse that will be made illegal on their behalf. Now that a few women have the tools to address the legal system on its own terms the law can begin to address women's experience on women's own terms.
> CATHARINE A. MACKINNON, *Sexual Harassment of Working Women*

If MacKinnon's vision of a dialogue between actual experiences of sexual harassment and the legal standards for defining conduct that constitutes sexual harassment is to become a reality, we need to analyze actual accounts of sexual harassment in detail. In this section we turn to an analysis of an actual account of hostile environment harassment. Based on this analysis, we suggest an alternative conception of harassment and expose some methods used to accomplish sexual harassment.

Anita Hill's testimony to the Senate Judiciary Committee provides a lucid account of how a hostile working environment was created and maintained. Hill described her harassment as the effect of the interactional dominance exerted by Clarence Thomas while she worked for him at the Department of Education and the EEOC. That is, Hill accounted for her harassment by describing the contours of their interactions: (1) his continual social invitations and his refusal to accept her justifications for declining his invitations; and (2) his control of topics for discussion and his refusal to acknowledge her attempts to shift the talk away from sexually explicit topics. Even though Hill did describe the content of Thomas's comments as pornographic in nature, her account of harassment turned on how Thomas manipulated the speech-exchange system to recontextualize their working relationship into one based on domination and thus recontextualized the workplace into a hostile environment.

Pursuit of Consent

The first method of harassment described in Hill's testimony is Thomas's *pursuit of consent* through repeated solicitations for social engagements even after she had declined them and his refusal to acknowledge as valid her accounts for declining his invitations. Hill (1992) described Thomas's initial invitation and her refusal: "I declined the invitation to go out socially with him, and explained to him that I thought it would jeopardize what at the time I considered to be a very good working relationship. I believe then, as now, that having a social relationship with a person who was supervising my work would be ill advised. I was very uncomfortable with the idea and told him so" (8–9).

Hill turned down Thomas's invitations and invoked their roles as subordinate and superior in accounting for her refusal. An invitation and its response form one common type of *adjacency pair* (Schegloff and Sacks, 1973). When a first speaker issues an invitation, the second speaker is constrained to give some response. Acceptances typically appear in brief, direct form. Refusals typically show delays, fillers, hesitations, and accounts for the refusal. In this example from a conversation between two friends, Pam issues an invitation. Gloria's decline follows a pause and the filler "well"; she constructs a lengthy account that reveals prior social arrangements and a paper she must write. (See the appendix at the end of this volume for an explanation of the symbol system used in this analysis.)

Pam: I'd love for you to come if you want to come.
         (0.4)
Gloria: pt Well, I would but I just talked to my sister a few minutes ago?=
Pam: =Yeah
         (0.4)
Gloria: And I promised her: ·hhh that I would u:m (0.4) you know- go over
         there cause I have the car cause I had to go take the ca:r- (0.2) over

this morning we had to have some junk fixed on it and to take it
over this mornin (.) and- she couldn't do it cause she works all day
so

Pam: O::h=

Gloria: =You know- I gotta go return the car and then she's b<u>a</u>bysittin so
we're am: we're gun take the little g<u>i</u>rl to go get her something to
<u>ea</u>t and some <u>i</u>ce cream or sum'm
(0.2)

Pam: ⎡O:::h h o w cu::te.   ⎤
Gloria: ⎣pt·hh so plus I have t-⎦
(0.2)

Gloria: Plus I have to type this stupid thing hh.

(UTCL A21:11, in Hopper, 1992, 159–60)

People commonly let such accounts pass unchallenged. Again, the conversational example shows this. Pam accepts Gloria's account for declining with
the "okay." Gloria then moves to close down the topic and talk about something else:

Gloria: Plus I have to type this stupid thing hh
Pam: <u>u</u>hhh hih hih
(0.4)

Pam: Okay well just thought ⎡I'd (call)⎤
Gloria: ⎣·hh↑<u>O</u>: ⎦ :w.
Gloria: I've to tell you something.

(Hopper, 1992, 160)

To challenge the basis for refusal is to cause trouble. Thomas did not accept Hill's refusal or her account; instead, he pursued the invitation. Hill
(1992) provided this report of that pursuit: "I thought that by saying no and
explaining my reasons my employer would abandon his social suggestions.
However, to my regret, in the following few weeks, he continued to ask me
out on several occasions. He pressed me to justify my reasons for saying no
to him. He began to show displeasure in his tone and voice and his demeanor
and continued pressure for an explanation" (9–10).

Thomas did not harass Hill by asking her out. Rather, she claimed that he
harassed her by continuing to ask her out after she told him no, dismissing
her justifications for saying no, and pressuring her to come up with a "real"
reason for not going out with him (i.e., a reason that Thomas would approve

because he could then provide a "better" one for her to go out with him). In a sense, Thomas refused to acknowledge Hill as capable of deciding whether she wished to see him socially and as capable of justifying her choices. (This refusal of her accounts also had the effect of extending talk on the topic— here, a nonwork topic about their relationship—thereby contributing to his control of the topic. This is the second device for harassment, described below.) Since she had not provided any "legitimate" bases for refusals, Thomas then had sequential grounds for pursuing her with repeated invitations.

Thomas's refusal to accept Hill's justifications for declining his social invitations forced Hill to repeat her refusals. Recipients of such pursuit may have a range of options available, including treating the pursuit as a joke, responding to it on a metatalk level, leaving the immediate interaction, or making it public. However, those having subordinate status or power in an organization may feel constraints against using these options since they may threaten the superior. We do not know if Hill tried any of these options; in any case, her description of Thomas's relentless pursuit suggests that even if she had tried any of these options, they probably would not have been effective. Hence, her only choices were to give in to Thomas, endure the harassment, or leave the relationship by quitting the job. Each of these options carried serious negative consequences for her. Giving in obviously would have been against her wishes. Continuing to endure, she believed, would have risked her being punished or fired, as her testimony shows: "He began to show displeasure in his tone and voice and his demeanor and continued to pressure for an explanation. At this point, late 1982, I began to be concerned that Clarence Thomas might take out his anger with me by degrading me or not giving me important assignments. I also thought that he might find an excuse for dismissing me" (Hill, 1992, 9–10). Severing the relationship with Thomas would have meant giving up a good job early in a promising career and damaging her opportunities for future advancement. Thus, within the superior-subordinate relationship, such pursuit sequences become particularly damaging: the victim's responses are limited and unsatisfactory. This pursuit by a superior creates an "invidiously discriminatory" condition of employment—she must give in or suffer the consequences. In this way, Thomas's pursuit of consent, in the superior-subordinate relational context, made Hill a victim of sexual harassment.

In a sexualized working environment, recipients of solicitations for sexual favors, sexually oriented jokes, or social invitations must monitor their behavior to determine if they are eliciting sexual attention. As the Court observed in the *Robinson* case, "They must conform their behavior to the existence of sexual stereotyping either by becoming sexy and responsive to the men who flirt with them or by becoming rigid, standoffish, and distant so as to make it clear that they are not interested in the status of a sex object" (1505). Hill testified that the intimidation, caused by having to decline Thomas's social suggestions repeatedly and to monitor her own behavior constantly, made both the Department of Education and the EEOC hostile working environments.

Control of Topic

A second method of harassment practiced by Thomas, as alleged in Hill's testimony, consists of his controlling the topic by unilaterally introducing sexual matters into the conversation and refusing to acknowledge her attempts to shift the topic away from those matters. Thomas, in effect, forced Hill either to listen to his sexually explicit comments or to refuse to engage in conversations with him. Since she could not very well refuse to engage in discourse with her immediate supervisor, Hill had no options other than to listen or to resign.

In this excerpt, Hill (1992) describes how Thomas would turn their conversations toward sexual topics: "After a brief discussion of work, he would turn the conversation to a discussion of sexual matters. His conversations were very very vivid. He spoke about acts that he had seen in pornographic films involving having sex with animals, and films showing group sex or rape scenes. Because I was extremely uncomfortable talking about sex with him at all, in particular in such a graphic way, I told him that I did not want to talk about this subject" (9). When we compare Hill's descriptions with research on the organization of topics in conversation, the intimidating nature of Thomas's control over the topic and its pursuit becomes clear. Generally in conversation, interactants mutually construct topics. One speaker may introduce a topic, but the other will ratify it in the next turn. Graham Button and Neil Casey (1984) found that in the course of three turns, speakers interactionally and mutually generate a topic for conversation. This sequence is illustrated in the following example:

1   S: What's new,
2   G: We:᷎ll? t °lemme see° las' ni᷎ght, I had the girls ov<u>e</u>r?
                                                [
3   S: Yea᷎h?=
(F:TC:I:1:12–13, in Button and Casey, 1984, 168)

First, S issues a "topic initial elicitor," packaged as an inquiry into the possibility of the other party's presenting a potential topic. Second, G responds to the topic elicitor and presents a newsworthy event. Third, S (who had issued the topic initial elicitor) topicalizes the newsworthy event. Topicalizers provide for the possibility for continued talk without developing talk on the topic. Thus, the speaker who presents the newsworthy event is in a position to begin talk about the "topic" at hand.

At each stage the current speaker allows the other to ratify the prior move and to initiate the next move in the sequence. This turn by turn negotiation makes the selection of topic a shared, interactional accomplishment. Mutual construction of a topic ensures interactional cohesiveness and some reciprocity of power between participants.

The sequence generated by a topic initial elicitor represents but one method for mutual construction of topics. The point is, however, that entry into topics generally is mutual, requiring ratification. For one participant to initiate topics unilaterally without the other's ratification creates an asymmetrical balance of power.

Thomas nominated topics for conversation and began speaking on them without giving Hill an opportunity to ratify the selection of the topic. In their interactions, talk of pornographic items was not the product of a sequence in which both parties mutually constructed sex as a topic. Rather, Thomas exercised complete control of the process.

When encountering an embarrassing or controversial topic, a conversationalist faces the problem of how to get off that topic. One method available to participants is to close the conversation (Jefferson, 1984, 191). Entry into a closing sequence does not ensure the conversation will end. It may, however, display the participant's orientation to troubling aspects of the topic. Hill (1992) testified that she dealt with Thomas's initiation of sexual topics by preempting the possibility of longer conversations: "My reaction to these conversations was to avoid them by eliminating opportunities for us to engage in extended conversations. This was difficult because, at the time, I was his only assistant at the office of education—or office for civil rights" (9).

Moving into closing preempts fuller development of conversational topics and thus provided Hill one possible remedy; however, this was difficult given their work relationship. A second method for getting off a problematic topic involves shifting to another topic. The vast majority of topic shifts are other-attentive; that is, they make the other person the focus of talk (Jefferson,

1984, 193–98). One common practice used to shift topics is for one of the participants to solicit relevant biographical information about the other participant(s). These other-attentive topic shifts preserve the interactional cohesiveness resulting from the practice of mutually constructing talk. Hill testified that she used this method when she attempted topic shifts. She noted, however, that such moves generally did not succeed: "I would also try to change the subject to education matters or to nonsexual personal matters, such as his background or his beliefs. My efforts to change the subject were rarely successful" (Hill, 1992, 9).

A third strategy for directing talk away from problematic topics is gradually to move the conversation away from the problem topic toward related matters. That is, a participant can make a *stepwise transition* from one topic to a seemingly unrelated topic by linking the next turn to some secondary aspect of the prior turn (Jefferson, 1984, 198–222). The effect of this stepwise transition is that participants starting an interaction by speaking about a particular topic may, by the end of the interaction, be speaking about a topic quite removed from the original without ever producing a disjunctive topic shift. The stepwise transition provides an effective means of getting off a problematic topic that still preserves the interactional cohesiveness of mutual topic construction. For Hill, however, introducing a stepwise transition somehow related to Thomas's sexually explicit talk would have been difficult to do without in some way implicating herself in such talk. In the light of the constant attempt to monitor her behavior to avoid giving off any signs of sexual interest, Hill would not have wanted to engage in any discussion (no matter how ancillary) with Thomas about sex. Therefore, Hill's only options to shift the topic away from sexual matters would have been to try to close the conversation or change the subject to something else of interest to him. Hill testified to having attempted both methods, without success.

Thomas's topic nomination and control practices constituted a radical departure from more collaborative topic selection methods. They did not allow for the mutual construction of a topic, nor did they produce the interactional cohesiveness found in conversation.

Hill did not claim that the presence of pornographic material constituted a hostile environment. In a conversation in which one party brings up a topic that the other party finds offensive, methods exist for changing to another topic. However, Hill testified that Thomas systematically refused to allow her to execute these methods, instead creating an environment in which he exercised complete control over topic. Hence, the coupling of topics perceived as pornographic (which in this case articulated an equivalence between Hill and the identity of a "woman" incapable of participating in the coconstruction of context) with the attending conversational practices (which excluded her from participating except in ways circumscribed by Thomas) constituted a hostile working environment.

Conclusion

Conversation differs from a lecture, interview, or interrogation in that participants try to maintain equal speaking rights (Wilson, 1987). That is, in a conversation, each participant may initiate such moves as nominating the topic, taking a turn, repairing a misunderstanding, and so forth. Clearly, Hill and Thomas did not share equal speaking rights. By refusing to accept Hill's justifications for declining his invitations for social engagements and by reissuing the invitations despite her insistence that those invitations were unwelcome, Thomas forced Hill into a position in which she had to monitor all of her actions and conform to a rigid sexual stereotype. By controlling all aspects of the choice and pursuit of a topic, Thomas created a relationship between him and Hill based on an asymmetrical balance of power. These practices forced Hill either to endure his sexual comments or to remove herself permanently from the workplace. Hill eventually chose the later option and found employment elsewhere.

Thomas could get away with controlling their interactions by virtue of the power he held over Hill as her employer. In the workplace context, norms typically exist that allow the superior to suspend ordinary conversational rules. An employer can pursue a response and control the topic by closing off avenues for employees to speak freely. Proponents of this configuration of context justify these practices by claiming that the primary objective of the workplace is the employee's efficient performance. Conversation is thus a luxury that cannot be "afforded" in the workplace. Yet this superior power is, in principle, limited to workplace topics, such as the nature of the task or employee performance. Thomas took advantage of this power and used it to force their discourse to sexual and personal matters. In so doing, he manipulated the context so that Hill was forced to endure his sexual harassment.

Superior-subordinate asymmetry is not an inherent or necessary characteristic of the workplace. Participants carry out the communicative actions that produce and reproduce asymmetry. A context founded on asymmetry may become frozen into practice and codified into a rigid set of procedures governing interaction. When this occurs the context becomes institutionalized. Hence, power and the abuse of power are often mistakenly explained as intrinsic characteristics of large scale institutions rather than effects of the practices of everyday social actors. However, the institution is an effect of those actors' communicative practices. We can imagine workplaces in which symmetrical conversational interaction is the norm between and among all organizational members.

Participants can and do operate outside of the "official" context. People carry out private conversations while no one is listening; develop alternate systems of identification, such as nicknames or acronyms; and modify normal methods for carrying out tasks by using systems of their own creation. However, these resistance strategies depend on the operation of the "official" context. Participants must always monitor their actions to avoid sanction. In the case of the sexual harassment Hill described, Thomas packaged his sexual discourse as conversational items to be discussed outside the constraints of the official context. Hill, however, was unwilling to participate in these "conversations." Thomas thus had to rely on the power given to him by his institutional identity as her superior and the attendant power of that position to manipulate the context so that he could control the choice and pursuit of subjects for conversation and force Hill to listen to his comments. That is, Thomas used the power afforded him by his position within the "official" context to suspend the conversational norms usually associated with talk about personal matters while at work.

The EEOC guidelines do not state that conversation should be the norm for interactions in the workplace. Nor do they state that workplaces should be democratically organized and be founded on a symmetrical power balance among all participants. The types of contexts normally associated with the workplace hold participants as a captive audience and allow for asymmetrical power relationships. However, EEOC guidelines stipulating that the conditions of one's employment cannot be altered on the basis of race, color, religion, sex, or national origin help protect employees from potential abuses of power in such contexts. If one's sexuality is used as the basis for an asymmetrical power balance, the conditions of employment have been altered and a hostile environment has been created.

We are now in a position to apply the methods of accomplishing sexual harassment contained in Hill's testimony to the legal conception of sexual harassment. Hill's account of sexual harassment turns on the pragmatic uses of sexual discourse rather than on its content, for an employer or a coworker could invite an employee or another coworker to a social engagement without committing harassment. The recipient may accept the invitation, or, if she or he declines, the other party may let the refusal pass without pressuring for an explanation. An employer and employee or two coworkers may mutually construct sexually explicit topics for conversation. Thus, it is not the presence of sexual discourse that constitutes a hostile working environment. Rather, a hostile environment results from manipulating the context so that the "victim" cannot freely accept or reject sexual discourse.

Compared with the current approaches the courts use, a communication-centered account of how a hostile environment is created and maintained through the pragmatic effects of communicative practices offers a superior basis for conceptualizing sexual harassment. First, since the uses and functions of the behavior in question are the focus, there is no reason to concentrate on the victim's psychological stability or occupational competence. The courts can therefore adjudicate claims of sexual harassment without resorting to a "reasonable woman" standard that entails "blaming the victim." Second, a communication-centered approach can account for harassing actions performed by coworkers as well as superiors; it can account for the noneconomic harm suffered in an intimidating working environment; and, because it is not centered on the intentions of the party performing the communicative actions, it does not have to look to the social mores of any particular group to determine what types of demeaning discourse are "reasonable." Third, because a communication-centered account shows the methods used to create and maintain a hostile environment, it also illuminates what needs to be done to transform a hostile working environment into a nonintimidating, noncoercive working environment.

Workplace training should focus on the pragmatic consequences of communicative practices rather than on a list of isolated behaviors or topics to be expunged from workplace interaction. Managers who assert that they can no longer talk with any employee about any personal matters without fear of being charged with sexual harassment can learn that it is their taken-for-granted methods of interacting (the pragmatic dimension) that need to be changed. To reiterate, it is not the sexual nature of interaction per se but the unwelcome pursuit of sexual matters through asymmetrical conversational practices that creates a hostile environment.

If a hostile environment is created by manipulating the workplace so that one is forced to endure unwelcome sexual advances and forced to participate in unwelcome sexual talk, it follows that the context could be redesigned to remove opportunities now existing for participants to create and maintain a hostile environment. In short, this process entails democratizing the workplace. By comparing nonintimidating, noncoercive workplaces with hostile working environments, we can discover exactly what changes need to be made.

A detailed analysis of Anita Hill's account of sexual harassment shows that a hostile environment is created, maintained, and transformed by communicative practices. No doubt there are methods of accomplishing sexual harassment other than the pursuit of consent and control of topics. Further analysis of individual accounts of harassing episodes can offer powerful bases for conceptualizing sexual harassment. Such research is needed if we are to uncover those methods necessary to transform a hostile environment into a noncoercive, egalitarian workplace.

REFERENCES

Button, G., and Casey, N. (1984). Generating topic: The use of topic initial elicitors. In J. M. Atkinson and J. Heritage (eds.), *Structures of social action: Studies in conversation analysis*, 167–90. Cambridge: Cambridge University Press.

Civil Rights Act of 1964, 42 U.S.C. sec. 2000e-17 (1982).

EEOC Guidelines, 29 C.F.R. sec. 1604.11 (1988).

Ellison v. Brady, 924 F. 2d 872 (1991).

Harris v. Forklift Systems, Inc., 114 S.Ct. 367 (1993).

Hill, A. F. (1991–92). Statement of Anita F. Hill to the Senate Judiciary Committee, October 11, 1991. *Black Scholar*, 22 (1–2): 8–11.

Hopper, R. (1992). *Telephone conversation*. Bloomington: Indiana University Press.

Jefferson, G. (1984). On stepwise transition from talk about a trouble to inappropriately next-positioned matters. In J. M. Atkinson and J. Heritage (eds.), *Structures of social action: Studies in conversation analysis*, 191–222. Cambridge: Cambridge University Press.

MacKinnon, C. A. (1979). *Sexual harassment of working women: A case of sex discrimination*. New Haven, Conn.: Yale University Press.

Meritor Savings Bank v. Vinson, 477 U.S. 57 (1986).

Pollack, W. (1990). Sexual harassment: Women's experience vs. legal definitions. *Harvard University Women's Law Review,* 13: 35–86.

Rabidue v. Osceola Refining Co., 805 F. 2d 611 (1986).

Robinson v. Jacksonville Shipyards, Inc., 760 F. Supp. 1486 (1991).

Schegloff, E. A., and Sacks, H. (1973). Opening up closings. *Semiotica,* 8: 289–327.

Strine, M. S. (1992). Understanding "how things work": Sexual harassment and academic culture. *Journal of Applied Communication Research,* 20: 391–400.

Taylor, B., and Conrad, C. (1992). Narratives of sexual harassment: Organizational dimensions. *Journal of Applied Communication Research,* 20: 401–18.

West, C., and Zimmerman, D. (1985). Gender, language, and discourse. In T. A. van Dijk (ed.), *Handbook of discourse analysis,* vol. 4, *Discourse analysis in society,* 103–24. London: Academic Press.

Wilson, J. (1987). On the topic of conversation as a speech event. *Research in Language and Social Interaction,* 21: 93–113.

Wood, J. T. (1992). Telling our stories: Narratives as a basis for theorizing sexual harassment. *Journal of Applied Communication Research,* 20: 349–62.

————. (1993). Naming and interpreting sexual harassment: A conceptual framework for scholarship. In G. Kreps (ed.), *Sexual harassment: Communication implications,* 9–26. Cresskill N.J.: Hampton Press.

The pressure to go out with him I felt embarrassed about. . . . [but] the
conversations about sex I was much more embarrassed and humiliated
by. The two combined really made me feel sort of helpless in a job situation. . . . I felt that [my job] was being put in jeopardy by the other
things that were going on in the office and so I was really, really very
troubled by it and distressed over it.

ANITA HILL

The scene is the executive director of the hospital, the chief of OB-
GYN [who was also my personal physician] and me in a public hallway,
and we're talking about something regarding public relations or development. And my boss says something about, "Well, you have the temperament of a redhead." And my doctor said, "Well, only her gynecol-
ogist knows for sure." And . . . I saw it as harassment, but I also saw it
as just plain bad taste, just awful, miserable bad taste.

INTERVIEWEE #7

12

"Giving" Voice to Sexual Harassment: Dialogues in the Aftermath of the Hill-Thomas Hearings

LEDA M. COOKS, CLAUDIA L. HALE, AND SUE DEWINE

Sexual harassment has existed for centuries, with victims[1] of harassment all
too painfully aware of the embarrassment and professional/personal jeopardy inherent in their situation. However, with the public airing of the U.S.
Senate Judiciary Committee hearings involving Judge Clarence Thomas and
Professor Anita Hill, the audience was "treated" to a variety of lessons concerning the challenges of not only defining but also responding to alleged
instances of harassing behaviors.

In an earlier analysis of those hearings (Hale, Cooks, and DeWine, 1994), we found that the senators who interrogated Thomas and Hill framed themselves as rational seekers of justice, citizens of a democracy devoted to fairness, and protectors of the truth. The outcome of the hearings depended on the ways these terms constituted the identities of Thomas and Hill and, in turn, the ways the audience framed the hearings through this discourse.[2]

The methods used in that essay positioned power as either present or absent in language itself. That treatment of power is somewhat problematic because it does not allow one to locate the spaces where power operates in both seemingly powerful and powerless behavior (witness the difficulty with which we determine who has power in situations where teachers claim to have been harassed by students or males have filed harassment complaints against females). Although a Marxist analysis points to the unseen (or what is hidden in policy disputes) and, in particular, the languaging of experience, such an analysis is limited in its ability to speak to an understanding of the possibilities for a new discourse.

Thus, the enthusiasm with which we continue to investigate the discourses surrounding the "trial of Anita Hill" (Hale, Cooks, and DeWine, 1994) is energy devoted to exploring the ways those most enabled in our society (corporate executives, academics, and members of the legal profession) are talking about sexual harassment. We are not interested in providing the ultimate definition of sexual harassment or in delineating the ways in which sexual harassment is experienced. Rather, we are concerned with the ways the hearings and discourse surrounding them have influenced discussion about harassment inside and outside the "boundaries" of the workplace. We are also concerned with the ways the hearings have affected awareness about what constitutes ethical behavior, as well as increasing attempts at legislating that behavior. Ultimately, though, we are interested in perceptions of power and empowerment (of employers, employees, men, and women) associated with perceived violations of body/self/identity.

The Construction of Power

Traditional treatments of power are dichotomous or hierarchical, emphasizing powerful versus powerless behavior. Foucault (1977), however, offers an alternative way of perceiving power and the experience of power. Through this alternative perspective, we find the potential for broadening our insights.

For Foucault, power is both/and rather than either/or. Power emerges from relations of domination and subordination and is employed in the discourses of knowledge (the defining of sexual harassment) and of experience (the ontological-epistemological relations of Otherness). From this standpoint, it would be impossible to speak of sexual harassment in the workplace without some notion of a woman's "natural" sexuality and of women as the objects of corporate (male) surveillance. The traditional view of power permits only a static analysis of oppositions; little attention is paid to the ways power relations are active and ongoing, constructed in discursive patterns of difference. By contrast, adopting and adapting Foucault's notion of power allow a focus on the exercise of power that moves away from the will or intentions of those identified specifically as powerholders.[3]

We chart the (dis)course about sexual harassment by means of two counterhegemonic codes (confession and discipline), which construct a larger narrative of power and domination. Each of these codes contributes to the construction of an ethical/moral line of reasoning that legislates the "corporate body" and influences the constitution of corporate identities. Both of these codes borrow from Foucault's study of power and from the ways that the self and other are constituted through the discourse of everyday life.

Confession

The first frame guiding this analysis is that of confession. Confession, for Foucault, implies a moral agency that regulates the behavior of individuals through the discourses of rationality and consciousness. The focus (post-Enlightenment) on the place of the individual within the framework of social practices positions individual actors as responsible for their moral and ethical behavior. Standards of behavior are constructed as guidelines (because, of course, the individual remains the agent capable of disciplined action).

Two ideas in confession are central. The first is the notion of individuality and, even more specifically, the individual paradoxically positioned as both the subject of (unique) and the object of (separated from) ethical codes of behavior. The second notion concerns sexuality. For Foucault (1978), sexuality was the product of social discourses that constituted individual identity. By privileging sexuality (as in Freudian analysis) as the "hidden-ness" of what is always present in discourse, the self-contained individual is pressed into *revealing/confessing* the truth about the self—the truth that lies within. Confession implies something-to-be-confessed (i.e., "bad" or "deviant" behavior) that is constructed against a norm of that which is "good" (i.e., conforming behavior). The constitution of self within the discourse of sexual harassment has positioned women who act "liberated" as deviant (in part, because they have raised the specter of sexuality), while women who conform to the norms of sexual repression are "healthy." Commenting on the construction of identity through confession, Ian Parker (1989) observes that "confession is organized into modern discourse in such a way that it becomes impossible for an individual to believe that she has developed a healthy identity without acknowledging troubling secrets about the self" (61).

Discipline

Where confession sheds some light on the ways we frame healthy and unhealthy responses to sexual impositions, Foucault's (1977) idea of discipline can provide a framework for looking at discursive patterns that constitute the identity of the "harassed." Discipline, in the Foucauldian sense, emerges from the need to make punishment a rational act. Just as truth implies falsity, the ideas of justice and fairness also must contain notions of what is not right and what is not fair. Foucault saw the movement from public to privatized punishment in the prison system as a corollary to the internalization of power in modern society. Foucault's notion of the panopticon (borrowed from Bentham's 1791 plans for building a guardhouse) best illustrates this point. Bentham's guard tower was positioned so that the guard could view any prisoner at any time. The mere possibility that a prisoner was being watched led the prisoners to believe that they were, indeed, the objects of surveillance. The power of the guard was thus present in the prisoners' internalization of surveillance. What then becomes important is not what is explicitly detectable as power (the guard); power is not reducible to the will of the powerful but instead is located in the control internalized by the self.

Approach to the Project

From our concerns about the ways sexual harassment is defined and experienced by men and women, we developed an interview schedule (see appendix A) that first asked participants for their definition of sexual harassment and then explored several issues arising from the proffered definition. Interviewees were asked whether they believed they had ever been sexually harassed and were invited to describe that experience. They also were asked to provide a metaphoric description of the experience and to indicate, given today's realities, how they would handle the situation should it occur again. Questions regarding participants' experiences of the Hill-Thomas hearings and discussions that took place at that time were included in the interview. Since each interviewee indicated that the Hill-Thomas hearings provided the impetus for the current focus on sexual harassment in the workplace, several of our questions concerned the perceived impact of the hearings on each interviewee's workplace environment.

Interviewees

Sixteen people (eleven women and five men), ranging from approximately thirty years to about seventy years of age, participated in the interviews. The individuals were selected for these interviews not so much because of their direct experiences with sexual harassment (or, at least, our immediate knowledge of their experiences) but because of our belief that the interviewee's personal background and corporate position would inform our understanding of corporate responses to concerns about sexual harassment. Each interview was tape-recorded and transcribed. Although the basic protocol for each interview was the same, the interviews themselves varied from twenty minutes to several hours. The interviews took place over three months.

Among the women we interviewed, one (#1)[4] was a key executive of an educational governing body, while a second (#2) had retired from an upper-level administrative position at a large university. One woman (#3) was a graduate student who served on a sexual harassment committee at her university. Another (#4) was a former administrative law judge at the Equal Employment Opportunity Commission (EEOC) and currently teaches law in a large southwestern university. One woman (#5) had an academic background in social work and currently serves as an ombudsperson for a large mideastern university, whereas another woman (#6) was an affirmative action officer for a moderate-sized mideastern university. Four of the women (#7, #8, #9, and #10) owned their own consulting firms (or serve as independent consultants) and were involved in presenting a variety of training programs, including, in at least one case (#9), programs on sexual harassment and male-female communication. The final woman (#11) interviewee was a vice president of a major corporation.

Of the men interviewed, all (with the exception of a military officer) were in positions to make corporate policy decisions on sexual harassment. Two of the male interviewees were CEOs, one (#12) with a charitable foundation that had nine employees and the other (#13) with a major corporation that had employees nationwide. The third man interviewed (#14) was a college professor and former chair of his department. The fourth (#15) was an officer in the military who had worked with males and females, both as a chief staff assistant and as a troop leader. The final male interviewee (#16) owned a small company with approximately eleven employees.

Most of the interviewees observed significant differences in the ways men and women talked about sexual harassment before and after the hearings. However, the nature of these differences and the extent to which the interviewees believed that their working environment had changed as a result of the hearings varied greatly. Although the hearings were only one of several events that have served as the genesis for legislation and the development of policy on sexual harassment, all of the participants except one pointed out that, compared with other events (e.g., Tailhook, the publicity surrounding Senator Robert Packwood), the hearings had the greatest impact on professional relationships and the working environment.

Approach to Analysis

Although the frames of confession and discipline guided our interpretation of power, this analysis is organized around several themes that arose in reading the transcripts, listening to the tapes, and discussing the similarities and differences among our perceptions of the meanings that emerged. Locating themes in the discourse involved finding those episodes that explicated the experiences of the participant and that spoke to the particularities of each instance, while simultaneously positioning sexual harassment and issues of body/self/identity as part of a larger puzzle. Themes were identified in one or both of the following ways: (1) identification of ideas about sexual harassment, the hearings, and power relations that were repeated in various interviews and (2) identification of experiences that were unique in that they located the text in context; that is, the description put the experience itself in play.

Analysis of Interviews

> . . . this is not a hearing about the extent and nature of sexual harass-
> ment in America. That question is for a different sort of meeting of
> this or any other committee.
> SENATOR JOSEPH BIDEN

> It [the experience of sexual harassment] is like drowning. Slow death.
> You can feel it, see it, you know it is happening.
> INTERVIEWEE #11

Identifying or defining sexual harassment is, ultimately, all about power. La-beling an action or behavior as symbolic is transformative and implies a cer-tain action or way of acting in the world (e.g., Crenshaw, 1992). To define a behavior as sexual harassment, then, would seem to be an empowering act in and of itself. However, as we have discussed earlier, power is located neither in language nor in people but is *discursively* constructed. Thus, our inter-viewees, while all familiar with the EEOC's definition of harassment, found the language to define the experience and the ability to vocalize that experi-ence to be two very different things.

Notions of personal discomfort, difference, and intimidation were common in the interviewees' definitions. There was less agreement on who makes the ultimate decision about whether a situation or action constitutes sexual ha-rassment. For one interviewee (#6) specifically, and others implicitly, whether an action or situation constitutes harassment rests with the individual who is on the receiving end: "We [her organization] make a real distinction between the intent of sexual harassment and the impact, and we assume that most people who are accused of sexual harassment probably don't intend to do that, but that's really immaterial as far as the recipient is concerned." Yet the in-terpretation of harassment often provides only an illusion of power because the power to "give" voice still rests with those in dominant positions in our society. That women in positions of power are "puzzled" by the silence of women who do not report sexual harassment reflects their integration into a patriarchal (hierarchical) system. As Carol Gilligan (1994) observed of the hearings, "Her [Hill's] voice flowed through everyone's life like a river and then through the filter of the 'expert' witnesses . . . it was, for me, the experience of hearing her and then hearing her not being heard."

Powerlessness

> In January of 1983, I began looking for another job. I was handicapped because I feared that, if he [Thomas] found out, he might make it difficult for me to find other employment and I might be dismissed from the job I had.
>
> ANITA HILL

> I've never been told that if I slept with somebody I'd get a promotion. Nothing as blatant as that. What I realize now is that I have tolerated a lot of personal comments about myself without objection because there just didn't seem to be any point in objecting.
>
> INTERVIEWEE #4

> You're prey. I mean, you've seen animals at bay. . . . If there is a wounded animal or an animal that is frightened, it will be sought out by the eagle with talons. You don't go after the strongest gazelle.
>
> INTERVIEWEE #1

Each of these statements speaks to feelings of powerlessness and thus to power-based relationships in corporations and society as a whole. Despite the fact that the definitions the interviewees offered did not specifically refer to power differences, comments at other points during each interview underscored the idea that power, or the assumption of power, is axiomatic to sexual harassment. As one interviewee (#2) stated, "It's power, perceived or real. When a woman feels powerless, she's susceptible to many kinds of things. . . . When you become fearful and you're powerless, you're very fragile."

Beyond the fundamental role power played in the definition of sexual harassment, interviewee statements spoke to the power of the Hill-Thomas hearings and attempts to separate the concept of "consent" from the positioning of individuals as "powerless."

Consequences of the Discourse

Several of the interviewees addressed the fact that it took an event such as the Hill-Thomas hearings to create visible corporate awareness of the problem of sexual harassment. Interviewee #9 noted, "The perception of power is the starting base. Why should a person in a position of power even think about what atmosphere they're creating; whereas, the person out of power is aware of that. That makes all the difference."

Assessments of the Hill-Thomas hearings reflected two dramatically different interpretations of a "trial." One interpretation focused on a theme of courage, whereas the other centered on fear. In both cases, interviewees spoke of "consciousness-raising"; however in the first there was an associated sense of empowerment, whereas in the second the overriding emotions were anger and defensiveness.

The theme of courage emerged in comments from most of the women interviewees and three of the five male interviewees. These interviewees described the hearings as having provided women with "the courage to stand up" (#8) and as being "a time when people felt free to discuss the issue of harassment" (#13). Of course, the significance of the hearings and the freedom to speak were not the same for everyone, as an experience conveyed to us by another interviewee (#10) illustrates:

> The week after the trial was completed and Thomas had been confirmed, I went into a local bakery. Two men standing at the counter were talking about the trial. "Good thing they figured out that b—— was lying. What is it with women anyway. They tease and go after men and then scream they've been attacked! What a crime that Thomas had to listen to that!" I could feel myself getting so angry I was unsure if I should say anything. . . . This incident made me angrier than I had been during the entire trial. They refused to hear what women are saying. . . .[5]

In this instance, as well as others, the specter of victim-blaming becomes a reality. Women are seen as having brought on themselves any problems they might experience. Silence, instead of speaking out, is advocated as the appropriate course of action.[6]

Although interviewee #11 understood the silence of many victims of sexual harassment, in her role as a corporate executive she expressed frustration with that silence. She described a situation in which, after dismissing a manager on the grounds of poor performance, "a number of women who were on his staff [informed the company] that they had been sexually harassed by him." Our interviewee asked, "How can I encourage people to step forward. . . . I don't know how to manage the problem [of silence]."

Discourse of Choice

> When Judge Thomas was made chair of the EEOC, I needed to face
> the question of whether to go with him. I was asked to do so, and I did.
> The work itself was interesting, and at that time it appeared that the
> sexual overtures which had so troubled me had ended. I also faced the
> realistic fact that I had no alternative job.
>
> ANITA HILL

> Probably the best way to describe how I felt was like an animal cowed
> into a corner. I was trapped, with few places to move and little room to
> maneuver.
>
> INTERVIEWEE #12

The cornered animal has few available options. Flight, although not impossible, is fraught with a variety of risks. A different option would be to fight. However, few fighters leave the ring unscathed, even if they are victorious, and total defeat is always a possibility. A third option is acquiescence. Individuals who either advocate or adopt acquiescence might rationalize this choice as minimizing potential harm while expediting the inevitable. The validity of such an argument, though, is debatable, and, as one of the interviewees (#3) noted, silent acceptance "probably just encourages more of this [harassing] behavior."

This theme of "choice" emerged quite strongly in the reactions and experiences the interviewees shared with us. The theme of choice found its voice in discussions of not only the presence or absence of options available to victims of sexual harassment but also the developing constraints and paranoia associated with individual—typically male—behavior. Each of the interviewees explored these issues to varying extents; however, their perspectives and concerns were by no means uniform. The comments and observations they offered underscore continuing areas of debate and disagreement.

Options for Victims

When discussing choices available to victims of harassment, three issues emerged. One issue concerned the very ability of an individual to label an experience as harassment. A second concerned the ability to act on the basis of that labeling. The third concerned the role of the victim in "inviting" victimization.

An uneasy sense of agreement existed among the interviewees about labeling an event sexual harassment. They seemed to realize that choice exists only when we are able to give voice to the experience. All of the interviewees spoke to their own, as well as society's, heightened awareness. In at least four instances, interviewees pointed to earlier periods, when the absence of an appropriate language system and the power imbalances inherent in patriarchal society effectively curtailed the ability of victims to talk about their experiences.

The interviewees recognized that the development of a language system for discussing sexual harassment does not make sexual harassment itself a recent phenomenon. Rather, the language system simply provides a mechanism for making public that which had been considered "private." For one interviewee (#5), the message had always been clear. Harassment was a fact of life and an intimate part of the history of her (African American) culture; however, harassment—sexual or otherwise—had not been considered a topic for open discussion. Another interviewee (#9) credited the strictures against open, frank communication to what she perceived as the development of "alternative" (i.e., nonverbal) communication skills on the part of women: "We've had to develop certain strategies and skills better than most males because we have not been privy and open to the same kind of direct discourse and direct options and choices that they have. It's survival." For another interviewee (#3), the decision to remain silent in the face of harassment was more an issue of priorities than a matter of corporate survival or even intimidation: "I know I could further the cause of the sexual harassment move, or whatever that's going on. But I don't. And it isn't my top priority. . . . I have, in the back of my mind, wondered if I'm doing a disservice by not reporting it because I know it probably just encourages more of his behavior. . . . I just feel like it's exhausting to me to think of one more conflict." She was not alone in alluding to the fact that the choice to remain silent can be motivated by a belief that the problems created by silence—by acquiescence—are less onerous than the prospect of the time and energy involved in voicing a complaint.

Discourse of Responsibility

> It would have been more comfortable to remain silent. I took no initiative to inform anyone. But when I was asked by a representative of this committee to report any experience, I felt that I had to tell the truth. I could not keep silent.
> ANITA HILL

> Lately, I've observed a situation where one of our new hires—a male—

> has been treating a fellow employee—a woman—more like his employ-
> ee than his colleague. I've spoken with her about this. She recognizes
> that this is occurring. I could step in, but I want her to handle it for
> herself. I think she needs to assert her position, and she knows that I
> will support her if she does.
>
> INTERVIEWEE #12

Choice does not come without responsibility. In these interviews, the discourse of responsibility emerged most strongly in statements made and stories shared about corporate reactions to sexual harassment. As with the issue of choice, the discourse of responsibility was marked by competing perspectives. The disagreements revolved not around whether a corporation had responsibility but around the practical impact of corporate policies. In essence, what emerged reflected differences between corporation-centered and victim-centered assumptions of responsibility and reactions to incidents of harassment. These differences are best illustrated through statements made by three interviewees: a male corporate executive, a female corporate executive, and a female ombud.

The male corporate executive (#13) referred to today's litigious society when he explained, "I think that's probably the biggest thing for a corporation—that they know that there's a vulnerability from litigation and, so great effort is made to be reactive very quickly. If anything is brought to the attention of a manager in our company, in the sexual harassment area, our instructions are very clear. They have to bring it up immediately to [Human Resources] and something is to be done in our company. They can never just let it go. Something has to be done and documented. . . ."

On the positive side, such statements would seem to underscore the fact that claims of sexual harassment are being treated seriously. Corporations have discovered that they cannot ignore problems or answer accusations (as did one high school teacher described by #6) by saying "boys will be boys." This assumption of responsibility, however, might create rather than solve at least some problems because the mandate to report effectively eliminates choices on the part of the victim as well as the others, whose assistance has been sought.

Discourse of Surveillance

> The accusation [of sexual harassment] alone is enough to end your
> career. . . . [It's] like walking across a mine field.
>
> INTERVIEWEE #15

One indication of the impact of the hearings on the discursive structures of power was manifest in the participants' discussions of surveillance. Just as Foucault's panopticon served as a mechanism for internal surveillance, so too did the discourse about harassment affect the awareness of body/space/identity. Although one interviewee (#6) indicated that "without constant monitoring built into this environment this behavior just doesn't stop," generally the discussions centered on the consequences of being monitored rather than on the need for external control. The internalization of control can be represented in the discourse in several ways: (1) the representation of the hearings (and sexual harassment) as a spectacle and (2) the separation accorded behavior (what I do) versus identity (who I am).

Several of the interviewees discussed the role of the media in creating a carnival atmosphere (and, by extension, making race and gender part of a spectacle for public consumption). Specifically, interviewee #14 noted that he found himself most interested in "the media effect and what was not immediately connected to the harassment charges themselves. . . . The extent to which this became a public issue rather than one which was actually chosen, but one that got forced in an odd way. At that point, I was more concerned and interested in the reactions that everyone else was having than I was with the hearings themselves."

The carnival atmosphere that surrounded the hearings and the public display of both Anita Hill's and Clarence Thomas's private lives before a confession-hungry audience reinforced the power of surveillance. The public viewing of the confession of sexual harassment reinforced the view that the powerful could play out the spectacle "off the backs" (#5) of the powerless in the name of entertainment.

That the hearings were represented as a media event did not change the value the interviewees placed on the hearings. Here, the entertainment value of the spectacle is recognized as being as important as the event/issue itself. Although the audience co-creates the story and believes it has the power of knowledge, in this instance those who monitored the activities of the audience were accorded power.

The second area in which surveillance became a salient issue is in the difference between discourse about behavior (what I do or don't do that is considered sexually harassing behavior) and discourse about identity (how who I am becomes the object of public scrutiny). All of the men and two of the women interviewed mentioned the heightened sense of paranoia that men experienced as a result of the hearings. One (#14) declared, "The most powerful experience I had after the hearings . . . was [in giving a presentation] to a male audience . . . the males very quickly got into discussion of the fear of being 'charged' when they weren't guilty. . . . The clearest thing was that you realize that a man being charged would be considered guilty and it would destroy his career. And of course the only response you could make is: do you realize what this could do to a woman?"

In this context, and in several others, conversation centered on the discomfort men feel when their behavior becomes the object of scrutiny. Interviewee #8 noted, "I think what many people fear that, you know, I think you and I have this thing going that sometimes includes these little sexual innuendos and all of a sudden ten years down the road you're in there getting me for it. I mean, I think there's a real fear."

Here an interesting dichotomy emerged. Whereas the discourse about the impact of the hearings on defining and regulating sexual harassment policy focused on the behaviors of men, the discourse about the impact on women centered on the perception of women's identities. As one interviewee (#5) pointed out, "You've got people standing there going, 'I'm appalled that you're talking about these things because they should not be talked about.' . . . But it's okay to talk about it because. . . . the ones who are carrying the message are those who we deem as less than us anyway, so it's okay. . . ." For the African American interviewees, issues of harassment were intricately tied to race and gender. Interviewee #5 observed, "For me, it's very inextricably linked. I can't separate out my African-American-ness from all that occurred. It's a very salient part of understanding who I am and understanding how, in fact, we, as women, are vulnerable to that. Understanding how I am particularly vulnerable and continue to be so." In other words, whereas the behaviors of (white) men were under surveillance as a result of defining and regulating sexual harassment, the very ways in which women are defined and define themselves have become the object of public scrutiny.

Although two of the men we interviewed (#14 and #15) said they had experienced sexual harassment, both indicated the experience held no meaning for them other than for purposes of illustrating the irrelevance of gender in situations of abuse of power. Interviewee #14 also indicated that "it is terribly difficult for any male, probably even a female . . . to say what the psychological impact would be in a harassing environment. Because men really treat it as relatively trivial in the sense of, 'oh yeah, I have had women come on to me.' But to forget the difference in their position, what sexuality is to a man and so on. . . . Generally, men dismiss these things as jokes, when they are in an uncomfortable environment because that is how they handle their sexuality." Yet another interviewee (#6) echoed this point in observations she offered: "There's no doubt in my mind that Anita Hill was saying what she thought was true . . . I also don't find it surprising that [Clarence Thomas said what he did] and I believe that some things about [the situation] he would not have remembered because I believe that they probably weren't important comments or behaviors to him."

The different ways that men and women handle their sexuality raise important implications for those who believe that sexuality is itself discursively constructed. Dismissing these differences as biological ignores the implications for understanding power relations in situations where work (commodified labor) and sexuality have traditionally been separated. Here, the distinction between behavior and identity is intimately bound to notions of the value of work (production) and the exclusion of reproduction (an important part of women's identities) as a form of labor.

Conclusion

Sexual harassment is not part of a larger, gendered circumstance; rather, it is a label that has certain effects and can be traced throughout the discourse that surrounds such concepts as the "professional" and the meanings of work and career in this country. Viewing the discourse on sexual harassment through the frames of confession and discipline allows the exploration of the ways the stories construct reality. Each of the four themes (power, choice, responsibility, and surveillance) revealed the complexity of power relations and the difficulties of imposing a structural overlay on experience.

As indicated in our discussion of the themes, the construction of the victim and the perpetrator, of the harasser and the harassee, is the result of a socially created discourse, maintained through corporate attempts to legislate against "offensive" behavior. Confession necessarily frames much of the discourse about sexual harassment, including the language of victim-blaming and "corporate" policy discourse that attempts to legislate individual behavior. Indeed, most of the research on sexual harassment and subsequent attempts to legislate policy has failed to look deeply into the consequences of not only the behavior itself but also the attempts to take communicative action—to redress wrongs or to enact changes in the company or the institution.

The conversations with men and women in positions to dictate or enact public/corporate policies on private identities led to new questions about the implications of this discourse. For instance, what happens (on an ideological level) when the corporation (re)discovers the political and artificial boundaries between work and sexuality and attempts to address these boundaries publicly? The ideological paradox for the corporation is that, in an ideal corporate environment, hierarchy remains intact while gender, age, and cultural diversity are somehow valued. Once the artificial divide between work and other forms of social and cultural life is politicized, what dictates future corporate policy?

Future studies in this area need to examine the ways power relations remain unaddressed in the new corporate policy on sexual harassment. Specifically, why is it so difficult for public policy to regulate private identities? The peculiar dilemma over regulating sexual harassment in the workplace is a problem specific to communicating a socially constructed position in the world: legislation cannot and does not speak to the "responsibility" inherent in confession.

Applying Foucault's notion of the panopticon to the discovery of truth or the achievement of justice implies that women and men have internalized standards of control that maintain power relations and constitute the identity of the "good" worker or the "competent" professional. Each standard and its application necessitates relations of power and control. The Hill-Thomas hearings serve as one catalyst for a series of events that have shaped new technologies of control. Common among several of the interviewees was the sense that their actions were no longer their own. Yet Foucault's panopticon seems to function on different levels and in differing ways. For some, the internalization of control has meant the objectification of identity—the public scrutiny of who they are. For others, it has meant the corporate (public) evaluation of behaviors that used to be legitimated as "private" and therefore not visible in the corporate space. As this study indicates, the emerging formations of power rely on the ideas of rights and equality to indicate a notion of "public" and "private" identities functioning in the "professional" domain of the workplace.

Nevertheless, what emerges in this discourse about harassment is a sense that the discursive power of language lies in the choice to communicate and the responsibility inherent in the symbols chosen. Anita Hill was "responsible" for giving voice to the accusation of harassment (as she repeatedly was told to "confess" Thomas's alleged statement to her that there was "pubic hair on my Coke can"). By giving voice to Thomas's actions, she became responsible for the words themselves. In a similar fashion, two of the interviewees (#7 and #8) emphasized the responsibility placed on women for the actions of men (commenting, for example, that there are those who believe that any woman who is raped must have done something to deserve it). In this manner, violence becomes the tie that binds women's identity to the behaviors of men. The symbolism of sexual harassment, rape, and other forms of abuse links who women are to what men do, reinforcing an assumption that women are forever the victims of an oppressive culture. Along with other victims, then, women are seen as a reflection of the objects and desires of those who are dominant.

Of course, how a "victim" raises the accusation of sexual harassment has personal implications. How can we escape being defined as victims when taking action against sexual harassment? How do we point out deviant behavior without being tainted by that behavior? Perhaps one answer that this study points to is through descriptions of appropriate behavior. Providing examples of behavior that is appropriate and affirms personal values can counter the self-defeating assumption embedded in the language itself: that, intuitively, I must really like this deviant behavior because I am talking about your actions and drawing public attention to them.

At this point, another troubling issue in communicating the nature of power, choice, and responsibility involved in relations between men and women in the workplace emerges. The fact that power is not a totalizing system in which the powerful acts against the powerless but rather a system that enables or handicaps people in different ways and at different moments presents extreme challenges for those who are trying to create an atmosphere of equality in the workplace. Here, power and equality/inequality are discussed in terms of the equity of relationships. Equity is measured by the division of power into property, through a system of costs and rewards that can be decided on in an economical, rational fashion. Yet, the division of power into property reifies the existing structural formation that delineates the allocation of resources to some and not to others as a measurement of control. Such terms as *empowerment* and *equality* thus use the same old yardsticks to determine successful integration of "difference" into the system.

Still, the theme of surveillance, as well as the "monitoring" of power relations through equity, implies a choice about how we define harassment and the ways we draw attention to it as a "spectacle" for public consumption. Recognizing the ways we internalize the symbols of our culture must become not the ends of understanding power relations in the workplace but the means toward a new comprehension of the power to change our lives through restructuring our language and thus our discursive identities. If, as many feminists have said, "the means become the ends," then change will occur only when we refuse to react to the same old symbols of power in the same old ways.

Any "truth" in sexual harassment lies in the intricacies of identity and language. Power relations are constructed in these moments and maintained in the structural overlays we seek to order our lives. Likewise, any "theory" about the nature of sexual harassment or gender relations necessarily perpetuates the social reality. As Sonia Johnson (1989) has stated, "What we resist persists." At the same time, as some of the interviewees noted, the failure to resist can be seen as lending credence to the behavior in question. Perhaps the best answer was provided by one of the interviewees (#6) in response to the question, "If that same situation were to occur again, how would you handle it?" "I will not allow myself to ever be that vulnerable ever again. It's just not going to happen. . . . I would not tolerate it on any level."

APPENDIX A: PROTOCOL FOR SEXUAL HARASSMENT INTERVIEWS

1.   How would you define "sexual harassment?
2.   What events in your life, the media, at work, etc., have brought about discussions or arguments concerning sexual harassment?
3.   The Senate Judiciary Committee hearings involving Clarence Thomas and Anita Hill created quite a stir. How did you feel while the hearings were taking place?
     a.   If you can recall any events which occurred or conversations you had at the time, please describe those events/conversations for me.
     b.   Was the general atmosphere at your office or in your company affected by the hearings? If so, describe that for me. What changes did you observe?
4.   Have you ever personally experienced sexual harassment?
     a.   Describe that situation for me. What was that experience like for you?
     b.   Can you describe your experience in terms of a metaphor? This experience was like . . .

    c.   If that same situation were to occur again, how would you handle it?

5.   Did the Thomas-Hill hearings make it easier to talk about sexual harassment in the workplace or more difficult? Describe what you mean.

6.   Did the Thomas-Hill hearings improve understanding or make workplace relationships more difficult to understand? Describe what you mean.

7.   Did the Thomas-Hill hearings help to open or close lines of communication?

8.   From your point of view as a manager/executive, what impact did the Thomas-Hill hearings have on the handling of (or the corporate response to) accusations of sexual harassment?

NOTES

Transcripts of the testimony from the U.S. Senate Judiciary Committee hearings for the confirmation of Justice Clarence Thomas were transcribed by Federal News Service and obtained from the Purdue University Public Affairs Video Archives, West Lafayette, Indiana.

    1. Although the term *survivor* is preferred by many writers, our use of the term *victim* is in line with the language of our interviewees. We do not dispute the appropriateness of the survivor label but instead prefer to respect the point of view of our interviewees.

    2. For a discussion of the ways in which the "victims" of sexual harassment frame their experience, see Clair, 1993.

    3. For other feminist works that take a Foucauldian view of power and the body, see Bartky, 1988; Harstock, 1987; Hekman, 1990; McNay, 1992; and Sawicki, 1988.

    4. We have assigned each interviewee an identification number (provided in parentheses) and maintained that number consistently throughout the essay.

    5. Ultimately, consciousness-raising comes at a price. We have already cited statements from one interviewee (#14) about the introduction of suspicion and mistrust into male-female corporate relationships. However, the reality of the consciousness-raising price tag was underscored for us by a story that a friend shared: "Three weeks after the Hill-Thomas trial, all the top level management received a memo saying, in essence 'Be careful around women with whom you work,' etc. Then, the CEO had a meeting with his direct reports. This included five men and three women. The issues generated by the memo were introduced into the conversation and he said, 'From now on, I will not socialize with any woman who works with me on a one-to-one basis.' When one of us asked, 'Will you continue to go out for drinks with your male reports?,' his answer was 'Absolutely. And furthermore, I will no longer have any closed door meetings with any

woman.' I said, 'Isn't that accusing us [i.e., the three women direct reports] of falsely bringing charges?' He mumbled something, but it was clear he was very unhappy with our raising that issue. . . . Of those three women, the only top level [women] executives in this organization, one has been 'eased out' with a buy out, one has taken a leave, and the third is currently interviewing for jobs with other organizations. This is one of the negative consequences of this trial. Instead of raising this male CEO's level of awareness, it has accomplished just the opposite—made him vindictive against women in the office."

6. The issue of silence was one that created a tremendous challenge for the U.S. Senate Judiciary Committee. For Senator Arlen Specter, in particular, there appeared to be a great deal of difficulty in understanding: "how could you [Anita Hill] allow this kind of reprehensible conduct to go on right in the headquarters without doing something about it?" (Hearings, 1991, 67–68). However, given that earlier silence, Senator Specter apparently believed that the only appropriate course of action for Professor Hill involved continued silence, as evidenced by the following question that Senator Specter asked Professor Hill: "In the context of the federal law limiting a sexual harassment claim to six months because of the grave difficulty of someone defending themselves in this context, what is your view of the fairness of asking Judge Thomas to reply eight, nine, ten years after the fact?" (Hearings, 1991, 81).

REFERENCES

Bartky, S. (1988). Foucault, femininity and the modernisation of patriarchal power. In I. Diamond and L. Quinby (eds.), *Feminism and Foucault: Reflections on resistance*, 61–86. Boston: Northeastern University Press.

Clair, R. P. (1993). The use of framing devices to sequester organizational narratives: Hegemony and harassment. *Communication Monographs*, 60: 113–36.

Crenshaw, A. C. (1992). Anita Hill goes to Washington: A Burkean perspective on race and gender differences. Paper presented at the annual meeting of the International Communication Association, Miami.

Foucault, M. (1977). *Discipline and punish*. London: Allen Lane.

———. (1978). *The history of sexuality: An introduction*. Trans. R. Hurley. Harmondsworth, England: Penguin.

Gilligan, C. (1994, August 1). Lecture on *voice* given at Smith College, Northampton, Mass.

Hale, C. L., Cooks, L. M., and DeWine, S. (1994). Anita Hill on trial: A dialectical analysis of a persuasive interrogation. In G. Bingham (ed.), *Conceptualizing sexual harassment as discursive practice*, 71–87. Westport, Conn.: Praeger.

Harstock, N. (1987). Foucault on power: A theory for women? In L. Nicholson (ed.), *Feminism/postmodernism*, 157–75. London: Routledge.

Hearings before the Committee on the Judiciary on the nomination of Clarence Thomas to serve as am associate justice of the Supreme Court of the United States. (1991, October 11, 12, and 13). U.S. Senate, 102d Congress, 1st session. Washington, D.C.: U.S. Government Printing Office.

Hekman, S. (1990). *Gender and knowledge: Elements of a postmodern feminism.* Cambridge: Polity Press.

Johnson, S. (1989). *Going farther out of our minds.* New Almaden, Calif.: Wolfe Video.

McNay L. (1992). *Foucault and feminism.* Boston: Northeastern University Press.

Parker, I. (1989). Discourse and power. In J. Shotter and K. Gergen (eds.), *Texts of identity*, 56–69. London: Sage.

Sawicki, J. (1988). Identity politics and sexual freedom. In I. Diamond and L. Quinby (eds.), *Feminism and Foucault: Reflections on resistance*, 177–91. Boston: Northeastern University Press.

This ain't about Anita Hill and this ain't about Clarence Thomas. This
is about a power struggle going on in this country between men and
women. This is the biggest thing you can imagine.
SENATOR JOSEPH BIDEN

13

Beyond the Hearings: The Continuing Effects of Hill vs. Thomas on Women and Men, the Workplace, and Politics

DIANNE G. BYSTROM

Years after the nationally televised hearings before the U.S. Senate Judiciary
Committee to evaluate Anita Hill's charges that she had been sexually harassed
by Clarence Thomas when she worked for him in the early 1980s, the controversy continues. The battle launched by Hill's allegations and Thomas's
vehement denial has moved from the Senate chambers to homes and businesses throughout the United States, pitting women against men, blacks against
whites, blacks against blacks, and employees against employers, as they grapple
with who was telling the truth and, perhaps more important, what the hearings revealed about how a predominantly white, male power structure responds to charges of sexual harassment.

The drama that unfolded live over network television, cable, and radio between October 11 and October 13, 1991, reaching an estimated 27 million homes (Rucinski, 1993, 576), and its aftermath continue to be debated in the popular and academic press. Between 1991 and 1994, at least six books were published on the hearings,[1] and two scholarly journals focused entire issues on the racial, sexual, and legal issues the hearings raised.[2]

Because the nationally televised hearings involved a black, politically moderate woman's allegations of sexual harassment by a black, conservative man before a committee of white male senators, it is not surprising that much of the analysis has focused on the political dynamics of the hearings, the racial and sexual stereotypes they revealed, and the divisive impact of the Hill-Thomas interaction on the black community.[3] The hearings also spawned three book-length investigations designed to determine who was telling the truth as well as essays assessing Hill's and Thomas's credibility or believability.[4] Less analysis—though much media speculation—has been devoted to the long-term effects of the Hill-Thomas hearings on work and politics: their impact on how men and women communicate, especially in the workplace; the new public awareness of and scholarly interest in sexual harassment; and the number of women elected to political office in the aftermath of the Hill-Thomas hearings.[5]

By focusing on the issue of who was telling the truth—or, more precisely, which one people believed—in the Hill-Thomas interaction, this essay first summarizes how race and gender have shaped the public's response to and construction of the sexual harassment allegations raised. It then argues that— no matter whom one believes—the Hill-Thomas hearings appear to have raised the nation's consciousness on the issue of sexual harassment, altered how men and women communicate in the workplace, and have been a factor in the election of a record number of women to political office.

To Believe or Not to Believe: Who Told the Truth?

Public opinion polls at the time of the hearings revealed that the majority of the American public, both men and women, believed Thomas and supported his confirmation to the Supreme Court (Rucinski, 1993). The eleven national polls that focused exclusively on the Hill-Thomas hearings conducted between October 8 and October 15, 1991, found that 46–60 percent of those polled believed Thomas was telling the truth compared with the 20–37 percent who believed Hill (Rucinski, 1993, 590–91). A small gender gap was revealed in the polls at that time; surveys showed that 42–63 percent of men and 38–57 percent of women believed Thomas (Rucinski, 1993, 590–91).

Although few polls focused on black opinion on the hearings, those that did found as much as 67 percent of the black population supported Thomas during and immediately after the hearings (cited in Staples, 1993, 146). As Robert Staples notes, the televised spectacle led many blacks to support Thomas "despite his philosophy, not because of it . . . their instinctual reaction was to support a black man besieged by whites in a nationally televised hearing" (146).

However, as Dianne Rucinski (1993) points out, none of the organizations that conducted the initial polls on believability "attempted to measure or control the influences of interviewer race or gender on responses" (584). Since both race and gender were key factors in the Hill-Thomas hearings, the interviewer's race or gender might have had an impact on the responses given. For example, blacks interviewed by whites might have been more likely to show solidarity with Thomas in the wake of his angry denouncement of the hearings as a "high tech lynching" (Rucinski, 1993, 585). As Rucinski notes, only a few polling organizations attempted the oversample of blacks necessary to test this hypothesis.

Some were surprised that public opinion had shifted toward believing Hill a year following the hearings. Embedded in three polls conducted in the final months of the presidential year election campaigns in 1992 were questions on the Hill-Thomas controversy (Rucinski, 1993). Two of those polls found that more people now believed Hill, and the third revealed that people were equally divided in their support for Hill and Thomas. Furthermore, these 1992 polls revealed dramatic shifts of opinion when compared with the 1991 surveys. For example, a poll conducted in September 1992 by the *Wall Street Journal* and NBC News found that 44 percent of registered voters surveyed said they believed Hill told the truth, compared with 34 percent who said Thomas did. The same poll conducted a year earlier had shown that Hill was believed by 24 percent and Thomas by 40 percent (Abramson, 1992, 1). The 1992 polls also showed a widened gender gap between men and women about which one they believed. Although a comparison of the 1991 and 1992 polls shows that Hill gained support from both men and women, the shifts of opinion were much more dramatic for female respondents (Garment, 1993).

Several reasons have been suggested for this shift in public support for Hill. Some researchers (e.g., Bowker, herein) as well as friends and supporters of

Hill believe that the public discussion of and education about sexual harassment in the months following the hearings caused the shift in public opinion. "Those earlier polls were taken in the middle of an earthquake," observed Emma Coleman Jordan, a Georgetown University law professor who served, pro bono, as one of Hill's attorneys during the hearings. "The profound charges brought up in the hearings hadn't been absorbed. The words 'sexual harassment' weren't words most people had heard before" (quoted in Abramson, 1992, A4).

However, the discussion of sexual harassment in the wake of the Hill-Thomas hearings might have affected women's opinions much more than men's. According to Suzanne Garment (1993), who found a widening gender gap between the 1991 polls taken during the hearings and the 1992 polls conducted after a year of discussion of Hill's case within the framework of sexual harassment, the "dispute has moved from a ground on which men and women find themselves in relative agreement to an area in which men and women disagree with each other more profoundly" (22)

Other friends and supporters of Hill have attributed her more positive evaluation in the 1992 polls to the "way she has comported herself in the wake of sudden celebrity," declining most interviews and focusing her public appearances on the issue of sexual harassment rather than on personal reflections on the hearings and comments on Thomas (Abramson, 1992, A4). Supporters of Thomas argue that Hill has benefited from the passage of time; "revisionist history" perpetuated by the "media elite," including popular television sitcoms; and Thomas's inability to defend his name in the "cloistered atmosphere of the Supreme Court" (Abramson, 1922, A4).

Or, as Rucinski (1993) persuasively argues, the differing results may reflect methodological problems with the instantaneous polls more than actual opinion change. That is, the initial support for Thomas might have been "soft or illusory—based on uncrystallized opinions" (576), whereas the 1992 polls "may be more indicative of opinion formation rather than opinion change" (586). "Fast reaction polls and the way they are reported by their media sponsors often give the impression that the public has opinions when it may not," Rucinski contends, warning that "pollsters must consider the fact that they sometimes make as well as measure opinions" (586).

In this case, the pollsters might have helped alter history. Since many senators cited these instantaneous polls in their decision to vote to confirm Thomas by 52 to 48, one could argue that the methodological problems helped place a sexual harasser on the U.S. Supreme Court, where he will have an opportunity to impact the law affecting women and minorities for years to come. At least it is interesting to speculate. If the polls conducted in 1991 had shown that the majority of the public believed Hill—as they revealed one year later—would the Senate have voted to confirm Thomas?

In addition to public opinion polls, three books written by investigative journalists have explored the events leading up to and through the hearings and take opposite views on the believability of Hill and Thomas. *The Real Anita Hill: The Untold Story* by David Brock (1993), an investigative journalist with the conservative *American Spectator,* attempts to cast doubts on Hill and her credibility by portraying her as a "zealot for the cause of civil rights" (333), who, at the persistent urging of Senate staffers and women activists, concocted her allegations of sexual harassment to explain her "disappointing relationship with Thomas and her failure to succeed at the EEOC" (333).

Conversely, *Capitol Games: Clarence Thomas, Anita Hill, and the Story of a Supreme Court Nomination* by Timothy M. Phelps, the *Newsday* reporter who broke the story about Hill's allegations, and Helen Winternitz (1992) takes a pro-Hill stance, portraying her as a reluctant witness who was victimized by a political process in which the nomination of a black conservative to the Supreme Court was more important to the Bush administration, conservative senators, and some leaders in the black community than learning the truth.

Similarly, the *Wall Street Journal* reporters Jane Mayer and Jill Abramson (1994) conclude—after more than two years of research—in *Strange Justice: The Selling of Clarence Thomas* that the "preponderance of evidence suggests" that "Thomas did lie under oath" (8). Through seemingly careful journalistic documentation, they poke holes in the public persona of Justice Thomas as sold to the American public by the religious right, White House handlers, and Republican patrons. Contrary to the image of Thomas presented to the Senate and public, the authors find evidence that Thomas—and the political process that led to his nomination and confirmation—mythologized his past; lied about, overlooked, or suppressed his penchant for pornography and vulgar language; and ignored information by others who corroborate Hill's testimony about key aspects of Thomas's behavior toward her and other women.

The Mayer and Abramson account also includes the first major on-the-record interview Hill granted about the hearings. Although they criticize Hill's ambition as a reason that she remained in contact with Thomas despite her allegations of his treatment of her, the authors find that "by all accounts, Hill had been scrupulous about being truthful all her life" (85). According to the authors, "Even [Hill's] strongest detractors suggested no pattern of dishonesty or unethical behavior. Indeed, no one could recall Hill's having ever told a lie" (85).

The *Court of Appeal: The Black Community Speaks Out on the Racial and Sexual Politics of Clarence Thomas vs. Anita Hill* (Chrisman and Allen, 1992), a collection of essays by prominent African Americans from across the political spectrum, shows deep divisions within the black community on many issues related to the hearings, including the question of who was telling the truth. For example, whereas Beverly Guy-Sheftal reports that she "encountered very few blacks, men or women, who believe that Thomas was telling the truth when he categorically and unequivocally denied having engaged in sexually inappropriate conduct" (73), Jacquelyne Johnson Jackson writes that her "black female and male friends and acquaintances (mostly social scientists) . . . all agreed that Hill lied" (101), and she suggests that Hill might have "come on" to Thomas.

Several contributors to the *Court of Appeal* collection who believe Hill (Guy-Sheftal, Hernton, and Staples) suggest that many members of the black community turned away from her because she broke her silence after ten years to publicly air allegations of sexual harassment before "whites in a nationally televised hearing" (198) to jeopardize a "black man getting his piece of the American pie" (89). This attitude is exemplified by the contributors Nathan Hare and Julia Hare, who assert that white feminists used Hill in an attempt to bring down a black man's advancement. "Many black women (including those who sympathized with Professor Hill) had mixed emotions and couldn't see why—as they themselves had done so many times—Anita Hill couldn't have put her hands on her hip, let her backbone slip, and told Clarence where to get off" (79), rather than publicly air her charges ten years later.

The few attempts by researchers to measure the truthfulness or believability of Hill and Thomas through analytical and experimental means have produced mixed results. Two studies—Curtis D. LeBaron's (herein) application of verbal deception detection techniques utilized by the FBI academy to Thomas's testimony and Dale G. Leathers, Laura Vaughn, Gregory X. Sanchez, and Jennifer L. Bailey's (1995) comparison of the nonverbal profiles of Hill and Thomas in their statements to the Senate Judiciary Committee—conclude that Thomas was deceptive. However, Valerie Cryer McKay (herein) found

no significant differences between Hill and Thomas when she examined videotapes of their prepared and spontaneous statements for nonverbal body,
facial, and vocal behaviors indicating deception. Although these studies shed
light on who may or may not have been telling the truth in their testimony,
they illustrate the difficulties in applying coding schemes to complicated communicative events.

The search for "truth" in the Hill-Thomas testimonies is further complicated by the passage of time between the alleged sexual harassment and its
public exposure at the hearings and by each person's internalization and ra-
tionalization of what occurred ten years ago. Especially for women who have
been harassed, it is not difficult to imagine that a male supervisor's unwanted sexual behavior could become engraved on a young woman's psyche, while
he has forgotten or dismissed it as unimportant or inconsequential.

Or, as Staples (1993) argues, the differences in Hill's and Thomas's construction of the event may be rooted in the black community's "historical
sexual liberality [which] mitigates against current definitions of sexual harassment" (146). That is, Hill—as an "upwardly mobile, quasi-Southern, religious
woman" (146)—might not have understood or appreciated the cultural context of Thomas's courtship style in which it is "customary for black men to
approach black women in a manner that openly expresses sexual interest"
(Kochman, 1981, cited in Staples, 1993, 146). However, this view about black
sexual politics is not held by other black men and women who believe, for
example, that "some black men . . . attempt to use their victimization by racism as an excuse for their dysfunctional behaviors toward black women" (Bell,
1992, 366).

Whereas it may be difficult to ascertain through experimental or analytical
means who was telling the truth during the hearings, research indicates that
the question of which one people believed seems split along gender, racial,
and political lines. For example, utilizing an experimental research design that
measured the effects of various segments of the hearings on the evaluations
of Hill and Thomas by three geographically dispersed groups of college students, Lynda Lee Kaid, John Tedesco, and Clifford A. Jones (herein) found
that women rated Hill significantly higher and Thomas significantly lower
than men did at every stage of the hearing process. However, gender differences were most pronounced before the subjects viewed an edited one-and-
a-half-hour segment of the hearings, when women evaluated Hill and men
evaluated Thomas most favorably, than at the conclusion of the viewing, when

both males and females evaluated Thomas more favorably than Hill. Similarly, Democrats—who were more positive to Hill at the outset—warmed to Thomas as the hearings progressed, whereas Republicans became more favorable to Thomas and more critical of Hill.

In another study using Q-methodology to investigate the public's reactions to the hearings, Dan Thomas, Craig McCoy, and Allan McBride (1993) found five alternative constructions of the same event based, in part, on the viewer's subjectivity, race, and gender. They found that women, particularly whites, identified with Hill and found her account more credible than Thomas's. Black women, however, appeared to be torn between loyalty to their sex and loyalty to their race. To them, whether Hill was telling the truth was not the issue; rather, Hill's public airing of allegations that happened ten years earlier led them to react protectively to a black man being attacked by a black women in front of an all-white, all-male jury.

White men also found Hill less persuasive than did white women, not because she publicly aired her allegations but because she "simply failed to make a case that a jury would find persuasive" (Thomas, McCoy, and McBride, 1993, 715). Black males, however, revealed dichotomous reactions to Hill and Thomas based on their personalized perceptions of who was villain and victim in this battle of black antagonists. The researchers also found that political persuasions affected people's reactions to the hearings. Liberalism correlated positively with pro-Hill sentiments, and conservatism covaried with pro-Thomas factors.

Reactions to Hill and Thomas along lines of gender, race, and political persuasion have subsequently transcended the hearings themselves as the debate over "who was telling the truth" has altered the way men and women communicate in the workplace, especially about the issue of sexual harassment, and how they reacted in the voting booth in the 1992 elections.

Raising Consciousness and Complaints about Sexual Harassment

Contrary to initial fears that the Senate Judiciary Committee's treatment of Hill's allegations would drive the issue of sexual harassment underground (Sandroff, 1992a), the Hill-Thomas hearings raised the nation's consciousness about sexual harassment and increased the number of complaints filed. In the nine months following Hill's testimony to the Senate Judiciary Committee, inquiries about sexual harassment to the Equal Employment Opportunity Commission (EEOC) increased by 150 percent (Sandroff, 1992a, 49), and a record-breaking number of charges (7,407) were filed, a 50 percent increase over the same period a year earlier (Abramson, 1992, 1). This flood of sexual harassment charges—which the EEOC attributed in 1992 to the debate over the Hill-Thomas hearings (Leatherman, 1992a)—has continued; more than 12,000 complaints were filed with the EEOC in 1993 (Nayyar and Miller, 1994, 50).

Hill herself has come to symbolize the issue of sexual harassment. "She is a national icon of women's awakening about the injury that sexual harassment inflicts," said Hill's friend Emma Coleman Jordan of Georgetown University Law School (quoted in Leatherman, 1992b). Declining most media interviews and numerous opportunities to comment on the 1991 hearings, Justice Thomas's subsequent confirmation, and his performance to date on the Supreme Court, Hill instead has focused on educating and enlightening the public about sexual harassment through her writing and speaking. During her 1992–93 sabbatical from the University of Oklahoma, where she specializes in commercial law, Hill conducted scholarly research on sexual harassment issues and, with Jordan, organized and sponsored a conference titled "Race, Gender, and Power in American Society" at Georgetown University Law School (Hill, 1993).

Hill continued to speak out on the issue of sexual harassment in 1993–94 while teaching full time at the University of Oklahoma College of Law and in 1994–95 while on unpaid leave from the university. Although some have criticized her for profiting from the hearings by giving speeches for fees up to $11,000 each at universities and before professional groups (Abramson, 1992; "A Year Later," 1992; Leatherman, 1992b), most of her public appearances related to sexual harassment have been unpaid (Abramson, 1992). According to the agency that books her speeches, Hill has "turned down several more lucrative speaking invitations from large corporations and other groups, as well as rich book and movie deals" (quoted in Abramson, 1992, A4).

Partly prompted by the articles and books that have attempted to discredit her testimony and personal integrity, Hill did sign a reported $1 million book contract with Doubleday in 1994 to write two books (Killackey, 1994)—a study of sexual harassment in historical and contemporary contexts and a memoir reflecting the impact of the Hill-Thomas hearings on contemporary legal and political issues—while on a leave of absence without pay from the University of Oklahoma in 1994–95 (Hill, 1994). Hill has said she will donate royalties from the two books "as a tribute" to her supporters at nine institutions, including the University of Oklahoma College of Law ("Give and Take," 1994, A29), where she returned to full-time work in the fall of 1995.

In addition to sparking Hill's own research on sexual harassment, the hearings have inspired other scholarship on the issue, including substantial interest in the communication field. Focusing their analysis on Hill's testimony about her interactions with Thomas in which his sexual harassment allegedly occurred, Darrin Hicks and Phillip J. Glenn (herein) show how communicative practices are used to create and maintain a hostile working environment. They call for "further analysis of individual accounts of harassing episodes" to "uncover those methods necessary to transform a hostile environment into a noncoercive, egalitarian workplace."

Prompted partly by the increased scholarly interest in and public acknowledgement of sexual harassment, the November 1992 issue of the *Journal of Applied Communication* featured twenty first-person narratives by communication professionals about their experiences with sexual harassment as well as two critical analyses. The purpose of this, according to the guest editor, Julia Wood, was to "discern how victims see themselves and sexually harassing encounters and to divulge discursive practices and frameworks with which it is embrangled and which subtly and/or actively legitimize it" (356).

Six of the narratives published include references to Anita Hill or the Hill-Thomas hearings, which some cite as reopening old wounds about the sexual harassment they had experienced—sometimes as many as ten to twenty-five years ago. "When Anita Hill went public, the incidents from my own past came back all too vividly—I understand intimately how someone could go years without telling anyone about such events, how shameful and painful they are to remember, why a woman would be reluctant to file a complaint," said one contributor, who explained that the hearings—and negative reaction to Hill's testimony—caused her to break her silence and share her personal experiences to expose and perhaps stop "this ugly behavior" ("Our Stories," 1992, 388).

Although many women and men have appreciated and applauded the spotlight cast by the Hill-Thomas hearings on the issue of sexual harassment, others have expressed concern about the effects of this public controversy on the relationships between men and women. According to a 1992 *Working Woman* magazine survey, almost half of some 9,000 readers and 106 human-resources executives of Fortune 500 companies thought that publicity about the Hill-Thomas hearings had reduced the "'comfort level' between men and women in the workplace" (Sandroff, 1992a, 49). One reader reported that she "could virtually hear the barriers to communication slam into place. We women confined ourselves to reassuring remarks and noncommittal comments . . . in order to preserve the rapport we've worked so long to build. The men closed ranks and, what is worse, closed their minds" (49).

Similar reactions were revealed in Leda M. Cooks, Claudia L. Hale, and Sue DeWine's study (herein) exploring the impact of the hearings and the discourse surrounding them on the discussion of sexual harassment within and outside the workplace by women and men with the power to enact and enforce corporate policies. All five of the men and two of the eleven women interviewed "mentioned the heightened sense of paranoia that men experienced as a result of the hearings." Men not only felt less comfortable talking with female supervisors, peers, and subordinates but also feared being unjustly charged with sexual harassment.

Whereas the hearings might have impacted the communicative comfort level between men and women in general, they seem to have created deeper tensions in the black community. As Staples (1993) observed, "The highly publicized cases of two black males, Clarence Thomas and [former black heavyweight boxing champion] Mike Tyson, have caused even black women to think of all black men as potential date rapists and sexual harassers" (147). Although Staples notes that black men are less often in positions to sexually harass women than white men are, he concludes that black men "may need to adjust to changing norms of male/female interaction" (147).

According to Staples (1992), Anita Hill may well become—as Jesse Jackson predicted—the Rosa Parks of her era. "Or, she may have sowed the seeds of an irreparable rift in the African American world" (147). Whatever place Hill eventually takes in history, the initial repercussions of the Hill-Thomas hearings not only affected communication in the workplace—and shed new light on the problem of sexual harassment—but also changed the face of electoral politics in the 1992 elections.

Translating Anger into Action at the Polls

Although the impact of the Hill-Thomas hearings on the women who sought—and won—elected office in 1992 may be impossible to isolate and ascertain empirically, it is widely accepted that anger over Hill's treatment by the all-white, all-male Senate Judiciary Committee translated into support for women candidates at the voting booth (Carroll, 1994; Rogers, 1993; Thomas, McCoy, and McBride, 1993; Witt, Paget, and Matthews, 1994). For example, more than one-half of the readers and one-third of the human-resources executives responding to the 1992 *Working Woman* survey said they intended to vote against their senator if he or she voted to confirm Thomas to the Supreme Court. The survey, conducted in February 1992, found that 70 percent of Democratic women and 37 percent of Republican women said the hearings would influence their vote in November 1992 (Sandroff, 1992a, 49).

Anger over the Hill-Thomas hearings frequently has been credited for helping engineer the upset victory of Carol Moseley-Braun, an Illinois Democrat who defeated the incumbent Alan Dixon, a Thomas supporter, in the primary and a former Reagan administration official in the general election to become the first black woman elected to the U.S. Senate. Moseley-Braun, formerly the Cook County recorder of deeds, has said her reason for challenging Dixon was the Hill-Thomas hearings, and exit polls showed that Republican women crossed over to vote for her in the primary because of that issue (Schwartz, 1992).

Eleanor Holmes Norton, who headed the EEOC under President Jimmy Carter and wrote the guidelines on sexual harassment in 1980, was emphatic about the reason for Moseley-Braun's candidacy and the support she received: "[Moseley-]Braun wouldn't have been in the race if it weren't for Anita Hill. She was virtually drafted by women to run as a vehicle of change, an expression of rage" (quoted in Sandroff, 1992a, 49).

Anger over the treatment of Hill—feelings of being excluded and misunderstood by the Senate's white male power structure—also contributed to the candidacies and campaigns of three other women elected to the Senate in 1992. Patty Murray, a Washington state senator who defeated U.S. Representative Rod Chandler after Senator Brock Adams decided not to seek reelection in the wake of sexual harassment charges, said she decided to run after she watched the Hill-Thomas hearings and "didn't see myself up there" (quoted in Abramson, 1992, A4). Similarly, Dianne Feinstein, one of two women senators elected in California in 1992, called the Hill-Thomas hearings the "galvanizing factor behind women candidates" because they helped people realize that there were only two women in the U.S. Senate (quoted in Wilkinson and Murphy, 1992, A23).

"And when they saw the egregious nature of the hearings, the questions that weren't asked, the support that wasn't given, the ignoring of certain elements of [Hill's] presentation, they began to realize how important it was to have more women who would be more sensitive to these issues and handle them in a much more forthright and direct way, rather than try to sweep them under the rug," said Feinstein (quoted in Wilkinson and Murphy, 1992, A23), who cited the "sense of rage" over "what they did to Anita Hill" in her fundraising letters (quoted in Mathews, 1991, A12).

Representative Barbara Boxer, who won a narrow victory over a conservative television commentator to join Feinstein in the Senate, used photographs of herself leading a group of congresswomen up the Capitol steps to protest the Senate's handling of Hill's charges in her campaign advertising (Abramson, 1992) and attempted to capitalize on outrage over the hearings in her fund-raising efforts and speeches (Mathews, 1991; Wilkinson, 1992). "They couldn't help her because they didn't get it. And they didn't understand it. And they didn't feel it," Boxer told a gathering of Democratic women. "Had there been one woman on that committee, it would have been different!" (quoted in Wilkinson, 1992, A12).

Anger over the Senate Judiciary Committee's treatment of Hill almost brought down the chief Republican interrogator, Senator Arlen Specter of Pennsylvania, when the political newcomer Lynn Yeakel ran against him in 1992. At the end of a television ad that showed Specter aggressively questioning Hill, Yeakel asked her viewers: "Did that make you as angry as it made me?" According to exit polls, Yeakel won 70 percent of the women's vote in the primary before narrowly losing to Specter in the general election (Schwartz, 1992, 12). "I think we'll look back in history at those hearings as the single most important event that finally galvanized American women to take the ultimate step into the public arena," Yeakel said after her primary victory (quoted in Leubsdorf, 1992, 1A).

Geraldine Ferraro, a former congresswoman and the 1984 Democratic vice presidential candidate, was another woman candidate who attempted to tap into the anger over the Hill-Thomas hearings in her bid to unseat the conservative Republican Senator Alfonse D'Amato of New York in 1992. Ferraro, who ran ads comparing herself with an embattled Hill, narrowly lost (by one percentage point) the Democratic Senate nomination to Robert Abrams in a four-person primary (Barone and Ujifusa, 1993).

Even women candidates who did not specifically use the Hill-Thomas hearings in their campaign rhetoric and advertising were given a boost at the polls, according to many political leaders, pollsters, and reporters. "The hearings really have motivated some women to run and other women to help them," said Harriett Woods (quoted in Cross, 1992, 6), president of the National Women's Political Caucus, which took out ads to channel the emotions they unleashed into electing more women in 1992 (Mills, 1991).

"We owe Anita Hill a great debt of gratitude because we can now spend time getting women elected instead of explaining why we need them," said Jane Danowitz of the Women's Campaign Fund (quoted in Rogers, 1993, 16). According to the pollster and political consultant Celinda Lake, "Anita Hill has become a metaphor for something a lot broader than sexual harassment. She has become a symbol for a system that's failed, that's become distorted and out of touch" (quoted in Ifill, 1991, B7).

It may never be proven that anger over the Hill-Thomas hearings led a record 150 women to seek seats in the U.S. House and another 20 to run for Senate in 1992 (Schwartz, 1992, 12). Or that the hearings helped elect 4 new women to the Senate, tripling the number of women who serve there, and 47 women to the U.S. House, an increase of 68 percent from the 28 elected in 1990 ("Women Break," 1992–93, 1). However, it is perhaps most significant that the media believed—and wrote—that anger over the hearings was a boost for women candidates in 1992.

"Call it the Anita Hill factor. Angry at the treatment Ms. Hill received last year during hearings of the Senate Judiciary Committee, women are running for Congress in record numbers," an article in the *Christian Science Monitor* on the 1992 primaries noted (Belsie, 1992, l). "Women's chances of victory are greatly increased because tens of thousands of other women are giving them money and working in their campaigns," wrote a reporter in the *New York Times*. "Many of them were drawn into electoral politics by their disgust at the behavior of the all-male Senate Judiciary Committee in the hearings on the nomination of Justice Clarence Thomas to the Supreme Court. Professor Anita F. Hill is their Joan of Arc" (Apple, 1992, 1).

A content analysis of the campaign coverage accorded to women congressional candidates by seven selected newspapers indicates that the Hill-Thomas hearings were cited frequently, especially by women reporters, as the primary reason more women were seeking—and, more important, why they might be elected—to the U.S. House and Senate in 1992 (Bystrom, 1992, 18–19). Although the closely related factor of electing outsiders (i.e., women and

minorities) to the political establishment was the top overall reason emphasized or mentioned in 65 percent of the 130 articles sampled, the Hill-Thomas
hearings were a close second, at 61 percent. When mere mentions were excluded from the analysis, the Hill-Thomas hearings were the most frequently cited reason for the candidacies of women. The hearings were the primary
focus in twice as many (35 percent) articles as the outsider theme (18 percent).
Other reasons for women's candidacies were voters' desire for change or an
anti-incumbency mood (11 percent) and financial backing or support for
women candidates (11 percent).

Consistent with the findings of previous research (Kahn and Goldenberg,
1991), this 1992 study found that the gender of the article's author appeared
to play a significant role in the reasons cited for women's candidacies. Of the
38 articles authored by female reporters, 76 percent cited Anita Hill or the
hearings as a reason women were running compared with 48 percent of the
73 articles authored by men (Bystrom, 1992, 19).

Women reporters also were more likely than their male counterparts to
credit the Hill-Thomas hearings in contributing to the campaign coffers of
women candidates in their coverage. Whereas 42 percent of the articles written by women said the hearings had an effect on the financial support women
candidates were receiving, only 11 percent of the articles written by men made
this connection (Bystrom, 1992, 23).

According to Mary Beth Rogers (1993), women candidates for the first time
did have the financial resources to make them serious contenders in 1992,
because of the specialized fund-raising techniques the major women political organizations developed and a "sense of financial solidarity among
women . . . fueled by fear and anger over [reproductive] choice and Anita Hill"
(18). Direct-mail contributions to established feminist groups swelled by 30–
50 percent after the Hill-Thomas hearings (Easton, 1992). EMILY's List, a
Democratic fund-raising group, collected a record $6.2 million in 1992, com-
pared with $1.5 million in 1990 (Rogers, 1993, 17).

Perhaps most important, the new financial solidarity of women, prompted
in part by the Hill-Thomas hearings, led them to contribute money for women
candidates who did not live in their states and whom they did not know (Rogers, 1993, 18). For example, Moseley-Braun—the Illinois candidate prompted
to run for the Senate by the Hill-Thomas hearings—raised $100,000 in Tex-
as and $60,000 from women in Massachusetts (Rogers, 1993, 18).

As the former Massachusetts Lieutenant Governor Evelyn Murphy has noted, "Money is the major measure of credibility to insiders, the media, to people who shape viable candidacies" (quoted in Rogers, 1993, 18). Also, media coverage of candidates—especially about their perceived viability—has been found to impact voters' assessment of candidates and the likelihood they will vote for them (Kahn and Goldenberg, 1991). Thus, if anger over the Hill-Thomas hearings prompted more financial contributions to women candidates and enhanced their coverage by the media—as campaign finance reports and Bystrom's 1992 study indicate—Anita Hill might have contributed significantly to the election of a record number of women to Congress in 1992.

At the very least, Hill has helped changed the face of the all-white, all-male Senate Judiciary Committee that she confronted in 1991. The committee's chair, Senator Joseph Biden of Delaware, "trying to make amends for allowing Republicans to arduously question Hill," insisted on having two new women senators—Feinstein of California and Moseley-Braun of Illinois—on the Senate Judiciary Committee in 1992 (Barone and Ujifusa, 1993). And, despite the Republican landslide in the 1994 elections—and the ouster of a number of incumbents, particularly in the House of Representatives—women managed to hold their own in Congress ("Women Hold Their Own," 1994–95). Of the record 112 women who ran in general election races for the U.S. House, 47 won their contests, to maintain the level of representation achieved in 1992. Of the 27 women who entered races for the U.S. Senate, 9 were candidates in general election contests. Three women—two incumbents elected in 1992 and 1993 to fill shortened terms created by resignations and one newcomer running in an open race—were elected to the Senate, bringing the total number of women who serve there to 8. ("Women Hold Their Own," 1994–95).

Conclusion

From all indications, the debate unleashed by the Hill-Thomas hearings is far from over. From the bedroom to the boardroom, from cocktail parties to campaign headquarters, and on the pages of the popular and academic press, blacks and whites, women and men, Democrats and Republicans, liberals and conservatives continue to talk about the hearings and their aftermath.

As this essay shows, many of the discussions and publications about the Hill-Thomas hearings to date have been preoccupied with the issue of who told the truth. Although continued analysis of recent works as well as Hill's own memoirs should shed additional light on the hearings and the motivations of its participants, such publications probably will not produce a definitive answer to this question. However, additional efforts by communication scholars to analyze and compare the testimonies of Hill and Thomas for deceptive discourse and nonverbal behaviors may help inject the rationality of social science research into this politically charged debate.

Future investigations also should move from the issue of who was telling the truth to the long-term effects of the hearings on the workplace, relations between women and men, and the political power structure. The dramatic rise in sexual harassment complaints to the EEOC and the increased attention to this issue by the media, businesses, and academicians suggest that Anita Hill has singlehandedly increased the public's awareness of sexual harassment and corporate America's response to the problem that for years was often ignored or laughed about as accepted behavior in the business world. She has been credited for encouraging thousands of the women who have broken their silence and come forward to tell their own stories of sexual harassment, file charges, and win multimillion dollar settlements (see, e.g., Nayyar and Miller, 1994; Sandroff, 1992b).

Although it may be too early to claim that Hill has become the Rosa Parks of her era, she has become a national symbol in the nation's newfound sensitivity to sexual harassment. As Wood (1992) and Hicks and Glenn (herein) suggest, communication scholars should respond to this increased interest in the phenomenon of sexual harassment with additional efforts to analyze individual stories by both victims and harassers to learn more about how sexual harassment is created, perpetuated, and often silenced through discourse, institutional practices, and cultural constraints. Through such research efforts, communication scholars could help empower victims of sexual harassment; educate those with the power to enforce policies prohibiting such behavior; and, eventually, change the corporate and cultural climates that allow sexual harassment to occur.

In addition to these lines of research, the Hill-Thomas hearings offer scholars an opportunity to explore further the dual impact of race and gender on issues of sexual harassment. As Wood (1992) notes, "While we know that there are generalizable differences in how women and men tend to perceive sexually related behaviors, we know far less about how race and class intersect with gender in patterns of interpreting and responding to sexual harassment" (355).

To learn more about these interactions, Wood advocates research that takes into account diverse social circumstances and their epistemological effects on individuals' perceptions of themselves, others, and personal interactions.

Finally, additional scholarship is needed to clarify the impact of the Hill-Thomas hearings on the political power structure of this country. Media coverage of the 1992 congressional campaigns involving women, increased contributions to organizations supporting women candidates, and the campaign rhetoric and commercials of the candidates themselves indicate that Anita Hill had a dramatic impact on the number of women who sought and were elected to political office in 1992. However, except for a limited study of seven newspapers' coverage of women congressional candidates in 1992 (Bystrom, 1992), researchers have not attempted to measure the impact of the Hill-Thomas hearings on political campaigns. Through surveys of voters, case studies of political candidates, and content analysis of political campaign communication, researchers should further explore the "Anita Hill effect" on the candidacies of women in 1992 and subsequent election years.

In the final analysis, Anita Hill's contributions to changing the corporate, legal, and public climate that has created, fostered, and ignored sexual harassment and altering the predominantly white, male political power structure through the election of more women and minorities to political office may overshadow whatever contributions Justice Clarence Thomas makes to American jurisprudence through his seat on the Supreme Court. If the five years following the hearings are any indication, it is Anita Hill who has been cheered, honored, and extolled, while Thomas has been largely ignored or criticized for his opinions on the Supreme Court (Abramson, 1992; Phelps and Winternitz, 1992). Time—and additional scholarly analysis of the continuing effects of the Hill-Thomas hearings on men and women, the workplace, and politics—will be the ultimate jury on the historical significance of this event.

NOTES

1. Bingham, 1994; Brock, 1993; Chrisman and Allen, 1992; Mayer and Abramson, 1994; Morrison, 1992; Phelps and Winternitz, 1992.

2. Chrisman, 1991–92; Escalante, 1992.

3. For analyses of the political dynamics of the hearings, see Darwin, herein; Leathers, herein; and Wiegand, herein. For analyses of the racial and sexual ste-

reotypes, see Allen, 1992; Beck, Ragan, and Kaid, herein; Bell, 1992; Bhabha, 1992; Burnham, 1992; Crenshaw, 1992; Feagin, 1992; Fraser, 1992; Giddings, 1992; Horne, 1992; Karenga, 1992; McKay, 1992; Noumair, Fenichel, and Fleming, 1991; Painter, 1992; Patterson, 1992; Pope, 1992; Roper, Chanslor, and Bystrom, herein; Stansell, 1992; and Wanza, 1992. For analyses of the divisive impact of the Hill-Thomas interaction on the black community, see Chrisman, 1991–92; Chrisman and Allen, 1992; Morrison, 1992; and Staples, 1993.

4. For book-length investigations of who was telling the truth, see Brock, 1993; Mayer and Abramson, 1994; and Phelps and Winternitz, 1993. For essays on credibility, see Leathers et al., 1995; and LeBaron, herein. For essays on believability, see Bowker, herein; Kaid, Tedesco, and Jones, herein; Rucinski, 1993; and Thomas, McCoy, and McBride, 1993.

5. For scholarly analyses of the hearings' impact on how men and women communicate, see Cooks, Hale, and DeWine, herein; and Hicks and Glenn, herein. For analyses of new awareness of sexual harassment, see Strine, 1992; and Taylor and Conrad, 1992. For analyses of the impact of the hearings on women elected, see Bystrom, 1992; Carroll, 1994; Rogers, 1993; and Witt, Paget, and Matthews, 1994.

REFERENCES

Abramson, J. (1992, October 5). Reversal of fortune: Image of Anita Hill, brighter in hindsight, galvanizes campaigns. *Wall Street Journal*, A1, A4.

Allen, E., Jr. (1992). Race and gender stereotyping in the Thomas confirmation hearings. In Chrisman and Allen (eds.), *Court of Appeal*, 25–28.

Apple, R. W., Jr. (1992, May 12). Steady local gains by women fuel more runs for high office. *New York Times*, 1, 4.

Barone, M., and Ujifusa, G. (eds.). (1993). *The almanac of American politics, 1994.* Washington, D.C.: National Journal.

Bell, E. L. (1992). Myths, stereotypes, and realities of black women: A personal reflection. *Journal of Applied Behavioral Science*, 28: 363–76.

Belsie, L. (1992, April 30). Primaries suggest 1992 may be "year of the woman." *Christian Science Monitor*, 1.

Bhabha, H. E. (1992). A good judge of character: Men, metaphors, and the common culture. In Morrison (ed.), *Race-ing justice, en-gendering power*, 232–49.

Bingham, S. (ed.). (1994). *The discursive construction of sexual harassment.* New York: Praeger.

Brock, D. (1993). *The real Anita Hill: The untold story.* New York: Free Press.

Burnham, M. A. (1992). The Supreme Court appointment process and the politics of race and sex. In Morrison (ed.), *Race-ing justice, en-gendering power*, 290–319.

Bystrom, D. (1992, November). From Anita Hill to Capitol Hill: A content analysis of factors contributing to the candidacies of women in the 1992 U.S. House and Senate races. Paper presented at the annual meeting of the Speech Communication Association, Miami Beach.

Carroll, S. J. (1994). *Women as candidates in American politics.* 2d ed. Bloomington: University of Indiana Press.

Chrisman, R. (ed.). (1991–92). The Clarence Thomas confirmation: The black community responds. *Black Scholar*, 22 (1–2): 1–2.

Chrisman, R., and Allen, R. L. (eds.). (1992). *Court of appeal: The black community speaks out on the racial and sexual politics of Thomas vs. Hill.* New York: Ballantine.

Crenshaw, K. (1992). Whose story is it, anyway? Feminist and antiracist appropriations of Anita Hill. In Morrison (ed.), *Race-ing justice, en-gendering power*, 402–40.

Cross, R. (1992, January 26). Hill effect: Political groups find their coffers filling. *Chicago Tribune*, section 6: 1, 6.

Easton, N. (1992, February 2). "I'm not a feminist but . . ." *Los Angeles Times Magazine*, 13–16.

Escalante, K. S. (ed.). (1992). *Southern California Law Review*, 65 (3).

Feagin, J. R. (1992). On not taking gendered racism seriously: The failure of the mass media and the social sciences. *Journal of Applied Behavioral Science*, 28: 400–405.

Fraser, N. (1992). Sex, lies, and the public sphere: Some reflections on the confirmation of Clarence Thomas. *Critical Inquiry*, 18: 595–612.

Garment, S. (1993, January–February). Confirming Anita Hill? *American Enterprise*, 18–22.

Giddings, P. (1992). The last taboo. In Morrison (ed.), *Race-ing justice, en-gendering power*, 441–65.

Give and take. (1994, January 12). *Chronicle of Higher Education*, A29.

Guy-Sheftal, B. (1992). Breaking the silence: A black feminist response to the Thomas/Hill hearings (for Audre Lorde). In Chrisman and Allen (eds.), *Court of Appeal*, 73–77.

Hare, N., and Hare, J. (1992). The Clarence Thomas hearings. In Chrisman and Allen (eds.), *Court of Appeal*, 78–82.

Hernton, C. (1992). Breaking silences. In Chrisman and Allen (eds.), *Court of Appeal*, 86–91.

Hill, A. F. (1993, September 17). *Sabbatical leave report.* (Available from the University of Oklahoma.)

———. (1994, June 15). Personal communication.

Horne, G. (1992). The Thomas hearings and the nexus of race, gender and nationalism. In Chrisman and Allen (eds.), *Court of Appeal*, 92–95.

Ifill, G. (1991, November 18). Female lawmakers wrestle with new public attitude on women's issues. *New York Times*, B7.

Jackson, J. J. (1992). "Them against us": Anita Hill vs. Clarence Thomas. In Chrisman and Allen (eds.), *Court of Appeal*, 99–105.

Kahn, K. F., and Goldenberg, E. N. (1991). Women candidates in the news: An examination of gender differences in the U.S. Senate campaign coverage. *Public Opinion Quarterly*, 55: 180–99.

Karenga, M. (1992). Under the camouflage of color and gender: The dread and drama of Hill-Thomas. In Chrisman and Allen (eds.), *Court of Appeal*, 125–35.

Killackey, J. (1994, May 4). Anita Hill taking unpaid leave from OU to write two books. *Daily Oklahoman*, 8.

Kochman, T. 1981. *Black and white styles in conflict*. Chicago: University of Chicago Press.

Leatherman, C. (1992a, October 14). Legacy of a bitter sex-harassment battle: Rising complaints, frustrations, fears. *Chronicle of Higher Education*, A17–A18.

———. (1992b, October 14). Once a little-known law professor, Anita Hill now is a "national icon." *Chronicle of Higher Education*, A18.

Leathers, D. G., Vaughn, L., Sanchez, G. X., and Bailey, J. L. (1995). Who was lying in the Hill-Thomas hearings: Nonverbal communication profiles. In P. Siegel (ed.), *Outsiders looking in: A communication perspective on the Hill/Thomas hearings*. New York: Hampton Press.

Leubsdorf, C. (1992, May 30). Women well represented in California's primary: State's voters may send several to Congress. *Dallas Morning News*, 1A.

Mathews, J. (1991, December 28). Courting voters with memories of Thomas: Seeking California's 2 seats, Feinstein and Boxer emphasize Senate's lack of women. *Washington Post*, A12.

Mayer, J., and Abramson, J. (1994). *Strange justice: The selling of Clarence Thomas*. New York: Houghton Mifflin.

McKay, N. Y. (1992). Remembering Anita Hill and Clarence Thomas: What really happened when one black woman spoke out. In Morrison (ed.), *Race-ing justice, en-gendering power*, 269–89.

Mills, K. (1991, December 1). Harriett Woods: Thomas hearings jolted Women's Political Caucus into action. *Los Angeles Times*, M3.

Morrison, T. (ed.). (1992). *Race-ing justice, en-gendering power: Essays on Anita Hill, Clarence Thomas, and the construction of social reality*. New York: Pantheon.

Nayyar, S., and Miller, S. (1994, September 12). Making it easier to strike back. *Newsweek*, 50.

Noumair, D. A., Fenichel, A., and Fleming, J. L. (1992). Clarence Thomas, Anita Hill, and us: A group relations perspective. *Journal of Applied Behavioral Science*, 28: 377–87.

Our stories: Communication professionals' narratives of sexual harassment. (1992). *Journal of Applied Communication Research*, 20: 363–90.

Painter, N. I. (1992). Hill, Thomas, and the use of racial stereotype. In Morrison (ed.), *Race-ing justice, en-gendering power*, 251–68.

Patterson, O. (1992). Race, gender, and liberal fallacies. In Chrisman and Allen (eds.), *Court of Appeal*, 160–64.

Phelps, T. M., and Winternitz, H. (1992). *Capitol games: Clarence Thomas, Anita Hill, and the story of a Supreme Court nomination.* New York: Hyperion.

Pope, J. (1992). The Clarence Thomas confirmation: Facing race and gender issues. In Chrisman and Allen (eds.), *Court of Appeal*, 165–68.

Rogers, M. B. (1993). Women in electoral politics: A slow, steady climb. *Social Policy*, 23 (4): 14–21.

Rucinski, D. (1993). The polls—a review: Rush to judgment? Fast reaction polls in the Anita Hill–Clarence Thomas controversy. *Public Opinion Quarterly*, 57: 575–92.

Sandroff, R. (1992a, June). The Anita Hill effect: Turning anger into votes. *Working Woman*, 49.

———. (1992b, June). Sexual harassment: The inside story. *Working Woman*, 47–51.

Schwartz, M. (1992, June 7). The no. 1 women's issue this year: Getting elected. *Washington Post*, 12.

Stansell, C. (1992). White feminists and black realities: The politics of authenticity. In Morrison (ed.), *Race-ing justice, en-gendering power*, 251–68.

Staples, R. (1992). Hand me the rope—I will hang myself: Observations on the Clarence Hill hearings. In Chrisman and Allen (eds.), *Court of Appeal*, 194–200.

———. (1993). Sexual harassment: Its history, definition and prevalence in the black community. *Western Journal of Black Studies*, 17 (3): 143–48.

Strine, M. S. (1992). Understanding "how things work": Sexual harassment and academic culture. *Journal of Applied Communication Research*, 20: 391–400.

Taylor, B., and Conrad, C. (1992). Narratives of sexual harassment: Organization dimensions. *Journal of Applied Communication Research*, 20: 401–18.

Thomas, D., McCoy, C., and McBride, A. (1993). Deconstructing the political spectacle: Sex, race, and subjectivity in public response to the Clarence Thomas/Anita Hill "sexual harassment" hearings. *American Journal of Political Science*, 37: 699–720.

Wanza, K. P. (1992). The three-ring circus of Clarence Thomas: Race, class, and gender. In Chrisman and Allen (eds.), *Court of Appeal*, 219–24.

Wilkinson, T. (1992, May 27). Will '92 be year of the woman? *Los Angeles Times*, A1, A12.

Wilkinson, T., and Murphy, D. E. (1992, June 4). Will be agents of change, say Feinstein, Boxer. *Los Angeles Times*, A1, A23.

Witt, L., Paget, K. M., and Matthews, G. (1994). *Running as a woman: Gender and power in American politics*. New York: Free Press.

Women break all congressional election records. (1992–93, Winter). *Women's Political Times*, 1, 3.

Women hold their own in Congress. (1994–95, Winter). *Women's Political Times*, 1, 4.

Wood, J. T. (1992). Telling our stories: Narratives as a basis for theorizing sexual harassment. *Journal of Applied Communication Research*, 20: 349–62.

A year later, Hill still talks about sexual harassment. (1992, October 8). *Norman Transcript* (Norman, Okla.), 1–2.

Appendix: Transcription Key

The following symbols are commonly used by practitioners of conversation analysis, a research methodology found in chapters 2 and 11 of this volume. Such symbols show timing, emphasis, vocal dynamics, nonverbal utterances, and other features of speech. Pronunciation is shown frequently by misspellings in addition to conventional English spelling. Nonverbal speech particles (e.g., uh huh, hah hah) are spelled in an attempt to indicate precise pronunciation. These symbols are adapted from Gail Jefferson's notation system as it appears in Harvey Sacks, Emanuel A. Schegloff, and Gail Jefferson's "A Simplest Systematics for the Organization of Turn-Taking in Conversation," *Language* 50: 696-735.

[ ]   Brackets indicate overlapping utterances. Left brackets designate the beginning of an overlap; right brackets end the overlap.

=   Equals signs at the end of one utterance and the beginning of another signify two contiguous utterances that "latch" onto each other but do not actually overlap.

_____ Underlining is used to represent stress or emphasis.

: A colon indicates an extending or stretching of the sound that it follows.

– A hyphen directly following a word or syllable marks a cutting off of sound (i.e., a glottal stop).

? Question marks are used to indicate rising intonation at the end of words or phrases; they do not necessarily mark a grammatical question.

. A period indicates a falling intonation at the end of words or phrases, not necessarily a grammatical sentence.

, A comma denotes continuing intonation that is too subtle to be indicated with a question mark or period.

↑ An upward pointing arrow shows a marked rise in intonation.

^ *or* ° Carat signs or degree signs preceding and following a word or phrase indicate that it was said more quietly than the surrounding talk.

(0.4) Single parentheses enclosing numbers represent pauses in talk, with the numbers expressing seconds and tenths of seconds. A pause too brief to be timed is shown as (.).

( ) Single parentheses enclosing words or a blank space represent doubtful or unintelligible hearings.

hhh The *h*s represent audible outbreaths, sighing, or nonverbal laughter.

·hh A superscripted period followed by *h*s denotes audible inbreaths.

pt This symbol indicates an audible lip smack.

» « Chevron brackets indicate talk that is spoken faster than the surrounding talk.

« » Reverse brackets indicate talk that is spoken slower than the surrounding talk.

Contributors

CHRISTINA S. BECK is an assistant professor in the School of Interpersonal Communication at Ohio University. Interested in television viewer behavior, interpersonal relationships, and health care interactions, she has authored numerous articles and papers.

JUDITH K. BOWKER teaches family and gender communication at Oregon State University. She has published several pieces about the Hill-Thomas hearings, the hearings involving sexual harassment allegations against Senator Bob Packwood of Oregon, and women's positions on reporting sexual harassment.

DIANNE G. BYSTROM is a research associate at the Political Communication Center at the University of Oklahoma. As an assistant provost, she has worked on equity, diversity, and workplace issues in higher education. She has presented numerous convention papers and has published articles in the *Political Communication Review* and *Communication Studies*.

MIKE CHANSLOR is an assistant professor of communication at Northeast Missouri State University. His research interests include the content and effects of political advertising. He has coauthored several journal articles, essays, and convention papers.

LEDA M. COOKS is an assistant professor of communication at the University of Massachusetts. She has presented numerous papers and has published in *Discourse and Society*, *Western Journal of Communication*, and *Howard Journal of Communication*.

THOMAS J. DARWIN is an assistant professor in the Department of Theatre and Communication Arts at the University of Memphis. His work has appeared in *Argumentation* and *Philosophy and Rhetoric*.

SUE DEWINE is a professor and the director of the School of Interpersonal Communication at Ohio University. She has published numerous articles, essays, and books, including *The Consultant's Craft: Coping with Communication Failures in Organizations*.

PHILLIP J. GLENN is an associate professor of speech communication at Southern Illinois University at Carbondale. His conversation analytic research has been published in *Research on Language and Social Interaction*, *Western Journal of Speech Communication*, *Repetition in Discourse*, and *Situated Order*.

CLAUDIA L. HALE is an associate professor of interpersonal communication at Ohio University. Her articles have appeared in *Communication Monographs*, *Journal of Language and Social Psychology*, *Discourse and Society*, and *International Journal of Conflict Management*.

DARRIN HICKS is an assistant professor in the Department of Human Communication Studies at the University of Denver. Interested in the philosophy of communication and conversation analysis, he has published several essays in edited collections.

CLIFFORD A. JONES is an attorney in private practice in Oklahoma City and recently received a master's degree from Cambridge University. He has published articles and books in the areas of antitrust law, campaign finance law, and constitutional rights litigation.

LYNDA LEE KAID is a professor of communication at the University of Oklahoma, where she is also the director of the Political Communication Center and supervises the Political Commercial Archive. She has coauthored or coedited twelve books, including *Political Campaign Communication*, *New Perspectives on Political Advertising*, *Mediated Politics in Two Cultures*, and *Political Communication Yearbook, 1984*.

DALE G. LEATHERS is a professor of speech communication at the University of Georgia in Athens. He is the author of five books, including *Nonverbal Communication Systems* and *Successful Nonverbal Communication*. He currently is studying the William Kennedy Smith and O. J. Simpson trials as impression management phenomena.

CURTIS D. LEBARON is a doctoral student at the University of Texas at Austin, where he is studying language and social interaction from a microethnographic and conversation analytic perspective. His master's thesis critiqued the FBI's approach to verbal deception detection.

VALERIE CRYER MCKAY is an associate professor in the Department of Speech Communication at California State University, Long Beach. Interested in mass communication and politics, communication and aging, and communication and instruction, she has published articles in a number of communication journals.

SANDRA L. RAGAN is a professor of communication and recently served as associate dean of the College of Arts and Sciences at the University of Oklahoma. Her recent publications include a coauthored book, *Communication Skills for Professional Nurses*, as well as articles in the *Journal of Language and Social Psychology* and essays in several edited volumes.

CYNTHIA S. ROPER is an assistant professor in the Department of Communication at Abilene Christian University and a doctoral candidate at the University of Oklahoma. She has coauthored articles and chapters on political debates, media coverage, and political advertising.

JOHN TEDESCO is a doctoral student of communication at the University of Oklahoma. Interested in political communication, political advertising, and social marketing, he has several publications, including articles in *Argumentation and Advocacy*, *Journal of Communication Studies*, and *Informatologia*.

ERICA VERRILLO is completing a doctorate in speech communication at the University of Texas at Austin. She has held positions as language supervisor for the Albany Chiapas Project, linguistics instructor at Dartmouth College, and assistant to the editor of *Mesoamerica*.

SHIRLEY A. WIEGAND is a professor of law at the University of Oklahoma, where she teaches civil procedure, alternative dispute resolution, conflicts, and gender-based discrimination. She is the author of *Library Records: A Retention and Confidentiality Guide* and numerous law review articles.

JULIA T. WOOD is the Nelson Hairston Distinguished Professor of Communication Studies at the University of North Carolina at Chapel Hill. She is the author of ten books, including *Gendered Lives* and *Gendered Relationships*, and fifty journal articles and essays and has coedited six books. The cofounder of the National Conference on Gender and Communication Research, she has served as a legal consultant on sexual harassment.

Index